Kevin S. Decker is Associate Professor of Philosophy and Associate Dean of the College of Arts, Letters and Education at Eastern Washington University. He has co-edited books on the philosophical significance of *Star Wars*, *Star Trek* and the *Terminator* films and television show.

Kevin S. Decker

WHO is WHO?

The Philosophy of Doctor Who

I.B. TAURIS

LONDON · NEW YORK

Published in 2013 by I.B.Tauris & Co Ltd
6 Salem Road, London W2 4BU
175 Fifth Avenue, New York NY 10010
www.ibtauris.com

Distributed in the United States and Canada
Exclusively by Palgrave Macmillan
175 Fifth Avenue, New York NY 10010

ISBN: 978 1 78076 553 2

A full CIP record for this book is available from the British Library
A full CIP record is available from the Library of Congress

Library of Congress Catalog Card Number: available

Printed and bound in Great Britain by Page Bros, Norwich

For Suzanne, with love,
for putting up with the chase cards
and everything else.

CONTENTS

PREFACE

I'm not exactly sure which was the first *Doctor Who* serial I watched, but I think it might have been Tom Baker's 'Terror of the Zygons', originally broadcast by the BBC in 1975 but watched by my younger self in syndication in 1982 on public television in St Louis, Missouri, United States of America. This story not only featured the flamboyant time traveller taking on shape-changing sea cucumbers (the eponymous Zygons) that had taken over part of Scotland but it also gave us a glimpse of the Loch Ness Monster. I was hooked! At the *first* peak of *Doctor Who*'s popularity in my home country, the mid- to late-1980s, the programme was considered nothing more than a 'cult' series. Nonetheless, even as it entertained, it offered substantive suggestions to its viewers about why truth and beauty are important and what constitutes living the good life (surely the attributes of what we call a 'classic'!). Interestingly, these are the same things that philosophy strives for, at least when it is done well.

Since those early days, *Doctor Who* has become an eclectic, trans-Atlantic success story and has repaid the patience of its long-term audience by earning several places in the *Guinness Book of World Records*: in 2007, it was named the 'longest-running science fiction series in the world', while in 2010 it was elevated to the 'most successful science fiction television series in the world'. This is all the more remarkable given two fundamentally mutable things about *Doctor Who*. First is the fact that 11 very different actors have played the titular role, differently emphasising elements of the Doctor's character, interests and morality, thus providing a built-in dramatic counterpoint in the series as the main character is changed every few years or so. When the process of 'regeneration' was dreamed up by the *Who* production team because its lead actor took ill, they could not have known how well the changing of the Doctor over time could map humanity's own divided consciousness between 'intuitive randomness' and 'scientific system' in the twentieth and twenty-first centuries. If this metaphorical mapping is accurate (and my analysis in this book rests on just such a view), then 'the apparently random alternation of Doctors is both appropriate and supported by the central emotional investment—that is, with being human—of the programme', as Tulloch and Alvarado write in their pioneering study of the show.[1] Second, there are also the different permutations of the programme's genre focus over the years: edifying children's show, adventure serial, politically subversive programme, horror, comedy, drama, even soap opera. Not even the control of a single 'show-runner' in the re-envisioned version of *Doctor Who* since 2005 has inhibited the inherent plasticity of the basic premise of a madman and his blue box.

That same pluralism has informed my approach to the philosophy of *Doctor Who* in these pages. I will be the first to admit that feminists, queer theorists and scholars of critical race theory and postcolonialism will find much to critique in *Doctor Who*. Students of Derrida who expect a deconstruction of the Doctor will be disappointed, and analytic Wittgensteinians will lament the lack of precision in my prose. Critical theorists will find that my treatment of the programme is far too optimistic and not judgemental enough. There is no doubt that *Doctor Who* was created as, and has always been, a commodity, Marxists will affirm, and this too I cannot deny. Eschewing all these methodologies, wherever I have found a parallel between the changing Western *Zeitgeist* or particular theories in philosophy – whether in continental, analytic, or American guises – on the one hand,

and the animating spirit of *Doctor Who* on the other, I have attempted to make the best case for the homology without emphasising any one approach to philosophy or intellectual history. In a sense, I feel this fits best with the Doctor's own protracted age and his multiple selves united by his self-understanding of being a person whose 'days [are] like crazy paving'. Observing the Doctor's admonition that a good quote's not worth anything if you can't change it, I have adhered to the Scottish intellectual David Hume's charge to 'be a philosopher, but first be a *Doctor Who* fan'. Thus I haven't limited myself to merely the evidence of the two televised series and the 1996 telemovie, but I have felt free to dip into novels, comic strips and audio adventures that also feature the Doctor. I have left discussions of canon, while interesting in their own right, to others.[2]

I would like to thank the following for their inestimable contribution to the fruition of this book: all the members of the former St Louis Celestial Intervention Agency and those involved with the making of the *Gateway to Time* 'zine (especially Jeff Morris); pop culture and philosophy comrades-in-arms Jason T. Eberl, Robert Arp, Richard Brown and Bill Irwin; my friends and colleagues in philosophy at Eastern Washington University: Kerri Sadowski, Terry MacMullan, Mimi Marinucci, Chris Kirby, Kathryn Julyan and David Weise. I also appreciated the thoughts and comments of the students in my 'Philosophical Voices and Popular Culture' classes of the 2011 and 2012 Winter Quarters. I want to offer special thanks to my time-travel research assistant, Sam Phelps, and to Ryan Weldon, who read the entire manuscript and offered comments that made it inestimably better. I should also like to thank Open Court Publishing Company, publishers of *Doctor Who and Philosophy: Bigger on the Inside*, and the books' editors, Courtland Lewis and Paula Smithka, for permission to reprint material from the chapter 'The Ethics of the Last of the Time Lords', which forms a substantial portion of the current book's Chapter 4.

My family gave me moral support and extra artron energy to finish this book: thank you Suzanne, Kennedy, Ethan and Jackson, and my mother, Carolyn Decker. Here's to more

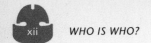

Doctor Who that my children can enjoy with their children! One caveat: 'Seriously, there is a tremendous amount of running through corridors involved.'

INTRODUCTION

'GERONIMO!'

The first question of many: why the philosophy of *Doctor Who*?

The parallels between philosophy and *Doctor Who* are legion. Like philosophical reflection, the Doctor's adventures are full of surprises; they develop through various twists and turns that could not have been predicted from the outset. The Doctor embraces mysteries of time and space; he fights ignorance and evil, and strives, in a complex universe, towards truth and the good.

More importantly, philosophy (the Greek roots of the word mean 'love of wisdom') and *Doctor Who* share a common origin: the experience of wonder. 'For this is an experience which is characteristic of a philosopher, this wondering: this is where philosophy begins and nowhere else', claims Plato's Socrates.[1] Aristotle, Plato's pupil, concurs: 'For it is owing to their wonder that men both now begin and at first began to philosophise.'[2] Hundreds of years before philosophy was kick-started in ancient Greece, Lao Tzu shared this wisdom: 'From wonder into wonder existence opens.'[3] *Doctor Who* has, from its very beginning, embraced this sense of wonder at every turn: fast-forward to 1963, when Coal Hill School science teacher Ian Chesterton steps into a battered police call box that is far bigger on the inside than it seems from the outside. 'Let me get this straight,' Ian intones, no doubt fighting off a certain intellectual dizziness. 'A thing that looks like a police box, standing in a junkyard … it can move anywhere in time and space?' 'Quite so,' chuckles the nameless Doctor, owner of the remarkable machine.

Fifty years later, the thing that looks like a police box still moves anywhere, its owner's guests still wonder how it can be bigger on the inside, and the question posed by the show's title is still a live one: 'Doctor *Who*?' The ethics and worldview of the Doctor, who is nearly immortal and the last of his kind, continue to evolve. So also has the philosophy that underlies this BBC production that has worn many hats since 1963: science fiction, fantasy, Gothic horror, weird comedy, tragedy. This book's explanation for the longevity of the longest-running science fantasy show in television history is that the whole interpretive approach of *Doctor Who* has changed faces more often than the Doctor himself.

A Brief History of Time (Travel)

At the beginning of his tenure as the 11th version of our favourite Time Lord, Matt Smith invited us to join him to see 'all of time and space, everything that ever happened or ever will. One question: where do you want to start?'[4] The Doctor's own story, on the other hand, begins with very little for us to go on:

> In the beginning, the Doctor was a mystery, an enigma. The title of the series – *Doctor Who*? – was a valid and very real question. We now know that he is a Time Lord from the planet Gallifrey who can change his form when he 'dies'. But this tells us very little about him.[5]

The creator of the character of the Doctor, as well as of details about the Doctor's first companions and his time machine, 'the ship', or TARDIS, was C.E. 'Bunny' Webber, of the BBC's Script Department. Three other individuals played a crucial role in the origins of the *Doctor Who* phenomenon: Sydney Newman (BBC Head of Drama), David Whitaker (the show's first story editor) and Verity Lambert (first producer). Whitaker was concerned that the episodes of *Doctor Who* should be action-packed and not too cerebral, and novice producer Lambert was keenly interested in doing something that the BBC had never done before. The philosophies of Whitaker and Lambert underwrote the BBC's new strategy of iconoclasm in the face of its incipient competitor, ITV, launched in 1955.[6] Newman's focus was to capitalise on an accessible time-travel premise 'exploring scientific and historical themes [...] which could be described as educational, or at least mind-opening, for the children watching'.[7]

Yet, contrary to the view that the new time-travel adventure programme was aimed specifically at children, Newman claimed, 'I wanted to bridge the gap on a Saturday between the afternoon's sports coverage, which attracted a huge adult audience, and *Juke Box Jury*, which had a very large teenage following. *Doctor Who* was never intended to be simply a children's programme, but something that would appeal to people who were in a rather childlike frame of mind.'[8] The label of 'children's adventure show' had less to do with the BBC's direction than with popular prejudices against 'pulp' science fiction (SF), particularly the space opera form that made use of mad emperors, spaceships and battles between the stars. Show chronicler Peter Haining writes:

> The main body of audiences in the Sixties were adults who tended to regard TV SF as either children's fare, or as trash: an unfounded prejudice probably stemming from unwarranted comparisons with the comic-strip science fiction movie serials of the 1930s and 40s, or with the UK-banned "horror" comics of the 1950s.[9]

In many ways, *Doctor Who* was created to be an 'anti-space opera'. The puzzling, misanthropic, elderly Doctor is an anti-hero and anti-authoritarian to boot. His fundamental interest is in travelling – not avenging wrongs – and when he does get involved in fighting evil, the weapons he uses are his wits.

That having been said, the technical advances that made early *Doctor Who* possible can be found in other ground-breaking British 'thriller' sci-fi vehicles: H.G. Wells's *The Time*

Machine (1949), a film based on what is arguably the best-known sci-fi novel and the world's first television science fiction production; the *Quatermass* serials (1953, 1955, 1958); and Sydney Newman's children's serials *Pathfinders in Space* (1959), *Pathfinders to Mars* (1960) and *Pathfinders to Venus* (1961). Like early *Doctor Who*, these programmes emphasised Newman's dictate to 'tackl[e] problems realistically with a strict observance of scientific laws'.[10] This worldview, suggesting that science and rational thinking could provide the solutions to the central dilemmas of the Doctor's world – and indeed, those of our own as well – is the essence of philosophical 'positivism', which largely dictated the ethical perspective of *Doctor Who* as well as other prominent television sci-fi shows of the 1960s like *Lost in Space*, Gerry Anderson's 'Supermarionation' programmes, and *Star Trek*. Yet, as we shall see in Chapter 1, *Doctor Who*'s positivism is tempered by other philosophical elements. In modern SF, the positivistic attitude generated plots that revolved around the theme of accepting modernism and the consequences of our increasing dependence upon technology:

> Science challenged man to rid himself of his illusions and face the true facts of existence [...] as science saw them. The soul of man was stripped away by science and discarded, and with it all of man's accustomed sense of worth and purpose. In its place, science offered man a new identity. Henceforth he was to be an orphan child in a universe vastly beyond his comprehension.[11]

This positivist outlook (called in written SF 'hard sci-fi') also supported Sydney Newman's desire to avoid preying on viewers' primal fears by featuring 'Bug-Eyed Monsters' on the new programme; one innovation of 1960s science fiction was the plot twist in which we are introduced to initially frightening alien beings, which are 'humanised' later in the story, usually through the rational inquiry of the protagonists.

The original crew of characters on board the TARDIS supports this mission well. Ian Chesterton (William Russell), a science teacher, is our guide to the right questions to ask about the future-oriented episodes. Barbara Wright (Jacqueline Hill), his fellow Coal Hill School teacher, relies on her historical knowledge to orient us when the TARDIS arrives in the past. Susan Foreman (Carole Ann Ford) is the 'unearthly child' who is the object of their interest since, as the original Writer's Guide to the series claims, she 'has a wide general knowledge and on some subjects she can be brilliantly factual. On others, she is lamentably ignorant.'[12] Susan is the ultimate 'insider', designed to attract the show's young core audience; her grandfather, simply 'The Doctor' (William Hartnell) or 'Doctor Who' as the Writer's Guide names him, 'has escaped from the Fiftieth Century' out of disillusionment with the lifestyle of that time. With strong intimations of his alien nature carried in his crotchety behaviour, he is the ultimate 'outsider'. The Doctor's alterity, his 'alienness' – quite different to Susan's – is eventually softened over the course of the first year's series. But the relationship between the Doctor and the TARDIS is the key MacGuffin that drives the series from episode to episode: 'insofar as his operation of the "ship" is concerned he is much like the average driver of a motor car in that he is its master when it works properly and its bewildered slave when it is temperamental'.[13]

Joined by a parade of fellow travellers scooped from past (the Trojan War), present (the club scene in 1960s London) and future (a space pilot marooned on the planet Mechanus, the natives of which are – wait for it – giant, mobile fungi), the Doctor careened through time and space, forging vaguely paternal relationships with his younger companions in weekly adventures that spanned, at least at first, the entire year. *Doctor Who* was neither the only nor the first BBC programme to use the approximately 25-minute episodic format, with story arc serials usually spanning from four to six episodes, yet it has become identified with the thrilling cliff-hangers that end each episode, and with a distinctive musical 'sting' and fade-out at the moment of imminent peril. From 1963 to 1966, the Doctor survived encounters with the Daleks, villainous Voords and bloodthirsty French revolutionaries, escaped from the 'security kitchen' of the monocular Monoids, and defeated a fellow time traveller in the year 1066. He ultimately met his fate after a harrowing encounter with the half-human, half-machine Cybermen.

But the Doctor doesn't die. Together with the time- and space-spanning TARDIS, the Doctor's surprising ability to *regenerate* – to change his physical form and personality while maintaining his identity and memories – is another distinctive hallmark of the programme. Although it is common to see different actors playing the same role (James Bond and too many soap opera characters come quickly to mind) no other television or movie series has featured the serial replacement of the protagonist as an integral part of the unfolding storyline. The programme's third producer, Innes Lloyd, developed the idea as a way to continue production of *Doctor Who* in the face of Hartnell's flagging health. In 1966, Patrick Troughton debuted as his replacement, and ratings immediately spiked upwards. Although Hartnell was himself less than enthusiastic about leaving the role he had originated, he had recommended Troughton highly.[14] Yet the appearance of a new face in the TARDIS control room left many viewers uneasy, a feeling echoed by companion Ben Jackson (Michael Craze), who finds on the ground the ruby ring that 'his' Doctor always wore. 'Now, look, the Doctor always wore this. So if you're him, then it should fit, now shouldn't it?' Ben accuses the curious, mop-haired fellow as 'the new Doctor' rises from the floor ('The Power of the Daleks', 1966).

Another new beginning for *Doctor Who* in 1966 was the concentrated effort to beef up the action-oriented elements of the programme. For the next decade, the show would appear less like a filmed stage production, taking greater advantage of location filming and more elaborate sets. Innes Lloyd and his story editor Gerry Davis (co-creator, with Kit Pedler, of the Cybermen) were keen to have the Doctor more physically involved in the adventures. The differences between the old and new Doctor are particularly obvious in two of Troughton's first few stories, 'The Highlanders' (1966–7) and 'The Underwater Menace' (1967). In both serials, the Doctor relishes the use of disguises, play-acting and accents in his quests to set things right. Whereas Hartnell's Doctor maintained an air of command and had exhibited a tempered respect for other authorities, Troughton's depiction was gleefully anti-authoritarian in tapping into the pulse of late 1960s youth culture. This often manifested itself in quips about how rational order always breaks down: 'Logic merely allows one to be wrong with authority,' he observes in spurning the efforts of the Brotherhood of Logicians to raise the Cybermen from their frozen tombs on the planet Telos.

During three years of running through corridors, Troughton's era of *Doctor Who* brought back the Cybermen four times and the Daleks twice. There was still plenty of room for new monsters that would quickly become iconic, the test being whether younger viewers were only able to watch them from the safety of behind the couch. The Ice Warriors, the Yeti, Macra, Chameleons, Quarks, Krotons and a carnivorous North Sea seaweed all menaced the Doctor and his Scots highlander companion Jamie MacCrimmon (Frazer Hines). Troughton's era mastered and refined the 'base under siege' motif of many future episodes, and during this period of relative innocence, there was no doubt in the viewer's mind that the show's monsters were the villains. The Doctor is surely right to claim, as he does in the face of a Cyberman invasion of Earth's moon, that, 'There are some corners of the universe which have bred the most terrible things. Things which act against everything we believe in. They must be fought!' ('The Moonbase', 1967). But precisely what is the nature of their evil, and what justifies the Doctor's interference in the 'web of time' to stop them? In the wake of the Troughton era, the Doctor's own motivations would sometimes become suspect to allies and companions, leading some to conclude that *he* is the monster.

Outer Space, Inner Time

The question of the Doctor's attitude towards evil would be further complicated in 1970 by another of the show's major transitions. For its seventh series, *Doctor Who* was moving to colour broadcasting and, with it, a flamboyant new Doctor (Jon Pertwee) was cast. Winning the role in part because his imposing height and mop of grey-white hair contrasted strongly with Troughton's appearance, the 'new new Doctor' emerged from the TARDIS after having been forcibly regenerated by his own people, the Time Lords of Gallifrey ('Spearhead from Space', 1970). Deliberately cast against type as a former radio and television funnyman, Pertwee found the role of the Doctor to be the first time he was able to emerge from underneath the actor's 'green umbrella' of 'character parts and eccentrics'. 'So eventually I just decided to play him as I felt,' he explained in an interview for the *Jon Pertwee Fan Club Newsletter*, 1975, 'so really what the Doctor liked was just an extension of what I like'.[15]

The narrative base that was to dominate the five years of Pertwee's time in the TARDIS was the Doctor's exile on Earth — his punishment for breaking Gallifrey's cardinal law of non-interference in the affairs of other times and worlds. Through adventures involving menaces both alien (the Axon energy vampires, the mannequin-like Autons) and home grown (the Silurians, intelligent reptilian predecessors to humankind on Earth), this acerbic, anti-authoritarian, often hedonistic Doctor was frequently accompanied by a military straight man, Brigadier Alastair Gordon Lethbridge-Stewart (Nicholas Courtney). 'The Brigadier' proved to be the Doctor's longest-standing friend, entering the show's canon through Courtney's repeated efforts in working with nearly all the actors portraying the Doctor, at least before his death in 2011. After the 1973 serial 'The Three Doctors', which served as a tenth-anniversary celebration reuniting the first three actors to play the role of the Doctor, it also became canonical to refer to individual incarnations of the Time Lord as 'the first Doctor' (Hartnell), 'the second Doctor' (Troughton), etc.[16]

Although Hartnell's and Troughton's Doctors had aligned themselves with the best and brightest of humanity in order to fight evil, the era of the third Doctor was more explicitly moralistic than theirs, engaging with real-life threats to the quality of life on Earth. The most pointed of its serials was 'The Green Death' (1973), which warned against ecological disaster. Pertwee-era producer Barry Letts shares:

> *The Green Death* came about after [script editor] Terrance
> Dicks and I had read a series of pieces in an environmental
> magazine, *The Ecologist*, about the pollution of the Earth by
> man. The articles were very disturbing and made me wish I
> could do something positive about it.[17]

The Pertwee era as a whole was also distinguished by the
strained relationships between a particular *troika* of players
– the Doctor, incessantly working to revive the TARDIS at all
costs to resume his life of wandering; the Brigadier and his
division of the United Nations Intelligence Taskforce (UNIT),
protecting Great Britain from alien invasions by shooting first
and asking questions afterwards; and the Doctor's jailers, the
Time Lords. Both sets of relationships are complicated by the
recurring interference of the Doctor's nemesis, the suave and
hypnotic Master (Roger Delgado). The Master understands
his fellow Time Lord's frustrations with humanity, yet holds
the Doctor's self-righteous morality in contempt. By the third
Doctor's final series of adventures in 1974, the insults and
resentment that he hurls at the Brigadier have softened into
trust and respect. Before this, the Time Lords had revoked
his exile (in the aforementioned 'The Three Doctors'), and
his attitude towards his own hyper-futuristic society is 'more
commonly presented as one of allegiance and loyalty'.[18]

But all this was to fall apart again with the Doctor's third
regeneration after an encounter with giant spiders and
radioactive crystals on the planet Metebelis III. The fourth
Doctor, played by Tom Baker, has enjoyed the most protracted
of the Doctor's lives so far (if we factor in both the time served
as the Doctor and the number of episodes starring him). Over
seven years, Baker fleshed out the character as a 'Bohemian
eccentric', with his trailing, multicoloured scarf becoming
one of the enduring icons of the programme. But Baker's
characterisation changed drastically, depending upon the
direction taken by the producers during his term. This ranged
from moody and prone to soliloquies (Philip Hinchcliffe,
1974–7); to over-the-top comedy and ad-libbing witticisms
(Graham Williams, 1977–9); to restrainedly mordant (John
Nathan-Turner, 1980–1).

The fourth Doctor shares little of his predecessor's loyalty to Earth, Britain and UNIT, and resumes his peripatetic career among the stars. Baker's era showcases one of the programme's more fruitful periods of experimentation, integrating wider themes from SF in general as well as playing to its own history. For example, the Doctor's first televised visit to his home planet of Gallifrey occurs in 'The Deadly Assassin', a 1976 *Manchurian Candidate*-style political thriller that reveals the vaunted Time Lords as both decadent and eminently corruptible.[19] Many of Baker's serials in the later 1970s reflect the show's evolving social conscience: no matter what planet he visits, the Doctor quickly assumes a position helping workers, the poor or socially marginalised to work towards reform or, in some cases, revolution. With regard to the show's format, these years also delivered outrageous scenarios from the mind of *Hitchhiker's Guide to the Galaxy*'s Douglas Adams, as well as a full year's story arc in 1978–9 with the quest of the Doctor and companions K-9 and Romanadvoratrelundar for the fabled 'Key to Time'. Christopher H. Bidmead, story editor after Adams, gave us mind-bending premises such as the 'Zero Point' between universes, a megalomaniacal cactus taking its revenge on a world of primarily deciduous forests, and the unravelling of the mathematical structure of the universe itself.

This final year of the fourth Doctor's adventures (1980–1) promised a more substantial transmogrification of the programme than had occurred with the transition to colour and the Doctor's exile on Earth. Throughout the 1980s, producer John Nathan-Turner helmed *Doctor Who* and initiated a distinctive second phase in the show's development. In hindsight, this decade would represent a harbinger of the show's feel when it returned in 2005 after cancellation for 16 years. The 1980s were characterised by a new, shiny TARDIS prop as part of a new, shiny look designed to compete in the *Star Wars* sci-fi market. They featured more frequent story arcs, and, most importantly, dramatically increased producer's control over the direction and marketing of the show. One thing that Nathan-Turner changed immediately was the way our protagonist was played, since he 'had never been particularly enamoured of Baker's portrayal of the

Doctor, considering that his increasingly assured and flippant interpretation made the character seem too dominant and invulnerable, detracting from the series' dramatic potential'.[20]

Flight into Danger

Increasing the risks and making the Doctor more vulnerable was precisely what Nathan-Turner was about, whether this meant getting rid of his problem-solving K-9 computer, destroying his sonic screwdriver, or reintroducing his arch-enemy, the Master (now played by Anthony Ainley). This strategy was reflected nowhere more clearly than in the choice of Baker's replacement in the youngest actor to have played the role yet, Peter Davison. Davison was cast against Baker's over-the-top portrayal. Now the Doctor was perceived as 'a rather slight, fair-haired young man with a pleasant, open face'.[21] Episodes were often fleshed out by squabbles between this old Doctor with a young body and his argumentative companions, like young mathematical genius Adric or Australian flight stewardess Tegan Jovanka.

The Davison era took a more serious look at itself – including the tragic death of TARDIS traveller, Adric (Matthew Waterhouse), whom the Doctor claimed it was impossible to save, even with a time machine. It also began to reopen certain ethical questions – seemingly shelved since the Hartnell era – about the desirability of interfering with established history. 1982's 'Black Orchid', the first purely historical story since 1966–7's 'The Highlanders', was a showcase for Davison's cricket-geared Doctor to play the game among the upper crust of the 1920s. In another episode, the TARDIS is used against its owner when it is revealed that the Doctor's companions will age to death if he attempts to escape. These escapades were capped by a television event in 1983, near the end of Davison's three-year tenure, when time turned back on itself four times over for a 90-minute special commissioned for the twentieth anniversary of *Doctor Who*. Like the tenth anniversary programme, this entry, 'The Five Doctors', emphasised the ability of Time Lords to take advantage of the special properties of time and allowed four incarnations – played by Davison, Pertwee, Troughton and Richard Hurndall (a stand-in for the late Hartnell) – to meet.

The deepening contrasts between appearances and personalities of the various Doctors in the 1980s may have been an effort by Nathan-Turner to recapture the 1960s and 70s phenomenon of audience identification with a particular actor, now called 'my first Doctor'. Criticisms of the Doctor's frailties, as well as worries about the level of violent themes in *Doctor Who*, were also amplified. In his première appearance, the sixth Doctor (Colin Baker) comments on his predecessor in a denigrating manner, almost as if he is speaking of another person. 'My previous self had a kind of feckless charm that simply *wasn't* me!' he blusters ('The Twin Dilemma', 1984). He proceeds, in a post-regenerative fit, to try to strangle companion Perpugilliam Brown (Nicola Bryant), then gives her over to alien kidnappers to try to save his own skin. While this instability of character is overcome within his first episodes, Baker's Doctor continued to be 'a highly volatile and unpredictable character. Theatrical, pretentious, arrogant, rude, impatient, irascible; all these adjectives could be reasonably used to describe typical aspects of his behaviour.'[22] Based on viewer outcry, this attempt by Baker to recapture some of the alien grumpiness that Hartnell had pioneered was significantly toned down in his second series of stories. Ultimately, discontent with his performance and with the whole tenor of mid-1980s *Who* left Colin Baker as the only actor who played the Doctor to be sacked by the BBC.

Before he left, however, Baker (in conjunction with his predecessor, Patrick Troughton) gave us 'The Two Doctors' (1985), a sprawling adventure set both on a station in deep space and on location in Seville, Spain. New alien costumes and effects accompanied the return of another perennial race of villains, the Sontarans, a clone race waging eternal war with their enemies, the shape-changing Rutans. As well as rehearsing familiar multi-Doctor jokes about 'who is the Doctor?', the episode raises questions about the persistence of the Doctor's identity through time and across regenerations.

Indeed, SF has always been a particularly fertile ground for speculations about whether significant physical, mental or spiritual changes leave personal identity unchanged.

Doctor Who is therefore not unusual in posing many questions about identity over time and how identity is challenged or reinforced by changes of society and environment.[23] At the level of social and political concerns, *Doctor Who* has always been a playground for the exploration of identities, from the appearance of the Doctor's 'evil twin' Salamander in the Troughton serial 'The Enemy of the World' (1967–8) to the self-conscious attempt to offer a more diverse TARDIS crew with the casting of a Doctor with a 'northern accent' (Christopher Eccleston) and non-white travellers like Rose Tyler's boyfriend Mickey Smith (Noel Clarke) and Dr Martha Jones (Freema Agyeman).

In the late 1980s, that diversification began with Sylvester McCoy, the first Scotsman and the seventh actor to play the Doctor on television, and his teaming with 'street kid' Ace (Sophie Aldred). After Baker's sacking, producer John Nathan-Turner found himself in the position of having to find a new Doctor. Having seen McCoy in the National Theatre's *The Pied Piper*, a play written especially for him, Nathan-Turner was impressed by McCoy's energy and the physicality of his performance. 'I definitely started off playing it for laughs,' claimed McCoy, whose style of comedy and his pseudonym (he was born Percy James Patrick Kent-Smith) originated from the Ken Campbell Roadshow. In this travelling group of madcap performers, he distinguished himself by 'setting light to his head, shoving ferrets down his trousers, exploding bombs on his chest, mentally combusting cotton wool and hammering nails up his nose'.[24]

The lightness of McCoy's touch barely lasted beyond his first season, as intimations of a darker nature in the Doctor were introduced in what would turn out to be the last two years of the programme's production. Under the guidance of script editor Andrew Cartmel, proposals were sought after that were not only more 'funky' (Cartmel's term), but also demonstrated more complex motivations from the central characters. Such episodes repaid multiple viewings, and were 'drama created for the video age, destined to be watched again and again rather than viewed and forgotten, as was so much television made ten years earlier'.[25] The series 25 opener, 'Remembrance of the Daleks' (1988), was seen by many critics and long-time fans of the programme as the strongest Dalek story since Tom Baker's 1975 'Genesis of the Daleks' (which also introduced their creator, Davros). The tale suggests that the Doctor is both older than we thought and possesses arcane knowledge of the universe. Again, because of Cartmel's influence, we saw the most drastic alterations to the Doctor's character yet – changes that directly paved the way for the portrayal of his later incarnations in the new show after 2005:

> The idea emerged of the Doctor as a master strategist, manoeuvring his adversaries and manipulating his allies like a galactic chess player—literally so in the case of [the villain] Fenric in 'The Curse of Fenric', although the chess motif was also made explicit in 'Silver Nemesis'.[26]

The development of this theme – especially in the 'Perivale cycle' of stories marked by a dramatic confrontation between the Time Lord and Ace, his unwilling pawn in 'The Curse of Fenric' (1989) – is particularly important for reinforcing the Doctor's status as an anti-hero, a badge he has worn proudly since the early years. It is also significant for contrasting the Doctor's attitude towards the ethics of means and ends with the plans of the scripted villains of each story. In 1989, the year the programme was cancelled, Anthony Ainley's Master made his last television appearance in the aptly named final episode of the classic programme, 'Survival'. Not only is this Ainley's finest performance in the role, but the episode also highlights by contrast the increasingly morally ambiguous nature of the Doctor and his aims.

Timing Malfunction

These late-term decisions to inject more pathos into the Doctor's relationships with his companions and pencil more mystery into the character were the smartest moves made in the 'middle' period of *Doctor Who*, the eight years of Nathan-Turner as producer. But they came to an end in 1989 with the indefinite 'resting' of the show, a decision made by the Controller of the BBC. More than six years passed, in which interval the Virgin series of novels *Doctor Who: The New Adventures* provided more thrills for disappointed fans.

In the cross-Atlantic-produced BBC/Universal Television/Fox Network telemovie *Doctor Who* (1996), these themes resurface dramatically: the Doctor cryptically reveals that he is half human and sizable segments of the plot devolve on the efforts of the eighth Doctor (Paul McGann) to make emotional appeals to a new friend, Dr Grace Holloway (Daphne Ashbrook), and an unlikely enemy, gang member Chang Lee (Yee-Jee Tso). Indeed, as Kim Newman has noted, there is a major shift in the characterisation of the protagonist with McGann's Doctor, who is 'impulsive, open (if the heart is the centre of feeling, this would explain why McGann has emotion enough for two), eager to share knowledge even if he knows he should keep it to himself'.[27] In hindsight, the elements of enhanced character background and relationship development, held in balance with the preservation of the essential mystery of the programme, would be the most significant guideposts as the storytelling of the programme moved into a new phase – a phase that began with a major transformation in how the show would be pitched to a new generation of viewers. One unfortunate consequence of this transformation is that 'many of the idiosyncrasies of the original *Doctor Who* are replaced with standardised tropes and terms' in a twofold effort to make the Doctor more approachable and heroic and to make his universe more comprehensible to fresh audiences.[28] For long-time fans, the 1996 telemovie represented a 'dumbing-down' of *Who*. But, philosophically, the new *Doctor Who* post-1996 shifts away from positivism and the reason- and progress-centred worldview of the Enlightenment and towards Romanticism and the importance of new experiences and diverse sympathies.

According to its most prolific historian, the Enlightenment 'burst upon the European scene in the late seventeenth century with terrifying force', creating an 'unprecedented and, for some, intoxicating, intellectual and spiritual upheaval'.[29] The twin brooms of rationalisation and secularisation not only swept aside magic and belief in the supernatural, but inspired a resurgence of scepticism and paved the way for the scientific revolution. For most of its time on the air, the first incarnation of *Doctor Who* took the prevalent Enlightenment values embedded in the very fabric of the meaning of science fiction as scaffolding for stories: witness stories in which the third Doctor fights against ecological crises on Earth ('The Claws of Axos', 1971; 'The Green Death') and those in which the fourth Doctor topples oppressive regimes on distant planets ('The Sun Makers', 1977; 'State of Decay', 1980).

The adjustment of these ideals and values works in favour of the themes of Romanticism, the period of Euro-American intellectual development usually taken to historically supplant the Enlightenment. It is aptly summarised as the view that 'abstract principle is hollow unless rooted in and expressive of concrete practice' and that 'reality is revealed in the first instance by lived experience, in the life world'.[30] This perspective is reflected not only in the eighth Doctor's Byronesque hair and clothing and the 'Jules Verne' chic of the new TARDIS console room design. It is present in the very reconceptualisation of the reason for the Doctor's wanderings as a voyage of self-discovery. This was affirmed in an unused theme for the adventure translated by telemovie scriptwriter Matthew Jacobs: 'Only when Doctor Who knows who he is will he be able to save us all. Only if you know yourself can you save yourself.'[31] The events that made many old-school fans uncomfortable with producer Philip Segal's *Doctor Who* (the infamous kiss between the Doctor and Grace – now unremarkable in the new version of the show; the Doctor's warnings about friends' and allies' potential futures; his 'hash science' about the beryllium clock and the Eye of Harmony) are precisely what characterises contemporary *Doctor Who* as the romantic's 'science fantasy'. Now, *Who* becomes concerned with the fates of individuals rather than embracing hard science fiction's concern with universal themes of progress or justice. One remarkable scene (of many) in the telemovie that underscores this shift occurs when a motorcycle policeman stops the fleeing Doctor and Grace on the verge of a traffic-jammed motorway. The Doctor pulls Grace aside to tell her, 'I held back death […] I can't make your dream come true forever, Grace, but I can make it come true today. What do you say?'[32]

The rebooted 2005 *Doctor Who* introduces a near-total loss of the Enlightenment ideal. The notion of making the universe a better place to live in is cast into doubt by the catastrophic series of events often referred to by the ninth and tenth Doctors (Christopher Eccleston and David Tennant) as 'the Last Great Time War'. The fallout from this war, together with the Doctor's status as its lone survivor,[33] are the most distinctive motifs of post-2005 *Doctor Who*, helmed by executive producers and 'show-runners' Russell T. Davies (2005–9) and Steven Moffat (2010–present). Davies, already well known for his Channel 4 drama *Queer as Folk*, had been a fan of the original programme since 1966 and, 30 years later, had authored *Damaged Goods*, an entry in Virgin Books' *New Adventures* series of original novels featuring seventh Doctor Sylvester McCoy. *Damaged Goods* provides a partial blueprint for reinventing a legend: 'the urban settings to firmly place the show in the real world, and the monsters and menaces that affect real people with real emotions'.[34] Careful management of the show along these lines, including subtle efforts at humanising the Doctor and his relationships with his companions and those affected by his actions, is largely responsible for the show's new popularity among the non-anorak-wearing set. Jane Tranter, then-Controller of Drama Commissioning for the BBC, explains the popularity in a different way:

> [I]n fact, it's barely sci-fi. *Doctor Who* is bigger than that. We're talking the biggest universal themes, we're talking the essence of who we are and where we live and what we stand for. We're talking about the basic fight between good and evil.[35]

This was a sentiment with which author and editor Harlan Ellison agreed in his introduction to the first US-published

Doctor Who novelisations from Pinnacle Books: 'You, too, can be Doctor Who. You, like the good Doctor, can stand up for that which is bright and bold and true. You can shape the world, if only you'll go and try.'[36]

Last of the Time Lords

But what if 'being Doctor Who' was a less than attractive proposition? Would the programme still be able to retain its lustre? *Doctor Who* from 2005 to the present has muddied this basic distinction between good and evil, producing more realism and greater dramatic effect. It has also sharpened its characterisation of the Doctor by using themes not only from Romanticism but also from philosophical and literary existentialism, represented by figures such as Jean-Paul Sartre (1905–80) and Simone de Beauvoir (1908–86). Homelessness, absurdity, the burdens of freedom, and the essential 'for-itself' isolation of the self are all existentialist themes that appear in the new *Doctor Who*.

The Doctor's good-natured but essentially rootless wandering has since been complicated by his existential *angst*. This, in turn, is largely fuelled by his bitterness over the losses of the Time War, in which he played an unclear but critical role. In Christopher Eccleston's second outing as the ninth Doctor, for example, he allows Lady Cassandra O'Brien – the 'last human' and the primary antagonist of the story – to die in an exceedingly unpleasant way. All he can offer by way of cold comfort is the epitaph, 'Everything has its time and everything dies' ('The End of the World', 2005). In a later episode, the Doctor's horror at being locked in the same room with the last surviving representative of his mortal enemies ('Dalek', 2005) is accentuated by the fact that he previously watched them all burn – along with his own people, the Time Lords. The Doctor's old and antagonistic relationship with the Master (John Simm) – who also apparently survived the Time War – takes on an entirely new dimension as the tenth Doctor, David Tennant, attempts to 'reform' him so that they might travel the universe together. Tennant's incarnation discovers that many of his people, led by the founder of Time Lord society, Rassilon, escaped from a time-locked state within the War and are still alive. However, the tenth Doctor makes the conscious decision to send them back to that state, based on the peril they pose to the cosmos that they once kept watch over. To date, the eleventh Doctor (Matt Smith) seems to have made a certain peace with his singular status, calling himself a 'madman with a box' rather than identifying with the more bellicose epithets 'The Oncoming Storm' or 'Destroyer of Worlds' (*Ka Faraq Gatri*, in the tongue of the planet Skaro). With Smith leaving at the end of 2013 (and intimations of the Time War resurfacing in 'The Name of the Doctor' [2013]), it remains to be seen how this tension will be resolved. For this more whimsical, eccentric version of the Time Lord, the end of the Time War was 'a bad day' when 'bad things happened' ('The Beast Below', 2010).

The programme's treatment of the nature of time itself has also changed dramatically, not only because of its turn away from hard-science positivism, but also because of the much richer, much more strange nature of the cosmos recently revealed to us by quantum physics. Quantum indeterminacy and quantum entanglement – the notions that extremely small particles do not, at any given point in time, have a set location in space, and that these particles influence other particles vastly distant without *causing* these different particles to change – have already begun to force scientists and philosophers to rethink our most basic ideas about the architecture of the universe. *Doctor Who* writers are not known (unlike hard SF writers) for agonising over 'getting the science right'. Yet we have seen progress from the show's early linear and causally deterministic notion of 'time's arrow'. Implications of this view of time include immutability of the past, found in such early episodes as 'The Aztecs' (1964) and 'The Reign of Terror' (1964), and the speculative concept of recurring closed causal time-loops ('The Claws of Axos'; 'Meglos', 1981). The pre-quantum understanding of time lends itself to a view of the 'space–time vortex' that the TARDIS uses to travel as a kind of hyperspace or hypertime. Steven Moffat, though, seems to favour a view of time that compromises between quantum strangeness and the Doctor's own intuitive understanding of his native element. 'People don't understand time – it's not what you think it is', the tenth Doctor claims in the Hugo and BAFTA Award-winning episode 'Blink', written by Moffat. 'People assume that time is a strict progression from cause to effect, but actually – from a non-linear, non-subjective viewpoint – it's more like a big ball of wibbley-wobbley, timey-wimey [...] stuff' ('Blink', 2007). Such are the slogans from which t-shirts are born.

The history of time, as well as the history and canon of *Doctor Who* itself, is not a straight line of unbroken continuity. Among the many intriguing themes explored by the world's longest-running science fantasy programme, its philosophical conundrums and insights simply cannot be summarised in a few pages. From the nature of personal identity to the essence of evil, from the possibility of time travel to the ethics of intervening in history, the philosophy of *Doctor Who* is bigger on the inside than it appears on the outside. Just precisely what goes on in the mind of a 900-year-old alien who adores jelly babies, little shops and Jammie Dodgers? Step through the double doors of that strange blue box that just materialised on your street corner, and we'll begin.

Allons-y!

1

LOST IN TIME

The Uncanny Experience of Wandering in the Fourth Dimension

Who made *Who*?

Answering this question is crucial to understanding the philosophy of *Doctor Who*. This BBC icon is quite different to other, equally long-standing and impressive science fiction franchises like *Star Trek* and *Star Wars*. Yet, from its very beginning, *Doctor Who* has been a child of multiple authors, unlike the sci-fi brainchildren of single creative figures such as Gene Roddenberry, Terry Nation, George Lucas or Joss Whedon. *Doctor Who* novel author, fan and critic, Lance Parkin, notes that the programme 'lacks a clearly identifiable creator', having 'no single authority' either to make rulings on the canonicity of diverse contributions to its 'Whoniverse' or to decide the ultimate direction in which the programme might venture.[1] There are only three stable elements in the programme – the Doctor, his TARDIS, and his 'days like crazy paving' that chart a course between itinerant wandering and saving the known universe. Besides these constants, the formula for good *Doctor Who* seems to rest on mutability, not invariance. To their credit, the creative influences stoking the fires of the programme at its inception were ahead of their time in meshing together an essentially unfathomed, if not unfathomable protagonist, and the premise of time travel. This would prove to be a plot device of potentially infinite permutations. What unique perspective does this afford the peripatetic Time Lord? What's the philosophy of the fellow who always comes first when the credits roll, this 'Doctor Who'?

A short but inestimably valuable document for answering these questions comes from Cecil Edwin Webber, a writer for the BBC's Script Department in 1963, who was little known save as a mutual copyright holder (with writer Anthony Coburn) to the first episode of the programme, 'An Unearthly Child'. Webber's 'General Notes on Background and Approach' – elaborations of the original ideas of then-BBC Head of Drama, Sydney Newman – are worth quoting at length:

> A frail old man lost in time and space. They give him this name ['Doctor Who'] because they don't know who he is. He seems not to remember where he has come from; he is suspicious and capable of sudden malignancy [...] he has a machine which enables them to travel together through time, through space, and through matter [...] He remains a mystery. From time to time the other three discover things about him, which turn out to be false or inconclusive [...] They think he may be a criminal fleeing from his own time.[2]

There are philosophical resonances here for anyone who seriously considers the meaning of Alfred North Whitehead's view that 'Philosophy begins in wonder. And, at the end, when philosophic thought has done its best, the wonder remains.'[3] Academic studies of *Doctor Who* attempting to conceptualise the deep meaning of the programme (compare, for example, *Star Trek*'s themes of humanism and exploration) have focused on the sense of wonder, born from a narrative dialectic of mystery and discovery, that permeates individual episodes, story arcs and even entire series of *Doctor Who*. The human propensity for conflict and change drives the dynamics of both philosophy and television drama. This has been true from the start for *Who*, in which it was conceived that 'the Doctor and his teenage companion would be the doyens of one alien culture, whose morality and attitudes would lead them into opposition with the two human characters'.[4]

What is most remarkable about *Doctor Who* – particularly the 'classic' programme (1963–89) – is how this sense of wonder, 'keep[ing] alive the awe and slight fear felt by strangers in strange lands',[5] is erected on seemingly the flimsiest of foundations – literally. The budget fixed in 1963 for one 25-minute episode was £2,500, roughly £90,100 today (adjusted for inflation, using average earnings) and therefore, as a budget for a half-hour time block, only 20 per cent higher than the *most cheaply made sitcoms* on British television today. And all this for a production that has always been much more technically demanding than its closest competitor programmes in the UK. One historian of the show, Jeremy Bentham, suggests that *Who*'s fragile birth-process typifies a more general grudging British attitude towards SF at the time:

> In Britain, more so than in other countries, science fiction has always had a stigma attached to it. Considering the technical complexities required, televised science fiction has frequently earned less than proportionately balanced critical response. The main body of audiences in the Sixties were adults who tended to regard TV sf as either children's fare, or as trash: an unfounded prejudice probably stemming from unwarranted comparisons with the comic-strip science fiction movie serials of the 1930s and 40s, or with the UK-banned 'horror' comics of the 1950s.[6]

Without a doubt, serials such as *The Quatermass Experiment* and its sequels, *Target Luna* and the *Pathfinders* series of broadcasts, formed the exception to this rule and, at the same time, were highly influential in the creation of *Doctor Who*. A 1962 BBC Survey Group Report on Science Fiction, examining the potential for the genre, noted that

> it is significant that SF is not itself a wildly popular branch of fiction – nothing like, for example, detective and thriller fiction. It doesn't appeal much to women and largely finds its

public in the technically minded younger groups. SF is a most fruitful and exciting area of exploration – but so far has not shown itself capable of supporting a large population.[7]

The writers of the report, Donald Bull and Alice Frick, noted that the most popular SF theme for a broad audience was 'Threat and Disaster' – which *Doctor Who* would later adapt into one of its most prevalent storylines, the 'base under siege' scenario that frames episodes from 1966's 'The Tenth Planet' to 2009's 'The Waters of Mars' and beyond.

Contrasted with their lacklustre appreciation for television SF, the BBC's audience had not quite yet ended their honeymoon period with edifying television, and the potential for *Doctor Who*'s pedagogical power outweighed any weaknesses the programme might have as a drama. 'At the beginning,' Tulloch and Alvarado claim, '*Doctor Who* was seriously concerned with helping to teach history and science.'[8] Upon close examination, only the original 1963–4 series' historicals ('Marco Polo'; 'The Aztecs'; 'The Reign of Terror') and one story each from the following two seasons, 'The Crusade' (1965) and 'The Massacre of St Bartholomew's Eve' (1966), earn high marks for teaching history seriously. While the production team in these instances clearly pays greater attention to detail and carefully avoids anachronisms, all these stories are told straightforwardly through the lens of dramatic conflict.

Yet, despite the Doctor's characteristic pro-science, anti-supernatural stance, *Doctor Who*'s own record on scientific education was not as robust. Tulloch and Alvarado explain this odd fact by noting that 'the programme has not been surrounded by the plethora of professional and university scientists that the early science fiction magazines in the USA had on their editorial boards'.[9] They also note that *Doctor Who*'s educative underpinnings can be traced far more clearly to 'the investigation of different cultures through space and time, rather than seeking an involvement with hard science'.[10] In turn, this is carried out in the context of a *Pygmalion*-like relationship of tutelage and coaching between Doctor and companion that resolves in the most memorable teamings: the second Doctor and Jamie McCrimmon; the fourth Doctor and Leela; the seventh Doctor and Ace; the ninth Doctor and Rose. While the admitted paternalism of this relationship diminishes as it evolves, it was first a clever way, in more conservative TV days, of teaming a male and female without reference to a romantic relationship. When confronted by 'the shock of the new', the difference in values and stances between the seasoned time traveller and the starry-eyed rookie has been another of the dramatic selling points of *Doctor Who* throughout its long run. It began with an itinerant wanderer through the universe who, because of his admiration for the human race, becomes a teacher to some of them, all within the context of an edifying television programme aimed at placing its young viewers squarely in the middle of the action. In its beginnings, at least, *Doctor Who* provided a perfect convergence of identification between the Doctor's young companions and its target audience.

A Positive Triumph

Like its American counterparts, adventurous British television SF of this period often framed its narratives not only in terms of educational impact but also in terms of the possibilities afforded by new technology. Particularly in *Doctor Who* episodes from the 1960s and 70s, the promises and pitfalls of applied technology – from oil drilling in the North Sea, to microcomputing, to nuclear power – drive numerous plots. The very premises of the show rely on the Doctor's credentials as 'every kind of scientist', and the Doctor's TARDIS[11] – a cross between a spaceship and a magic portal to distant worlds – presents itself as the ultimate expression of the expectation of rational solutions to society's problems. This is the basis for scientific empiricism and its modern philosophical programme, *positivism*.[12]

The first positivist was the philosopher of science and self-described 'sociologist', Auguste Comte (1798–1857). Previous to Comte's work, philosophical examinations of changeable human nature had been considered mere 'anthropology', inferior to what we today would call the physical sciences. Comte created a periodisation of humanity's efforts to explain strange phenomena and gain further control over its environment. According to him, we have passed through two stages – the religious and the metaphysical – and are embarking on the last stage: the scientific.

The question then was, according to Comte, what to do with religious or metaphysical claims that might compete with scientific claims? The critical tool that many positivists found most useful for advancing a 'science of human nature' was Hume's Fork, named after the Scottish philosopher, historian and *bon vivant* David Hume (1711–76). Hume claimed that all assertions – for example, 'TARDIS is an acronym having six letters' or 'The Sontaran clones number in the billions' – could be separated into two classes. The first example is what Hume calls a 'relation of ideas', which comprises definitions and mathematical-geometrical formulae that are axiomatic, necessarily true and tautologous. The relation of ideas specified by 'All triangles have three internal angles' is true of every triangle, past, present and future, but it gives us no new information about triangles that we didn't already know from the definition of 'triangle'. On the other hand, the second example regarding Sontarans is a 'matter of fact', an assertion that is neither axiomatic nor necessarily true, and which requires observations of states of affairs in the world to determine its truth. Thus, every statement we could make about the world – scientific, theological, ethical – would either be a relation of ideas, a matter of fact, or neither, in which case the statement could be classed as meaningless.

This would provide a tool capable of dethroning (but not destroying) theology and metaphysics. In its methods, positivism 'was both descriptive and normative, describing how human thought had in fact evolved and prescribing norms for how our thinking [...] should proceed'.[13] Its nineteenth- and twentieth-century appeal was rooted in the popularisation of the fruits of the scientific revolution, before there was any critical public understanding of the difference between 'science' and 'non-science'. Perhaps Comte was naively optimistic when he claimed that in the medieval and early modern periods of Western intellectual history, 'the primitive speculative exercises of mankind originated a theological philosophy which was modified more and more, and at length destroyed, without any possibility of its being replaced'.[14] But, historically, his view not only retrieved the promise of the French Revolution from its nadir in the Reign of Terror; it also bound together two *Weltanschauungen* – two worldviews – that dominated European thought in the nineteenth century. One of these was the belief in inevitable human progress; the other was a kind of evolutionary ethics, which at that time implied that the intellectual elite ought to explicitly support broad social processes (like Herbert Spencer's 'social survival of the fittest') that were going on in any case.

The development of societies and economies through stages expressing a coherent, logical vision was not unique to Comte, but also distinguished the thought of the Germans Georg W.F. Hegel (1770–1831), Johann Fichte (1762–1814) and, of course, Karl Marx (1818–83). While this theme of the upwardly progressive movement of history might have been lost by the twentieth century, its normative force as an idea critical of non-empirical metaphysics and theology was sustained. In his short book *Language, Truth and Logic*, A.J. Ayer (1910–89) popularised and succinctly summed up a distinctly 'logical' positivism as the view that 'there is no field of experience which cannot, in principle, be brought under some form of scientific law, and no type of speculative knowledge about the world which it is, in principle, beyond the power of science to give'.[15] The slogan of the 'Vienna Circle', a formal working group of logical empiricist philosophers and scientists founded in 1924, was 'the scientific world-conception serves life and life receives it'.[16] The most general aim of the group was an essentially Comtean one: to permeate culture with the ethos of logical argumentation and the explanatory power of science in an effort to replace metaphysical or theological *Weltanschauungen* with a scientific 'world-conception'. What positivism and logical empiricism were advocating was no less than a new phase to the Enlightenment.

Of course, there are always at least six degrees of separation between how an idea is deployed in philosophy and how it appears in popular culture. Nonetheless, philosophical positivism and empiricism in SF literature are foregrounded as the master ideas behind what is often called 'hard science fiction', a term coined in 1957. The nursery for hard science fiction was found in the exponential scientific and technological growth of the early twentieth century. Its proving-ground was the 1950s and 60s, when *Sputnik* and Project Mercury seemed to confirm that space was 'viewed as the forefront of active life, the region where the future is made rather than talked about or run away from'.[17] In the view of David G. Hartwell, co-editor of the *Year's Best Science Fiction* anthologies and an historian of science fiction, hard SF can be recognised by the following characteristics:

- It is didactic, making points about contemporary life through a radical distancing from the here and now, although its conclusions are made 'not usually through insight into human character but through insight into the mechanics of the universe, true in all times and places'.[18]
- It rests firmly on the conception of a determined universe, structured by scientific laws and facts, and known by scientific method.
- Its appeal to its audience supports their faith that 'knowledge has meaning', that 'the universe is ultimately knowable and that human problems [...] are solvable through science and technology'.[19]
- Finally, it often assumes its audience can take the same point of view as it is written from – a 'god's-eye' point of view that, according to Hartwell, requires 'great aesthetic distance'.[20]

Positivism was ably represented in the period of *Doctor Who*'s genesis by American authors such as Isaac Asimov and Hal Clement, and in British SF by Sir Arthur C. Clarke. Many of their successes can be attributed to the way in which their fiction capitalised on the potential for secular salvation represented by technology and a scientific understanding of human nature. This was a dream that, while appearing desperate in tone in SF of the 1930s (for example, Jack Williamson's 1938 *Legion of Time*, which made accessible the ideas of causal determinism and alternate futures), became increasingly more upbeat over the next three decades. It was fuelled, no doubt, by the novelty of American and Russian space missions, which represented a transformation in human abilities not merely of scale, but upwards towards an entirely different stratum.

Elements of the positivistic or empiricist worldview abound in early *Doctor Who*, particularly in the period from 1963 to around 1974, when a pro-science, pro-technology attitude was seen as the key philosophical guidepost available to the scriptwriters charged with making future-based *Doctor Who* stories edifying. Many plots were driven – especially in the Hartnell and Troughton years – by the Doctor's scientific superiority as well as his curiosity. Take this exchange from 'An Unearthly Child', for instance. Ian and Barbara have entered the TARDIS for the first time, and Ian claims that it all must be an illusion:

DOCTOR: *(coughing)* You don't understand, so you find excuses. Illusions, indeed? You say you can't fit an enormous building into one of your smaller sitting rooms?
IAN: No.
DOCTOR: But you've discovered television, haven't you?
IAN: Yes ...
DOCTOR: Then by showing an enormous building on your television screen, you can do what seemed impossible, couldn't you?
IAN: Well ... yes, but I still don't know ...
DOCTOR: It's not quite clear, is it? I can see by your face that you're not certain. You don't understand. *(He laughs.)* And I knew you wouldn't! Never mind. Now then, which switch was it ...? No, no, no ... Ah yes, that is it! *(He flips the switch.)* The point is not whether you understand ... *(He turns back to Ian.)* What is going to happen to you, hmm?[21]

Typically, the Doctor's sense of scientific superiority is used to break technological deadlocks that other characters have failed to deal with. In the episodes 'The Sensorites' (1964) and 'The Ark' (1966), the Doctor crafts remedies for poisons and viruses that manage to confound the scientifically advanced civilisations he visits. On the planet Vortis, he deals with the unusual phenomenon of organic technology and the mind-control of giant insects ('The Web Planet', 1965). The Doctor's eccentric, yet brilliant problem solving is characteristically deployed in the face of force used in vain and the defeatism of others in 1964's 'The Dalek Invasion of Earth'. Trapped in a cell aboard the enemy's space-going saucer, the Doctor and Ian are filled in by another prisoner, Jack Craddock, as to how the monstrous Daleks invaded the Earth in the twenty-second century. Rather than give up, the Doctor analyses a device in the cell obviously made for Dalek manipulators, and concludes that it must hold the key to their escape. The Doctor struggles to find the 'correct refractive index' for the device, while Craddock derides his efforts. 'They have only contempt for human intellect,' the Doctor says to him, referencing their alien captors, 'and if all their prisoners are like you, I'm not so sure they're wrong.'[22] Stories from later Hartnell seasons provide instances of other familiar positivistic hard SF tropes, from the epic space opera and temporal shenanigans of the 12-part story 'The Dalek Masterplan' (1965–6) to the 'life-force' draining machines and the Doctor's strange 'Reacting Vibrator' of 'The Savages' (1966).

Throughout, the Doctor steadfastly defends the scientific method and espouses philosophical naturalism: the view that the methods of philosophical inquiry ought to more or less align with those of science. He is also a harsh critic of supernatural or occult explanations for phenomena. In 1971's 'The Dæmons', companion Jo Grant sets the third Doctor a difficult problem that illustrates the 'anti-metaphysical' arguments of positivism: 'Suppose something was to happen and nobody knew the explanation,' she says, trying to convince the Doctor that the magical 'age of Aquarius' has finally arrived. 'Well, nobody in the world – in the universe! Well, that would be magic, wouldn't it?'[23]

Jo's position has the flavour of what is often called a 'god of the gaps' argument. These arguments infer the need to posit a supernatural force because of the possibility of inexplicable, yet very real occurrences (like miracles). There are two immediate problems with Jo's view: first, it needs to be shown (and not merely assumed) that mysterious phenomena are *inexplicable* rather than merely currently unexplained. The Doctor makes a counter-argument by demonstrating the ability of his yellow roadster, Bessie, to drive around the tarmac seemingly on its own. Jo's amazement is short-lived when the Doctor reveals a remote control device as the source of the illusion, converting the 'inexplicable' to the easily explained.

The second issue with Jo's argument is philosophically more interesting. In the case of a genuinely dumbfounding occurrence, how would we know that there is no one in the entire universe who knows an explanation for it? And would the lack of a known explanation necessarily imply that there was no explanation? These questions became the focus of key twentieth-century European thinkers influential to positivism and the logical empiricists of the Vienna Circle. These included Ludwig Wittgenstein and his book *Tractatus Logico-Philosophicus* and Rudolf Carnap, author of *The Logical Construction of the World*. Wittgenstein and Carnap utilised the conceptual resources of logic and science to erect a systematic approach for addressing what could and could not be counted as legitimate explanations. The approach, widely popularised as 'logical positivism' by Ayer's *Language, Truth and Logic* but also called 'logical empiricism', was based on Wittgenstein's 'principle of verifiability'. In effect, this principle responds to Jo Grant's appeal, saying (a) that any claim regarding a mysterious phenomenon, to be meaningful, would have to meet strict 'rules of observation' in its description, and (b) that a meaningful potential explanation of that phenomenon would have to be, in principle, verifiable by exacting logical or empirical standards. The focus on meaning here replaces the early modern epistemological question asked by figures such as John Locke and René Descartes: 'How do we know with certainty that something is the case?'[24]

Wittgenstein claimed (and Moritz Schlick of the Vienna Circle coined the slogan) that 'the meaning of a proposition is the method of its verification'.[25] The mere possibility that a particular proposition, such as 'The Doctor restarted the universe using the Pandorica and a second Big Bang', could be actualised is no proof that it is meaningful. For Wittgenstein, 'it is the deep logical grammar of language that governs how its elements combine to form propositions and also which propositions follow from which others'.[26] We can see this in his *Tractatus*, wherein 'names' are the fundamental units bearing meaning while each such name correlates with an 'object' in the world. At a more complex level in which names are conjoined in logically well-formed sentences, propositions 'picture' certain states of affairs in the world. Meaningful propositions are not only those that 'picture' true states of affairs, but also those that, while not directly *observed*, can be *inferred* from other true propositions. This, then, is the idea of verifiability in Wittgenstein and the Vienna Circle. Meanwhile, Ayer's 'modified verification principle' takes on board the scientific virtue of recognising human fallibility – our ability to get it wrong even in the best of times. It doesn't demand that every proposition be 'conclusively verifiable', but instead,

> that some possible sense-experience should be relevant to the determination of its truth or falsehood. If a putative proposition fails to satisfy this principle, and is not a tautology, then I hold that it is metaphysical, and that, being metaphysical, it is neither true nor false but literally senseless. It will be found that much of what ordinarily passes for philosophy is metaphysical according to this criterion, and, in particular, that it can not be significantly asserted that there is a non-empirical world of values, or that men have immortal souls, or that there is a transcendent God.[27]

While Wittgenstein was to write a later book (*Philosophical Investigations*) picking apart his own theory, particularly its reliance on the idea of propositions 'picturing' reality, and while Ayer eventually resolved that the main problem with logical positivism was that 'nearly all of it was false',[28] it is important to remember that logical positivism or empiricism is a philosophical position that reflects a longitudinal segment of the empiricist mindset in general. It not only represents an active force of cultural secularisation, but also proposes a 'logical', if not wholly scientific, approach to Western ethics, which seemed increasingly poised to slide into relativism in the later twentieth century. Its own drawbacks alone do not show that philosophical analysis ought to avoid focusing on language as the carrier of meaning, or that the reduction of complex fields of phenomena to simpler ones cannot be the task of a critical philosophy.

Doctor Who has proved that it is comfortable holding its own positivist origins in tension with its respect for limits of experience and the potentially unverifiable. In the early stages of what could be called its 'post-positivist' era (from 1974 to the present), the programme's production staff often went to great pains to ridicule the idea of the kind of organised scientific hegemony proposed by the supporters of Unified Science as a replacement religion or, worse, as a cult. 'Robot' (1974–5), Tom Baker's first outing as the Doctor, demonstrates that even the most helpful and informative members of the 'Think Tank' organisation can turn out to be little more than scientifically literate fascists – here in the form of the Scientific Reform Society. Closer to the end of Baker's tenure, the society of the planet Tigella in 'Meglos' is divided between deeply devotional Deons and scoffing, rationalist Savants. Uncharacteristically, the Doctor doesn't land on Tigella by accident, but is summoned by the planetary leader to head off a potential culture war because the Doctor 'sees the threads that bind the universe and mends them when they break'. Much earlier than these stories, though, the strongest anti-positivist story from *Doctor Who*'s first decade must be counted as 'The Tomb of the Cybermen' (1967), starring Patrick Troughton. The villain of the piece, Eric Klieg (George Pastell), finances an archaeological expedition to the planet Telos, reported to be a base of the Cybermen, who have largely disappeared from the galaxy. When Klieg schemes to revivify the Cybermen from their icy hibernation in the bowels of the planet, he informs the expedition leader that he is a member of the 'Brotherhood of Logicians' and thus his motivation is 'logic, my dear Professor, logic and power. On Earth the Brotherhood of Logicians is the greatest intelligence man ever assembled. But that is not enough, we need power. Power to put our ability into action. The Cybermen have this power.' Klieg's logic in thinking the Cybermen will prove reliable allies is faulty, and the Doctor knows better:

> **DOCTOR:** Yes, as you say, such a combination between intelligence and power would make you formidable indeed! Why you'd be commander of the *universe* with your brilliance! It … it makes the imagination *reel* with the possibilities!
> **KLIEG:** Why Doctor, if I had only known you shared my imagination. You might even have worked for me!
> **DOCTOR:** Perhaps it's not too *late*?
> **JAMIE:** *Doctor!*
> **DOCTOR:** No Jamie, don't you see? Don't you see what this is going to all mean to those who come to serve '*Klieg the all powerful*'? Why, no country, no person would dare to have a single thought that was not your own! Eric Klieg's own conception of the … of the way of life!
> **KLIEG:** Brilliant! Yes … yes you're right. Master of the world! *(He smiles, gazing into the distance.)*
> **DOCTOR:** And now I *know* you're mad, I just wanted to make sure.[29]

Again, the Doctor sees further. What separates *Doctor Who* from hard SF – indeed, the programme is more properly called 'science fantasy', with the only SF elements in some episodes being the alien Doctor and his time vehicle – is the consistent *de jure* commitment of the production team to science and physicalist explanations, while *de facto* they take full advantage of Arthur C. Clarke's famous 'Third Law': 'Any sufficiently advanced technology is indistinguishable from magic.'[30] However, this blurring of the lines between hard-headed rationalism and the fantastic limits of the possible is better epitomised, in my own estimation, by how Clarke's 'First Law' resonates with the first Doctor's adventures: 'When a distinguished but elderly scientist states that something is possible, he is almost certainly right. When he states that something is impossible, he is very probably wrong.'[31]

The Doctor regularly flirts with sufficiently advanced pseudo-science like the trusty 'slightly psychic paper' and the sonic screwdriver. He manifests a kind of practical knowledge that seems to be uncanny for a human. Before he has even set foot in the new Post Office Tower, where he meets the supercomputer WOTAN in 'The War Machines' (1966), the first Doctor has a small fit, telling his companion, 'You know, there's something alien about that tower! I can sense it!' He claims that he gets the same feeling whenever the Daleks are near. Much later, the fourth Doctor will ape his own heightened sensibilities by pronouncing that his hair curling is a sign that 'it's either going to rain ... or that I'm on to something'. The ability of the Doctor to take in far more knowledge than seems feasible from a simple examination of his environment echoes the notion from early modern philosophy of an 'intellectual intuition'. This would be an act of perception in which one gains seemingly inscrutable knowledge directly from the five senses without the necessity of coming to a judgement about them or applying concepts to them. It is a bit of narrative genius that firmly places *Doctor Who* in the science fantasy camp, and yet it is philosophically troublesome.

Into the Uncanny

Readers who are very familiar with the programme under discussion, particularly in its rebooted form from 2005 to the present, have probably been struggling for an understanding of precisely how to characterise the Doctor as a positivist. Admirers of the Doctor's romantic, humanist side might note the significant variance between the Doctor's status as an advocate of science, on the one hand, versus the slip into *scientism*, on the other. This is, of course, a variance that depends on any particular Doctor's era. Scientism, a view at least some positivists held, claims that the methods of science, applied to any area of human inquiry (including politics and ethics), can produce better results than a non-scientific approach. In contradistinction to many pieces of hard SF-inspired fiction, *Doctor Who* often subverts scientistic pretensions: in the first series alone, the plot strands of 'The Daleks' (1964) are woven through the almost crystallised, neutron-bomb-devastated landscape of the planet Skaro, highlighting writer Terry Nation's fascination with the outcomes of technological warfare, while 'The Edge of Destruction' (1964) – still the programme's only 'bottle show' confining all the action to the interior of the TARDIS – surprised viewers with the intimation that the Doctor's ship is not merely an implausibly complex machine, but has a degree of sentience and intentionality. In 'The Massacre of St Bartholomew's Eve', the humanist side of the Doctor emerges at the end of a harrowing adventure in which a young Protestant girl, Anne Chaplet, is left to the mercy of the Catholic guards on the eponymous eve. '[H]istory sometimes gives us a terrible shock, and that is because we don't quite fully understand. Why should we?' he asks Steven Taylor (Peter Purves), his companion. 'After all, we're all too small to realise its final pattern. Therefore don't try and judge it from where you stand.' The corruptibility of chemical scientists was explored in the *Silent Spring* storyline of 'Planet of the Giants' (1965), and in 'The Macra Terror' (1967), on a colony world controlled by mutant crabs in the future, the second Doctor claims that 'reason is the last thing you must expect in this or any other world'.[32] While none of these instances demonstrates a complete rejection of the reliance on scientific methods, the history of Western philosophy is often written as if its audience must come down on one side or another of a tradition, supporting either positivism or pure faith.[33]

For another thing, the Doctor is as much a *phenomenologist* as he is a physicist or computer scientist. He is not only attentive to the phenomena or, in simpler terms, 'extremely good at recognising things so obvious that nobody else sees them at all',[34] but he derives great pleasure and significance from the simplest elements of experience. Against the leader of a platoon of Cybermen, creatures that have engineered emotions away entirely, the fifth Doctor rails, 'When did you last have the pleasure of smelling a flower, watching a sunset, eating a well-prepared meal?' The Cyber-leader claims, 'These things are irrelevant', to which the Doctor replies, 'For some people, small, beautiful events is what life is all about!'[35]

As a way of philosophising, phenomenology questions what is taken for granted in scientific observation and generalisation. Edmund Husserl's (1859–1938) method for phenomenology makes a fundamental discovery: the world that positivism 'strips bare' through the principle of verifiability is not the world as it really is, but is an abstraction from a common, 'lived' world. The practices of scientific and mathematical modelling of the world presuppose a meaningful yet transparent 'natural standpoint' of experience:

> Perhaps I am busied with pure numbers and the laws they symbolise: nothing of this sort is present in the world around me, this world of 'real fact'. And yet the world of numbers also is there for me, as the field of objects with which I am arithmetically busied [...] *The arithmetical world is there for me only when and so long as I occupy the arithmetical standpoint.* But the *natural* world, the world in the ordinary sense of the word, is *constantly there for me*, so long as I live naturally and look in its direction. I am then at the '*natural standpoint*', which is just another way of stating the same thing.[36]

Husserl contributes a new understanding of what constitutes *awareness*, emphasising not only the need to 'shift frames' to take in detail properly (he calls this 'bracketing') but also our attentiveness to the 'life-world', a layer of pre-theoretical experience 'to be inserted between the world of nature and the world of culture (or spirit)' that should be seen as 'the ultimate horizon of human experience'.[37] While the Doctor can play the role of the alien, he is also able to isolate portions of the human life-world obscure to the rest of us for further inquiry. In 'The Beast Below', the eleventh Doctor repeatedly uses *Sherlock*-like inference to the best explanation to draw startling conclusions from the appearance of a crying child, urging companion Amy Pond, 'Look closer. Secrets and shadows. Lives led in fear.' A porcelain mask and perfectly still glasses of water on a moving starship also prove to be important, if unlikely, clues to the mystery at the heart of the episode.

Beyond Edmund Husserl's focus on the distinctive type of knowledge that phenomenology brings to the table, a crucial phenomenological element in *Doctor Who*'s formula is our sense of the *uncanny*, or what Kingsley Amis generally calls 'a non-rational sense of insecurity'.[38] If positivism proceeds as though the underlying structure of the universe is fundamentally rationally ascertainable, the phenomenological philosophy of Martin Heidegger (1889–1976) plumbs the dark possibility that our being is fundamentally irrational (or, at best, *a*rational). Heidegger's frequent use of the term *unheimlich*, the 'uncanny',[39] underscores the sentiments of Susan Foreman's teacher Barbara Wright as she waits in the fog outside a lonely junkyard in 'An Unearthly Child': 'It's silly, isn't it? I feel frightened … as if we're about to interfere in something that is best left alone.' The specific nature of Barbara's fear is intriguing, Heidegger would say, because it has no object – it is *of the unknown*. '*All fear finds its ground in dread*,' he claims, and 'dread can "befall" us right in the midst of the most familiar environment.'[40]

Barbara was more or less correct. She and Ian would soon be meeting the Doctor, the 'ultimate outsider', a character possessing an alien *je ne sais quoi* that Verity Lambert, the first producer of the programme, called 'totally anti-establishment' – even to the extent of alienating those more traditionally against the establishment.[41] As Jim Leach observes, 'Although the Doctor is a scientist, he has an ingrained distrust of technology, and his use of the scientific method is much more flexible than those human scientists who simply dismiss anything that cannot be explained rationally.'[42] As a result, he is also deeply humanistic in his attitudes. Even when he occasionally plays the mythological 'trickster' role (Patrick Troughton's high jinks in 'The Highlanders' as the German 'Doktor von Wer' and Matt Smith's 'I'm a monk' scene in 'A Good Man Goes to War' [2011] come immediately to mind), the Doctor struggles to reconcile the limited cosmological perspective of his (usually twentieth-century-human) fellow travellers with his greater knowledge and technological prowess. A potential new companion's acid test is when she first steps through the TARDIS doors and attempts to wrap her mind around the impossibility of a larger space contained inside a smaller one. We must imagine that the discontinuity (were it real) would be wrenching enough to be felt viscerally. One fellow time traveller who required rather less support after entering the Doctor's ship was Leela (Louise Jameson), a member of a 'primitive' tribe from the far future which was really the remnants of a degenerated human colony. In 'The Robots of Death' (1977) the fourth Doctor explains trans-dimensionality to Leela by placing a large box on the TARDIS's central console some distance from where she holds a considerably smaller box. This forced perspective brings her to acknowledge that the larger box *appears* smaller, just so long as it is further away:

> **DOCTOR:** Now which one is larger?
> **LEELA:** *(pointing to the large box on the console)* That one.
> **DOCTOR:** But it looks smaller.
> **LEELA:** Well, that's because it's further away.
> **DOCTOR:** Exactly. If you could keep that exactly that distance away and have it here, the large one would fit inside the small one.
> **LEELA:** That's silly.
> **DOCTOR:** That's trans-dimensional engineering, a key Time Lord discovery.[43]

The Doctor often claims that he is 'of no fixed abode', and the TARDIS's status as a mobile headquarters for the wanderings of Time Lord and companions is a further gesture towards the *unheimlich* themes of *Doctor Who*. Efforts at fleshing out the daily life of the TARDIS crew by showing bedrooms, food machines – even a swimming pool – never seem to last for long. Just as the location of the Doctor's vehicle is constantly in flux, so the interior seems to be as well.

Companions and enemies alike boggle at the capacities of the Doctor's TARDIS, which is the most advanced piece of scientific equipment they've ever seen. Yet this 'Time and Relative Dimension(s) in Space' machine is capricious, erratic, unreliable and (sometimes, quite literally) seems to have a mind of its own. This lack of fit between the ultra-sophisticated device and its anachronistic-looking operator is exploited profitably in *Doctor Who* to motivate a variety of storylines, particularly the creepy telepathic presence driving the TARDIS crew to violence in 1964's 'The Edge of Destruction'. The TARDIS's ability to travel anywhere in time and space has a contestable value – blessing or curse? – that is increasingly presented as the most important theme of the show. Evidence of this tension ranges from the very first episode in which the Doctor protests to a companion, 'But you can't rewrite history. Not one line!'[44] to the remarkable story arc of the 2011 series, in which the Doctor is shot and killed in the first act of the first episode and the rest of the series is spent trying both to save him and to find out 'whodunnit'. Of course, the uncanny nature of time travel, both in the inscrutability of its premise and in its wildly unpredictable consequences, is not an original theme. It dates back to *The Time Machine*, H.G. Wells's 1895 novella that was also the inspiration for the Doctor's exploits.

One of the most poignant themes of Wells's *Time Machine* is the anxiety that the time traveller faces whenever he contemplates how far he is from home and whether he will ever see that home again.[45] It seems that SF's time machines are constructed not merely as vehicles but as vehicles of radical *emigration*. The TARDIS takes young people yearning for adventure away from their homes, occasionally makes them homesick, often deposits them in new homes, and allows the Doctor to avoid a home that he despises and that he later claims he destroyed. The centrelessness of the Doctor's travels is one of the programme's unique charms. But why all this not-being-at-home is significant as a *phenomenological* theme may not be immediately clear.

As this discussion of the uncanny indicates, phenomenology, while just as concerned with truth and knowledge as positivism, treats the question of the nature and justification of knowledge as an occasional focus within a far wider field of human experience. Phenomenologists don't circumscribe the range of human experience narrowly, as was done by earlier theorists like Locke and Immanuel Kant, both of whom claimed to have found the limits of our capability to know the world and ourselves. However, Husserl often referred to the human ability to be affected by our environment in rich and diverse ways as 'transcendence', and referred to the limits of the life-world as a 'horizon', which is constantly shifting temporally and culturally. Existential phenomenologists like Heidegger, Simone de Beauvoir and Jean-Paul Sartre described human existence (as opposed to biology or psychology) in terms of the fundamental attitude towards change and 'becoming'. This is the attitude of projecting cares and projects into the not-yet-determined future: a comportment unique in the world because of the promise of human freedom and the recognition of the fullness of one's possibilities. The human way of being, what Heidegger calls *Dasein*, is sketched richly and suggestively, if not always clearly or comprehensively, by the existentialists' foregrounding of concepts like 'freedom', 'existence' and 'authenticity'. Other examinations of theirs falling outside the remit of science (at least that of the time) focused on the understanding of fundamental 'structures' of first-person subjectivity: moods and emotions. Despite the fact that he is not human, the Doctor amalgamates and concentrates some of the most distinctive phenomenological elements of Heidegger's *Dasein*. The Doctor is ontologically akin to *Dasein* because he '*is*, though as the *being-on-the way* of itself to *itself*', in Heidegger's words. In a constant flurry of action – particularly in his younger-looking incarnations – the Doctor is always ahead of himself. The preternatural drive in the Doctor's being to seek out danger is *unheimlich* itself, in the sense that he is always taking an 'anticipatory leap forward: not positing an end, but reckoning with being-on-the-way, giving *it* free play, disclosing it, holding fast to *being-possible*'.[46] Heidegger was undoubtedly thinking of the Doctor when he approvingly quoted Søren Kierkegaard: 'Life can be interpreted only after it has been lived.'

The existential phenomenologist's view of what is most foundational in human experience contrasts rather starkly with that of the positivists using Hume's Fork. The latter are concerned with answering the question 'How are our assertions about the world meaningful?' in terms of cognition and truth, while existential phenomenology takes a pre-cognitive stance, one we might call 'practical-orientative'. So, when Heidegger writes, 'To the everydayness of being-in-the-world there belongs certain modes of concern', he means not only that authentic existence requires no proof of the external world but also that our 'way of being-in-the-world' is characterised by the dually cognitive *and* affective stance of concern or 'care'.[47] We are 'always already' living in a world shot through with meaning and significance, even before we start to make or assess claims to knowledge.

It goes without saying that the Doctor's curiosity and extended sense of care (particularly for planet Earth) has placed him and his companions in trouble innumerable times. He also waxes existential from time to time; when the fourth Doctor is asked whether he is from outer space, he replies, 'I'm more from what you would call inner time' ('The Stones of Blood', 1978). Most often, however, the Doctor simply sighs in the face of his Heideggerian homelessness. There seem to be three chapters to the Doctor's dispossession. Throughout the 1960s, the Doctor offers few details of his origin. The place in which he would belong is a blank, a pure negation. Both where he comes from and the source of his authority are constantly in question, particularly at key points when he engages foes of cosmic proportions like the Monk, a less benevolent fellow time traveller, and the mad, surreal Celestial Toymaker. In 'The Massacre of St Bartholomew's Eve', he proposes that a cure for his melancholy could be to return home, but he simply cannot.

With the second Doctor's trial at the conclusion of 'The War Games' (1969) and his forcible regeneration, his relationship to his fellow Time Lords (now revealed) transforms into an adversarial one. Now the Doctor must play the role of anti-authoritarian agent. He is set against both his own people and the martial excesses of UNIT, the paramilitary organisation introduced in 'The Invasion' (1968). Thus the programme's central character is recast as a renegade or pariah, with the Time Lords representing an advanced yet officious, stagnant and ultimately corrupt culture.[48] This representation of the Doctor reaches its apogee in the avant-garde figure of the fourth Doctor, who uses the Time Lords' own Byzantine political code against them to allow alien invaders to occupy Gallifrey ('The Invasion of Time', 1978), and in the breathlessly active fifth Doctor, running away from his homeworld yet again despite the Time Lords' professed need for him to step in as president in 'The Five Doctors'.

For twenty-first-century, 'new' *Doctor Who*, producer Russell T. Davies would change the dynamic of home and homelessness for the Doctor yet again, giving the eponymous Time Lord the credit (or blame?) for entirely destroying Gallifrey at the conclusion of the Last Great Time War. This was a radical change in the show, but it had been tried before, namely in the novel series published by BBC Books between 1997 and 2005. A particularly baroque entry in that series by Peter Anghelides and Stephen Cole, *The Ancestor Cell*, has the eighth Doctor confronting Faction Paradox, a voodoo-like cult of Gallifreyans, and destroying Gallifrey as a result. For the new television series, Russell Davis opined:

> I wanted the Doctor to be a loner [...] That's why the Time Lords had to go, it was a programme coming back with an awful lot of mythology and back story, and I wanted to give it a background in which fans and brand new viewers would be on a level playing field.[49]

Russell believed that audiences would be more existentially empathetic when watching a lonely traveller than when seeing someone claiming, 'I come from a great big planet full of powerful people.' Little is said about Gallifrey until 'Gridlock' (2007), when the tenth Doctor finally opens up to fellow traveller Martha Jones, a cathartic moment when he mentions losing 'family and friends' in the Time War. 'Oh, you should have seen it! That old planet,' he sighs. 'The second sun would rise in the south, and the mountains would shine.

The leaves on the trees were silver, when they caught the light, every morning it looked like a forest on fire. When the autumn came, a brilliant glow through the branches.'

While the Doctor exhibits melancholia for an actual *place*, existential phenomenology posits an analogous *metaphysical* homelessness that has the potential to affect anyone, even those of us who haven't locked the last members of our species in a time-loop for eternity. *Doctor Who*'s sense of the uncanny is tied to the metaphysical homelessness of its protagonist in at least two ways. Because the Doctor and company always pull up stakes at the end of each adventure, there is a pervasive lack of closure to his involvement in affairs and a lingering sense of the unfinished and absent. For the existential phenomenologist, how we face this lack of closure determines the degree to which our response to our own freedom is authentic. Simone de Beauvoir explains:

> One may hesitate to make oneself a lack of being, one may withdraw before existence, or one may falsely assert oneself as being, or assert oneself as nothingness. One may realise his freedom only as an abstract independence, or, on the contrary, reject with despair the distance which separates us from being.[50]

We can also understand the other sense of the Doctor's homelessness in terms of Heidegger's idea of 'the worldhood of the world' and the distance from that 'worldhood' that time travel creates for the traveller. While the uncanny can be equated with absence, Heidegger conceives 'worldhood' as what is *present*, in the sense of what constitutes a 'referential totality' of 'everyday concern'. From the perspective of positivism and of 'Laplace's demon', though, the character of the 'worldhood' of the world is precisely what goes missing. This 'demon' is an iconic figure in the history of philosophy and mathematics representing the perspective of a 'god's-eye point of view'. Pierre-Simon Laplace (1749–1827), an astronomer and advisor to Napoleon Bonaparte, spoke of an intelligence that could perceive the framework of the universe as a three-dimensional matrix of objects and events, all moving forward in regular tempo towards the future. 'We may regard the present state of the universe as the effect of its past and the cause of its future', Laplace comments. He continues:

> An intellect which at a certain moment would know all forces that set nature in motion, and all positions of all items of which nature is composed, if this intellect were also vast enough to submit these data to analysis, it would embrace in a single formula the movements of the greatest bodies of the universe and those of the tiniest atom; for such an intellect nothing would be uncertain and the future just like the past would be present before its eyes.[51]

For this 'demon' (imagine a cross between the aforementioned Klieg of the Brotherhood of Logicians and the Beast imprisoned in 'The Satan Pit' [2006]), the universe is the sum total of all spaces, and cause and effect neatly regulate the transmission of matter across spaces. This is, above all, an orderly universe, one that completes the vision of Laplace's fellow Frenchman, René Descartes, of the cosmos as a well-oiled machine.

However, according to Heidegger, this is a world deprived of its essential 'worldhood', or the presence of a primordial level of meaning in which things make sense because they refer, in our experience, to other things, events and experiences. Our experience, for Heidegger, is one of constant and unreflective interpretation of the world as a 'referential totality' – converting, for instance, 'spaces' into 'places' and 'objects' into 'tools' – that is, as opportunities in the service of needs and projects. What worries Heidegger is that 'environmentality', that nested sequence of relationships and dependencies in which one tool is 'ready-to-hand' for the purpose or function of another, is simply dissolved by the rigorous application of mathematical-logical structure. Heidegger writes,

> When space is discovered non-circumspectively by just looking at it, the environmental regions get neutralised to pure dimensions. Places—and indeed the whole circumspectively oriented totality of places belonging to equipment ready-to-

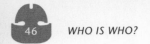

hand—get reduced to a multiplicity of positions for random Things.[52]

With this in mind, the deeper sense in which the central character of *Who* is homeless can be found in the fact that he is only a temporary visitor in the 'worldhood' of each world he visits. His typical rejection of assimilating to any culture – even British culture – is often contrasted with his companions' ties to place, relationships and, sometimes, family. In 'An Unearthly Child', this contrast is strikingly drawn in the Doctor's decision to leave Earth despite the resistance of Ian and Barbara, while Susan complains about having to leave the referential totality of cultural meaning that she has adopted as her own:

> **DOCTOR:** *(taking off his cloak and scarf)* You have heard the truth. We are not of this race. We are not of this Earth. We are wanderers in the fourth dimensions of space and time, cut off from our own planet and our own people by aeons and universes that are far beyond the reach of your most advanced sciences.
> **SUSAN:** It's true. Every word of it's true. You don't know what you've done coming in here. Grandfather, let them go now. Don't you see they don't believe us? They can't do us any harm. I know these Earth people better than you. Their minds reject things they don't understand.[53]

The trope of alienation from the worldhood of the world in *Doctor Who* appears everywhere, from Hartnell's portrayal of the Doctor as the alienated, eccentric professor, to the inability of Peter Davison's younger and more emotive Doctor to relate to his younger, more emotive companions. The phenomenon can also be used to comic effect, as Matt Smith's eleventh Doctor demonstrates when he finds himself unable to stomach even the blandest of human foods ('The Eleventh Hour', 2010) and when he awkwardly pecks those he meets on either cheek with 'Gallic air kisses', asking, 'That's how we greet each other nowadays, isn't it?' ('The Lodger', 2010).

Before us, then, are two uncanny aspects of the Doctor's homeless existence. The open-ended nature of his travels, unburdened by any particular puzzle at the heart of the programme to which everything else must lead is one of these. The other is his conscious distancing of himself from even the closest of his travelling companions. These components of *Doctor Who* are just as important to its mutable formula as are the pro-science Doctor and the hypertechnological TARDIS itself. Together with the critical, inquiring edge that this renegade Time Lord cultivates, itself the heritage of science fiction's commitment to the values of the Enlightenment and the rationalistic spirit of the positivists, these strands gesture towards some of the more unique charms of wandering in the Fourth Dimension.

2

EXTERMINATE!
Evil Must Be Fought

Is the Doctor merely a wandering 'madman with a box'? Is his role to counterbalance 'necessary' evils? Is the Doctor, as some of his companions have suspected, a source of evil himself? Or is the Doctor (to borrow a phrase from Friedrich Nietzsche) 'beyond good and evil'?

Doctor Who emerged as ahead of its time in its messages about the relationship of human nature and evil, whether personal, institutional or cosmic in nature. This may be surprising for a television programme originally designed – at least in part – for children. But, as Jeremy Bentham's history of the early years of *Who* points out, the fresh memories of continent-wide war and post-war austerity in Britain explain its unique position to use fantasy to explore the depths to which human beings might sink:

> 'I don't think *Doctor Who* is a children's programme at all. It is an adult's programme addressed to adults via children. Many stories – *Alice*, *Gulliver's Travels*, *The Wind in the Willows* – are like that', commented Brian Jackson, Director of the Advisory Centre for Education. Turning specifically to one of the Dalek serials, Mr. Jackson went on to say, 'With its undefined echoes of Hiroshima, concentration camps, and Kafkaesque corridors it was very much out of the stuff of our time.'[1]

In *Evil in Modern Thought*, Susan Neiman gives a similar list of events and circumstances that we may call 'evil' in a distinctively modern sense: these include natural calamities, like the 1755 earthquake that destroyed Lisbon, Portugal and several thousand of its inhabitants; political and military tragedies, like the Reign of Terror and Hiroshima; and institutional evils such as Stalinism and, of course, Auschwitz.[2] Certainly cruelty, dehumanisation, misrecognition, and misfortunes without any meaningful 'silver lining' deserve to be spoken of as evil. Aggression and self-destructiveness, terrorism and war, unquestioned obedience, and hatred are allied concepts to evil, as is a certain 'banality' ascribed to it in the wake of the Holocaust by Hannah Arendt (1906–75).

To speak of good and evil may sound as though we are beginning a discussion of ethics, which is the topic of the next chapter. This essential dualism also has a *metaphysical* cast because of the disproportionately great influence on Western thinking of the system of Plato of Athens (*c.*429–*c.*347 BCE), of Christian theology, and of syntheses of the two in Fathers of the Church such as St Augustine (354–430). As a result, much of the structure of Western intellectual life – and both SF and *Doctor Who* are no exceptions – exploits the possibility that reality itself is divided in two, with individuals having to choose which side they will serve. Augustine himself was familiar with this narrative, as, before he converted to Christianity, he had flirted with Manicheanism. This was a younger religion that taught about a World of Light and a World of Darkness that became intermingled through 'three creations' and syncretically found a place for many familiar Judaeo-Christian figures, such as Adam and Eve and Jesus, who, like the 'Great *Nous*' or 'Great Intelligence', emerged from the third creation.[3]

From his complex characterisation and mysterious origins we examined in the last chapter, the Doctor in the late 1960s developed into a dependable force for good, exercising a protective and fatherly relationship with his companions while expounding a Manichean view of the world. 'There are some corners of the universe which have bred the most terrible things. Things that act against everything we believe in,' the Second Doctor intones gravely in 'The Moonbase'. 'They must be fought.' The Doctor is, of course, referring to the Cybermen, who after the Daleks continue to be the most infamous sources of evil in the Whoniverse. The Cybermen were co-created by Gerry Davis, who served as the programme's script editor during the period of transition between William Hartnell and Patrick Troughton. Together with his successors, Peter Bryant and Derrick Sherwin, and producer Innes Lloyd, Davis not only solidified the appeal of Troughton's time as the Doctor in terms of the chills and thrills of watching the 'good guys' run from Yeti, Ice Warriors and Quarks, but also helped create a dialectical relationship between Doctor and monsters that would define the entire course of the show. As David Howe writes:

> *Doctor Who* would not be *Doctor Who* without the monsters. It is almost impossible to think of the series without experiencing a heady rush of nostalgia at all those times when the programme scared viewers witless and sent thousands of children hurrying behind the sofa, out of the room or into the safety of their parents' arms.[4]

The focus on tense, exciting scenarios and memorable alien menaces (which might quickly return to menace humanity again) demonstrated the production team's response to the appeal of both the American 'Universal Monsters' classic films as well as Hammer horror productions.[5] And although enthusiastic viewers of today's Weeping Angels or the Silence might scoff at the scare factor of black-and-white *Doctor Who* aliens, it became quite popular in the 1960s to watch the programme from behind one's sofa. While we were concerned about the uncanny in the preceding chapter, this and the following chapter focus on the philosophy of evil, monstrosity and 'the Other'.

Nothing in Ze World Can Stop Me Now!

The most basic distinction in the architecture of philosophical theories about evil is that between irrational and rational evils, and is modelled on the 'nature versus culture' distinction that lies at the basis of much Western thought:

> Culture, in its anthropological senses, is an attempt at creating some kind of order out of relative chaos. Or, perhaps more precisely, culture is an attempt to carve some kind of order out of the vast chaos that is nature. The way humans go about carving out order is to impose it onto the environment. They arrange themselves and their belongings in ways that signify—to themselves and to nature—that this is cultural space. Humans map onto the environment their own theories of the cosmological order.[6]

Nature is the formidable Other facing the earliest cultures: in Greek thought, this opposition is conceived in terms of *physis* and *nomos*: that is, nature-as-chaos and law-as-order. Irrational evil, like intransigent nature, defies our best attempts to explain its causes and thus to control it. It appears in descriptions of natural catastrophes like the Lisbon earthquake, which motivated Kant, Voltaire, Rousseau and Goethe to consider the possibility of 'the collapse of the most basic trust in the world, the grounds that make civilization possible'.[7] It also takes *human* form in unbridled emotional or instinctive reactions – often, those from fury – that have damaging consequences, whether to self or other. This is the model of conflict that drives many Greek tragedies, including Euripides' *Medea* and Aeschylus's *Oedipus Rex*.

There is a third type of irrational evil, however, which is of more interest to the philosopher. This is evil defined not in terms of harm, but as a perverse will, and this is a view that obtains in light of the historical failure to causally explain where our worst intentions come from. Examples of this kind of evil seem to abound in *Doctor Who*, particularly in the form of powerful, immoral characters who harness technology for apparently unnatural purposes. The creator of the Cybermen in a parallel universe, John Lumic ('Rise of the Cybermen'/'The Age of Steel', 2006), seems to be one of these, as does Max Capricorn, who will stop at nothing – even destroying Buckingham Palace and most of London – to sink the spaceship *Titanic* and his own company with it ('Voyage of the Damned', 2007). On closer inspection, Lumic's and Capricorn's fiendish schemes are rather easily explicable as motivated by a desire for immortality and revenge on a treacherous board of directors, respectively. Additionally, both antagonists demonstrate *cruelty* – a path for harm often thought to be irrational and one that plays a special role in modern theories of evil – as we will see later in this chapter. For his part, however, Augustine lays out for us the puzzle of what Kant later called 'radical evil':

> If one seeks for the efficient cause of their evil will, none is to be found. For, what can make the will bad when it is the will itself which makes an action bad? Thus, an evil will is the efficient cause of a bad action, but there is no efficient cause of an evil will.[8]

Immanuel Kant (1724–1804) spilled much ink showing that an admittedly metaphysical concept of freedom was the necessary precondition for morality. If we are presented with voluntary choices between acting on good maxims (those principles that accord with moral law) and bad maxims (those principles that don't so accord), we may be tempted to choose the latter, and in just this case our action might be called 'evil', our intention 'immoral' or 'wicked'. But not every case in which I act wrongly is also evidence that *I* am evil, or that it makes sense to speak of *radical* evil. One of the master ideas behind Kant's moral law is that motivating others through force or fraud is never morally acceptable, although this might seem to be required by prudence or efficiency. For instance, despite the fact that the first Doctor acts coercively in leaving his granddaughter Susan behind in 'The Dalek Invasion of Earth', we should not quickly draw the conclusion that there is any 'radical' evil involved. Perhaps it is the case that if someone's actions consistently lead to harm, especially to others, the label of 'radical evil' fits (this would suit the Master or the Daleks). However, Kant's ethics are resolutely anti-consequentialist: it is not what the will – good or bad – *achieves* by action, but a person's *intention*, or choice of maxim, that is morally relevant. It is entirely possible that the wicked intentions of a figure like Matron Cofelia, in promoting the use of Adipose capsules, could lead to the beneficial effect of Adipose's million London customers losing weight as 'the fat just walks away' ('Partners in Crime', 2008). But, for Kant, this would not excuse Cofelia's intention to surreptitiously use the bodies of the overweight as breeding grounds for Adipose young.

To settle the issue, Kant helpfully distinguishes between different degrees of the capacity to do evil:

> First, there is the weakness of the human heart in the general observance of adopted maxims, or in other words, the *frailty* of human nature; second, the propensity for mixing unmoral with moral motivating causes (even when it is done with good intent and under maxims of the good), that is, *impurity*; third, the propensity to adopt evil maxims, that is, the *wickedness* of human nature, or of the human heart.[9]

The Doctor's refusal to let Susan into the TARDIS seems a clear case of 'impurity' of motive, in which his benevolence for a relative who is ready to settle down conflicts with force and fraud. Only someone who consistently, and of their free will, chooses evil maxims for their own sake can be classed, for Kant, as 'wicked' or radically evil.

A better example of such a phenomenon than Lumic or Capricorn could be the ethereal creature 'Light' from 'Ghost Light', a story in the final season of classic *Who* (1989). A powerful alien creating a catalogue of life forms, Light had collected species from all over Earth when, for some unexplained reason, he went into hibernation in his stone spaceship. In the nineteenth century, the mansion of Gabriel Chase would be built on the site, and Light's seemingly supernatural powers (as well as two subservient agents of his survey, Josiah Samuel Smith and 'Control') would convince generations of visitors – welcome and unwelcome – that the house was haunted. By the time the seventh Doctor finally solves the mystery of Gabriel Chase and confronts Light, the creature has sent several people insane, dismembered a maid, changed a reunited mother and daughter into stone, and chemically reduced the investigating Inspector Mackenzie to 'the cream of Scotland Yard'. Because the Doctor is unsympathetic to both the end represented by Light's catalogue and the means by which it is accomplished, he views every deliberate action of Light as contrary to even a minimal morality; in other words, Light wills harm on others without a flicker of conscience. Recognising that the ethereal surveyor is too powerful to defeat by normal means, the Doctor calls attention to Light's failure to accomplish his sole mission:

> **DOCTOR:** You missed the dragons, the bandersnatches. Then there are the slithy toves and the crowned Saxe-Coburg.
> *(Light appears. He's not as bright and golden as he first was.)*
> **LIGHT:** Where are these items?
> **DOCTOR:** I can't think how you missed them. You have to complete the catalogue before you can destroy all life here.
> **LIGHT:** Control?
> **DOCTOR:** She's no use to you now. She's evolved as well.
> **LIGHT:** No! All slipping away.

Soon after, Light simply stops being. Much of what separates Light from Lumic or Capricorn is that even Light's own basic survival does not stand in the way of his urge to destroy what does not suit his project or fit in his catalogue. Since the evil will is either uncaused or the cause of itself, it has nothing to appeal to in times of a crisis of conscience, as those of good will can and must do.

The exact source, then, of evil is questionable since for Augustine it is not a creation of God, and for Kant it cannot be a cause overriding our free will as the instinctive urge to self-defence or overpowering lust or hunger might be. When Kant speaks about humanity as a species, and not merely a collection of moral agents, he says that radical evil is 'as a natural propensity, *inextirpable* by human powers, since extirpation could occur only through good maxims, and cannot take place when the ultimate subjective ground of all maxims [i.e., human will] is postulated as corrupt'.[10] Elsewhere, he agrees with Augustine that one condition of having freedom of the will *must* be the 'inscrutable' possibility of choosing evil, perhaps consistently and resolutely so. The wills of individuals, for Kant, are not merely potentially *radically* evil because of their choices; they are so *from birth* as an irremediable residue of either our anthropological or autonomous makeup – or both. Regardless of whether this type of theory of evil can be saved or not, even Kant does not see those who regularly exercise their radically evil propensities as irredeemable persons (and one of the themes of the new *Who* is the Doctor's constant efforts to 'save' those, like the Master, who often act irredeemably wickedly). As philosopher Richard Bernstein summarises Kant's position: 'All human beings are radically evil—that is, possess the powerful propensity to become morally evil—but only some persons *do* become morally evil, and develop a morally evil character or disposition. But even such wicked persons can be reborn and become good.'[11] To draw the conclusion, therefore, that the 'irrational' horn of evil represents the side of *intrinsic* malevolence does not deny, with the second Doctor, that it must be fought; it does, though, raise questions about whether the war may ever be won outside of the conflicts of the gods.

Diabolic or demonic characters in folklore and SF have often represented the dimension of 'rational' evil, the other horn of the dual interpretation of wickedness introduced above. 'Rational' evil excludes natural calamities, so it can be explained in terms of its meaning and significance for a wider plan of intelligent action; it is also chosen for the sake of something other than itself, usually a perceived good. What might be called 'instrumental' evil, or colloquially 'the lesser evil', is one of two types here, and is typically analysed in terms of consequential *harms* rather than intentions, as Kant did. The very term 'lesser evil' assumes that harms are not incommensurable – that they are comparable or quantifiable in some way – and this rests on the common-sense notion that, all other things being equal, our morally relevant decisions ought to at least minimise evils done to those involved. Most importantly, the idea of choosing the least harmful of courses of action, all things considered, is not merely a personal judgement of comparison or quantity of harms and goods, but is also a judgement that is subject to evaluation and criticism in a public forum, large or small. As Michael Ignatieff says, '[H]uman beings can justify anything as a lesser evil if they have to justify it only to themselves.'[12] And if simply any course of action can be subjectively so justified, then the very idea of a 'lesser evil' seems conceptually empty, just as the idea of an action being 'morally good' is descriptively bankrupt if the only criterion for moral goodness is subjective, individual preference. Thus, talk about weighing evils and choosing the lesser evils is a form of communicative action, an essentially public discourse that acknowledges that although individuals may privately rationalise anything as being good, 'they are less likely to carry it out if they are forced to do so in adversarial proceedings before their fellow citizens'.[13]

Hence *secrecy often conceals* visions of the good that may be highly controversial as lesser evils in zero-sum situations. This formula neatly encapsulates the projects of the archetypal mad scientist, among the ranks of whom we must count Professor Zaroff, who, despite being 'the greatest living scientist since Leonardo', cannot help crafting over-the-top lines such as the infamous 'Nothing in ze world can stop me now!' ('The Underwater Menace'); Solon, the would-be-resurrector of the mad Time Lord conqueror Morbius, played with manic intensity by Philip Madoc ('The Brain of Morbius', 1976); and Professor Richard Lazarus, whose experiments have the grandiose yet sinister goal of 'chang[ing] what it means to be human' ('The Lazarus Experiment', 2007). The breathtaking scale of the criminal biochemical experiments of the Doctor's fellow renegade, the Rani (Kate O'Mara), illustrates that even the officially neutral Time Lords are not beyond making calculations of greater and lesser evils when it comes to introducing more harmony into the universe. In 'Time and the Rani' (1987), the inaugural story of the seventh

Doctor, the newly regenerated Time Lord and friend Melanie 'Mel' Bush discover the Rani's plan to turn the planet Lakertya into a 'time manipulator':

> **DOCTOR:** This monstrosity will give you the ability to change the order of creation.
> **RANI:** Creation's chaotic. I shall introduce order. Wherever evolution has taken the wrong route, I shall redirect it. That planet you're so obsessed with, Earth, I shall return to the Cretaceous age.
> **MEL:** The Cretaceous age?
> **RANI:** The potential of the dinosaurs was never fully realised.[14]

The Rani's plans exemplify (to the point of absurdity) the notion that, in private, we may rationalise anything as a lesser evil (or a greater good).

Rational discourse around the weighting of 'lesser evils' typically presumes a fairly broad cultural consensus about values that can motivate and sustain the discourse in the first place. However, there is another type of 'rational' evil – often raised in discussions of war, torture and terrorism – in which pain and suffering result from the deep incommensurability of visions of what is good. When the fourth Doctor accuses the Osirian Sutekh of using his power only for evil, Sutekh replies, 'Your evil is my good' ('Pyramids of Mars', 1975), returning us once again to a Manichean opposition wedded to an almost Newtonian reciprocity. Every good act the Doctor performs causes pain to Sutekh; everything that Sutekh values, such as leaving 'dust and decay' everywhere he walks, diminishes the Doctor's pleasure. Although we will undoubtedly side with the Doctor on this one, the 'your evil is my good' view has the possibility to entail genuine tragedies, especially if those trying to make sound moral judgements are third parties standing outside a local conflict. This is the type of moral conflict that motivates many of scriptwriter Malcolm Hulke's stories for classic *Doctor Who*, including 'Colony in Space' (1971), in which an Earth Adjudicator (really the Master) must decide whether colonists from an overpopulated Earth or the

IMC Mining Corporation have rights to the planet Uxarieus. To illustrate how these conflicts might occur, Colin McGinn offers us a streamlined thought experiment that keys 'visions of the good' to pleasure and the absence of pain, and is rather worthy of being adapted into a *Doctor Who* plot:

> Imagine the following two species of beings—call them the G-beings and the E-beings. The G-beings are such that when another member of the species experiences pleasures they too experience pleasure, while when another experiences pain they feel pain. The interpersonal laws of feeling preserve pleasure and pain, so that cause and effect will be of the same hedonic type. The E-beings, on the other hand, exemplify the opposite laws of social psychology: pleasure in one causes pain in another, and pain causes pleasure [...] Now, supposing that members of both species pursue their own pleasure, what will we expect of their behaviour? [...] The answer is obvious: the G-beings will promote and seek out pleasurable sensations in others, since this contributes to their own pleasure; while the E-beings will promote and seek out painful sensations in others, since—given the way they are hooked up—this will contribute to their pleasure.[15]

The key conceit in this scenario is the unexplained but direct way in which the pleasure or pain of one member of these societies is transmitted to others – if this were always true of humans, ethics would be a much more intimate and pressing concern than it already is! We might also ask ourselves these questions: is there any such thing as morality (at least as 'doing the right thing no matter what') in the G-being species, since any G can reliably count on a hedonic 'reward' as the result of bringing good to other Gs? Further, are the E-beings even possible? While it is true that Es will cause pain to others because they seek their own pleasure, their pleasure will bring pain to other Es unconnected with their actions, which of course will bring pleasure to still other Es. The question here is one of consistency: how will we know whether any given E-being will feel pain or pleasure (assuming they won't feel both at the same time) when a particular E harms another E? As opposed to the morality-free Gs, the Es seem to have an overly complicated, if not chaotic, moral life. The motivation to do evil in such a world is entirely rational, as it is based in the self-interest of E-beings who are hard-wired by nature in a certain way and who prefer pain over pleasure; like Sutekh, the evil of others is their good. E-beings would need a moral conception beyond simply maximising their own pleasure in order to overcome this rational self-interest. They would, in fact, need some sense of sacrifice, as prevails upon the Master in 'The End of Time', Part Two (2009), as well as upon the Doctor when he saves Wilf Mott in the same tale. And although evil is more than merely the causing of pain, McGinn's story is evidence that a *thoroughly* evil society – at least one that might obtain under the terms assigned above – is a contradiction in terms.

The View from Behind the Sofa

Contemporary philosophers are generally uncomfortable discussing 'evil', probably because, in a discipline that seeks clarity, evil wells up from an obscure nexus of metaphysics and ethics. Ethically, it is not uncommon to discuss a person's character as 'base' or 'vicious' (for Aristotle, the opposite of 'virtuous'); but the metaphysical flavour of the way in which 'evil' is commonly used suggests two notions that many thinkers, particularly contemporary secular ones, reject. One is that a person could be, in their essence, irredeemably wicked. The other is – as Manicheanism suggests – that evil is itself a force independent of human action and desire, capable of swaying, or indeed engulfing, individuals. Gary Gillatt has correctly argued that the employment of this sense of evil functions as a limiting concept for fiction:

> The concept of fundamental 'evil' has always been a useful moral get-out clause for *Doctor Who* writers – or writers of fantasy in general [...] No further meaningful psychological study or character insights are required, and all the heroes can pitch themselves, without hesitation, into the thrill of the chase and the inevitable execution.[16]

Augustine – who, as I mentioned earlier, has been historically identified with the 'privation' theory of evil – claims that there are degrees of goodness (leading towards God) but no absolute, unfathomable badness, only a lack of this goodness (as a hole in the ground is merely a lack of dirt, not something of itself). He claims, 'Thus, good things without defects can sometimes be found; absolutely bad things, never [...] for the simple reasons that a defect exists only where harm is done.'[17] Augustine's full argument explaining the idea of evil as a deficit of goodness in *City of God* implies something fairly subtle: there can be no 'natural evil'. This is because 'defects' in the natural order only exist in the value judgements of those capable of making them – and because 'doing harm' is an intentional act, anything without the capability for such acts can't be productive of 'evil'. Only moral agents may cause 'evil' in the world, and every such evil – as 'sin' – is also a deduction away from the fundamental goodness of the 'absolute', or, in Augustine's case, God. Evil is a greater or a lesser *hollowness*, or lack of being.

The writers of *Doctor Who* seem unfamiliar with Augustinian ethico-metaphysics, since it seems rather common for the Doctor to meet up with foes who are advertised as the epitome of evil itself: leaving aside the Daleks and the Master (whom we'll get to presently), this must include at least the Great Intelligence, the Dæmons, the fourth Doctor himself (in 'Face of Evil' [1976]), the Black Guardian, the Mara, the tortured Sharaz Jek *or* the vile Morgus (from 'Caves of Androzani' [1984]), the Valeyard, the Gods of Ragnarok, the Destroyer, Fenric, and the Beast in the 'Satan Pit' (2006). Philosophically, the abstract idea of evil as a cosmological force or problem that must be explained was quite alien to the ancient Greeks and emerges when we depart from the pre-Christian polytheistic pantheon of competing, anthropocentric, limited divinities, and move to the position represented by the syncretism of Judaeo-Christian divinity and a Platonic conception of the absolute. Here we find the notion of one God as sole creator and supreme being, unlimited in perfection and providential power. As a philosophical problem, the existence of evil in the world (think of easy cases such as infants born anencephalic or disastrous tsunamis) seems incompatible with the existence of an all-powerful, perfectly good God. In settling this incompatibility, a believer may choose to reject God's omnipotence, therefore claiming that God is good but unable to stem all incidences of evil, or reject God's omnibenevolence, and similarly claim that God is all powerful but doesn't wish to eliminate all deleterious events. Perhaps the more radical solution is to accept the existence of evil and draw the conclusion that there is no god whatsoever. Versions of these criticisms have occasionally been levelled at the Doctor, whose ability to transcend time, space and his own death have appeared godlike to some of his travelling companions. After the fifth Doctor's young friend Adric is killed in an exploding space freighter, we witness this tragic exchange:

TEGAN: Aren't you forgetting something rather important? Adric is dead!

NYSSA: Tegan, please.

DOCTOR: *(softly)* We feel his loss as well.

TEGAN: Well you could do more than grieve! You could go back!

(The Doctor looks startled.)

NYSSA: Could you?

DOCTOR: No.

NYSSA: Surely the TARDIS is quite capable of ...

TEGAN: *(cutting Nyssa off)* We can change what happened if we materialise before Adric was killed!

DOCTOR: And change your own history?

TEGAN: *(persuasively)* Look, the freighter could still crash into Earth, that doesn't have to be changed. Only Adric doesn't have to be on board ...

DOCTOR: *(stridently)* Now listen to me, both of you! There are some rules that cannot be broken, even with the TARDIS!

NYSSA: Doctor ...

DOCTOR: *(speaking over Nyssa)* Don't ever ask me to do anything like that again! *(more softly)* We must accept that Adric is dead. His life wasn't wasted, he died saving others like his brother Vash.

('Time-Flight', 1982)

Similarly, Donna Noble petitions the tenth Doctor to save 'just one family' in Pompeii from the eruption of Vesuvius in 79 CE, with rather more success. In each case, the argument is that if one has the power to prevent or reduce evil, one should use it – and a conundrum results when the evil is allowed to occur nonetheless.

A believer's response to the problem of evil typically takes the form of a *theodicy*, or an argument demonstrating the compatibility of evil with god's omnibenevolence and omnipotence. This sort of response to 'natural' evil – death, famine, disease and deformation – makes one of its earliest appearances in Irenaeus's (second century CE–c. 202) theology, which offers a sophisticated response to the problem of evil. Irenaeus claimed that evil is part of the natural order in at least two respects. First, deficits in optimal human functioning, like pain and hunger, provide knowledge about our own condition and that of others, knowledge that can be used to improve our estate. Second, our perception of these deficiencies as 'evil' is a kind of confusion that results from the collision of our perceived needs and desires with the natural laws of the universe.[18] Finally, and perhaps most importantly, Irenaeus believed that suffering through bad events and hard times shapes character, or is essential to what philosopher of religion John Hick calls 'soul-making'.[19] Theodicy-like arguments also abound in *Doctor Who*, not only in the ninth Doctor's grim elegy 'Everything has its time, and everything dies.' One features even more prominently in one of the best-known scenes from the classic programme, centring on fourth Doctor Tom Baker's question 'Have I the right?' posed as he is about to explosively avert the 'Genesis of the Daleks'. 'You see, some things could be better with the Daleks,' he agonises in the final episode of the story. 'Many future worlds will become allies just because of their fear of the Daleks!' So, as he holds the wires rigged to destroy the Dalek mutant incubation chamber, the Doctor's moral reflections signify a desire to avoid committing evil to fight evil only at the most basic of levels. It is moral reflection that the universe can ill afford, as the Doctor's companion Sarah Jane Smith reminds him. After all, the Daleks are neither to be pitied nor reasoned with. They are *Doctor Who*'s essential 'Other', as this description makes clear:

> Secured within tank-like life-support machines, the Daleks were genetically engineered on the planet Skaro to be emotionless killers – their primary function to simply conquer and destroy all other life across the universe and to ensure the survival and purity of the Dalek race. Bred as soldiers, the Daleks lived for commands, and elected designated controllers to coordinate units via a military computer.[20]

At a higher remove, the Doctor's moralising could be interpreted as an act of ethico-political redemption, 'revisit[ing] the isolated stand against evil [in World War II] that cost an empire – to disavow Britain's ongoing history of colonial violence, oppression, and expropriation' and thus – at least metaphorically – justifying the evil that the Daleks do as contributing to an incomprehensibly wider good.[21]

Few viewers watching 'Genesis of the Daleks' in 1975 would have been worrying about the ethics of doing evil to prevent evil, and would probably have sided with Sarah Jane Smith, who replies to the Doctor's moralising that he cannot doubt that destroying the Daleks is the right thing to do. They would have been thinking about the Daleks as threatening, shrill-voiced aliens, motivated by the same desires as power-obsessed humans, but characterised by the 'total inhumanity' of their robotic appearance, which in turn hides a grotesque mutation inside that was never fully revealed to the viewer until 2005's 'Dalek'.[22] The writer of the scripts that first featured the Daleks in 1964, Terry Nation, described them thus:

> Four hideous machine-like creatures. They are legless, moving on a round base. They have no human features. A lens on a flexible shaft acts as an eye. Arms with mechanical grips for hands. The creatures hold strange weapons in their hands. One of them glides forward. It speaks with an echoing metallic voice.[23]

Although this was not always made clear in his later scripts for *Doctor Who*, Nation was very much a 'big ideas' writer. His first story for the show, 'The Daleks', elaborates the dualistic opposition of Doctor and Daleks by using SF tropes familiar from H.G. Wells's *The Time Machine* and Jules Verne's *A Journey to the Centre of the Earth* and *Around the World in Eighty Days*.[24] He also pioneered the deployment of space-time travel to distant locales as constructive metaphors for historical movements as well as contemporary social criticism:

> Something of a keen student of modern history [Terry] Nation had two main preoccupations – technological warfare and the ideals of the European dictatorships in the Thirties and Forties. In particular Nation had long held a morbid fascination with the horrors of contemporary warfare: gas attack, chemical shelling and especially with the effects of nuclear weapons. Recently, he had been intrigued by a paper proposing the development of an atomic weapon designed to kill people through massive exposure to radioactive fallout, but with a limited blast capacity, thereby keeping buildings relatively intact – the Neutron Bomb. He decided to base his *Doctor Who* story ['The Daleks'] around a world where this nuclear nightmare had already happened. The heat flash of an enormously powerful neutron bomb had carbonized a planet with the ensuing radioactive fallout condemning its survivors to the full horrors of atrophy and mutation.[25]

As Bentham suggests, the nature of the Daleks – and the dimensions of the evil they embody – has always been tied closely to particularly modern fears, not only of nuclear war and Nazism (the culture of the humanoid 'Kaled' progenitors in 'Genesis of the Daleks') but also of bio-technological dehumanisation in general. Crucial to this latter theme is that the Daleks have no individual self-consciousness; the only differentiation between them is strategic and functional. Within the context of a programme that has always focused on the distinctiveness of each of its main character's multiple personae, and on the particularity of what each new companion brings to the weekly adventure, this depersonalisation represents the most significant way in which an adversary can be an 'Other' to the protagonists. In turn, the dramatic distance between protagonists and Other, their conflicts and reconciliations, can be understood in terms of a developing movement – from episode to episode, series to series – between the strange and the familiar.

Viewers of long-running science fiction television like *Who* or *Star Trek* will be familiar with the dialectic of estrangement and familiarisation that typically occurs when a recurring alien race of enemies like the Klingons or the Borg is developed, sometimes over generations of elapsed time. We can see this dialectic operating in microcosmic perspective in how episodes 1 and 2 of the introduction of 'The Daleks', written by Nation, are filmed. In the first movement of this dialectic, the dissimilarity of aims, values, beliefs, and even biologies between antagonist species, is drawn in as great a relief as possible in order to establish conflict for dramatic effect. (A fine example: the first Doctor's companion Barbara, lost in gleaming corridors of irrational architectural metrics, is confronted by something – we only see the Dalek eyestalk as if from behind the creature – and she screams.) In the second movement (which again, for dramatic effect, ought not to occur too quickly or too easily), conflict is defused because commonalities between former antagonists are formed (the Daleks are fully revealed as it becomes clear they also have the Doctor, his granddaughter Susan and Ian Chesterton as prisoners). Sometimes, the shift from strange Other to the comprehensible and familiar occurs through forces outside the control of the scriptwriters and production crew. So, in the case of the Doctor's robot-like nemeses:

> By 1966 the novelty of the Daleks' initial appearance had worn off [...] Mr. John Bennett, a member of the committee of the Society for Education in Film and Television, expressed the opinion that the Daleks were losing their power now that much of the mystery surrounding them had been cleared up.[26]

The macrocosmic application of the dialectic occurs in terms of outright space wars, like that brewing between

Earth and Draconia in 'Frontier in Space' (1973), or a 'survival of the fittest' contest for a contested ecological niche, as demonstrated between humans and Tractators in 'Frontios' (1984). The result is what the German idealists J.G. Fichte and G.W. Hegel first called 'recognition', in the seventeenth century, and what contemporary philosopher Paul Ricoeur explains as 'acting consciousness and judging consciousness confront[ing] one another: the "pardon" resulting from the mutual recognition of the two antagonists who admit the limits of their viewpoints and renounce their partiality denotes the authentic phenomenon of conscience'.[27] Even the resolution of the dialectic can be creatively exploited by restarting it again, perhaps through the actions of an insurgent fraction of one of the parties ('Doctor Who and the Silurians', 1970) or through the revelation of some new, disturbing fact about one of the former antagonists (cf. the actions of the High Council of Gallifrey on Thoros-Beta in 'Mindwarp', 1986, or the genocidal intentions of Rassilon and the other freed Time Lords in 'The End of Time', Part Two).

Davros was the chief scientist of the Kaled people in the Kaled–Thal war forming the background for 'Genesis of the Daleks. He becomes a kind of mediating factor between the Doctor as familiar protagonist and Daleks as utterly alien adversaries. The struggle for recognition is also highly significant to Davros's character. Played variously by Michael Wisher, David Gooderson, Terry Molloy and (in the newer programme) Julian Bleach, Davros is typically portrayed as the intellectual equal of the Doctor, but also as his crazed mirror-image. Davros has been twisted and deformed (ever a sign of evil in Western narrative) by a bomb blast during the war against the Thals, an event that has also left him blind and totally dependent on the life-sustaining equipment built into his wheelchair, which resembles exactly the base of a Dalek. As Ronson, a fellow scientist in 'Genesis', tells the Doctor and companion Harry Sullivan, Davros's goal in creating what were originally called 'Mark III Travel Machines' was patriotic, if not entirely benevolent:

RONSON: You see, the Elite was formed to produce weapons that would end this war. We soon saw that this was futile and changed the direction of our research into the survival of our race. But our chemical weapons had already started to produce genetic mutations.

HARRY: And the mutations were banished out into the wastelands.

RONSON: Yes.

DOCTOR: The mutos.

RONSON: Now Davros, he believed that there was no way to reverse this trend and so he started experiments to establish our final mutational form. He took living cells, treated them with chemicals and produced the ultimate creature.[28]

Davros, together with the Doctor's fellow renegade Time Lord, the Master, represents the purest form of what Tulloch and Alvarado identify as the 'Gothic' villain in *Doctor Who*, a nemesis who is an 'indefinably close shadow' of the hero, and the paradigmatic goal of whom it is 'to convert the world into [his] own passion for identity'.[29]

Davros's own identity seems to lie at the convergence of his cyborg nature (physically, he is a hybrid of humanoid and Dalek) and his overweening ambition, which mixes thirst for personal power with a perfectionist obsession to recreate the Daleks over and over. The motivation for this continuous work stems from a more insidious personal desire to refine 'their instincts [to] be as accurate as a scientific instrument' ('Genesis of the Daleks'). As a pawn within a Dalek 'Civil War' storyline that was developed over three episodes in the 1980s, Davros receives nothing but misrecognition from his brainchildren: he is either useful or a non-Dalek, and therefore impure and fit to be 'exterminated'. The situation allows Davros to hone his guile, but also moves him to engineer new Daleks who actually accept him as their creator, if not superior. It's an almost Frankenstein-like twist on the dialectic of strangeness and intimacy: if I have made everyone my enemy, I must simply *make* new allies whose orders include recognition of me. However, as Hegel might have pointed out, since Davros and his Daleks differ in the morally relevant statuses of freedom and equality, the programmed recognition will never satisfy someone like Davros. In both Peter Davison's 'Resurrection of the Daleks' (1984) and Colin Baker's audio drama 'Davros' (2003) the Dalek creator turns on the charm – what little is left – in order to impress the Doctor with the cosmic significance of his work. Seeing the Doctor as an intellectual equal, Davros seeks his recognition. Again, this is a touch of the Victorian Gothic that is still at work in *Doctor Who*: ultimately unable to make the transition from alien to familiar in terms of being acknowledged as 'father' to his own children, Davros seeks out validation from his own 'indefinably close shadow'.

Gods and Monsters

Whichever story we follow – the emergence of the deformed Daleks and the Aryan-like Thals from a neutron bomb explosion on Skaro ('The Daleks') or their creation by Davros ('Genesis')[30] – it seems that military supremacy and racial purity are the two pillars of Dalek culture, such as it is. The Dalek ideology of superiority, which Nation created as an analogue to the Third Reich's pronouncements of Aryan destiny, plays itself out in stories such as 'The Dalek Invasion of Earth', 'Planet of the Daleks' (1973) and 'Destiny of the Daleks' (1979) in ways that Nazism, if it hadn't been routed in World War II, might have done. The Daleks ruthlessly strip the planet of natural resources, often utilising a terrified and oppressed local populace to do the work. As 'Planet' shows, they are not above biological experimentation on others (indeed, they see certain of their ranks as expendable as well), and in 'Dalek Invasion' they instrumentalise the entire Earth in an effort to turn it into a vast, mobile platform for conquest. Mind-controlled 'Robomen', analogous to brainwashed Hitler Youth, do some of the dirty work for the Daleks. What the Robomen cannot do falls to monstrous and imbecilic mercenaries like the Ogrons, or quislings such as the human Dalek Controller ('Day of the Daleks', 1972). Because their ultimate goal is the subjugation of all other life forms, the Daleks seem to subscribe to what Michael Ignatieff sees as the basis for the logic of terrorism in the twenty-first century, expressed in French as *la politique du pire*. This 'politics of the worst' has the purpose of 'mak[ing] things worse so that they cannot become better'.[31]

Nation and other Dalek scriptwriters had to be clever with how to use the Daleks, since creative and budgetary constraints on the production of classic *Doctor Who* never allowed more than a handful of the creatures (with their operators folded inside on tricycles) to be seen on screen at any one time. However, original novels published by BBC Books after Nation's death in 1997 and Big Finish's *Dalek Empire* series of audio adventures did what modest television budgets could never do and censors could never allow – increase both the number and malevolence of the Dalek armies.

As the most iconic Others of the Doctor, the Daleks were radically upgraded in the 2005 series in their ability to 'conquer and destroy'. They were carefully redesigned to look more solid, more intimidating – like small tanks, complete with a tank's armour and weaponry – and allowed more firepower, mobility and force of numbers through the magic of convincing postproduction effects and computer-generated imagery (CGI), courtesy of the Mill's special effects. By 2005, the Daleks were upgraded so much that they not only achieved a wider believability in the eyes of a more cosmopolitan and mainstream audience; they achieved a kind of apotheosis. Series 1 of the Russell T. Davies-helmed reboot of *Who* fulfilled the long-anticipated return of the Daleks not once but twice, in two vastly different contexts that, when considered together, forced viewers to see the Daleks in a new light.

The first of these was 'Dalek', written by Rob Shearman and based on his exquisite, blackly comedic meditation on cruelty and propaganda, the 2003 Big Finish audio drama 'Jubilee', starring Colin Baker as the Doctor. The second was the two-parter 'Bad Wolf'/'The Parting of the Ways', penned by Davies himself. 'Dalek' presents us with what appears to be the lone Dalek survivor of 'The Last Great Time War', an obscurely described event that apparently occurred in the continuity of the Doctor's 'timestream' after the 1996 telemovie. 'The War erupted through every time and no time and left the universe in an infinite state of temporal flux, yet no one knows how it started, few know what happened, and only one man [the Doctor] truly knows how it ended', claims *The Dalek Handbook*.[32] The Time War between the Daleks and the Time Lords, which ended in the apparent mutual annihilation of both sides, was intended by Davies and his co-executive producers to serve as a MacGuffin on a massive scale. It allowed the new *Doctor Who* to distance itself from its predecessor for a new audience, while keeping selected links, by positing the existence of an event that has literally rewritten (and re-rewritten) the history of the moving present. The Time War – and, in particular, the reasons why it came about – also suggests that plausible accounts of the narrative continuity of both the old and new series are far more complicated than they appear at first glance. Some licensed reference sources for the new *Who* suggest a connection between the outbreak of war and the aforementioned 'Genesis of the Daleks'. 'Across time, Dalek aggression has led to interstellar wars and encouraged alliances against them. The Time Lords became so fearful of the Daleks' potential for universal domination that they attempted to tamper with their creation, sparking the Last Great Time War', write Steve Tribe and James Goss.[33] The fullest accounting for the conflict's events suggests not only that it encompassed atrocities and catastrophic consequences for many unallied races, but also that its strategies and tactics must have been conceived on a mind-numbingly complex four-dimensional galactic chessboard. The nature of the conflict implies that history has been altered and restored, and altered again on a scale unknown in *Doctor Who* save for the 'Faction Paradox' storylines of several Virgin novels encapsulating adventures of the eighth Doctor after his single telemovie appearance.[34]

At the close of the 2005 series, and planned in conjunction with Christopher Eccleston's regenerative departure from the show after one year, the Daleks again emerged from the depths of space – in their *billions* – revealing that more than one Dalek had survived the Time War. This is the first time that viewers of *Doctor Who* have had the until-then allegedly superior might of the Daleks *shown* to them rather than implied, again through the magic of CGI.[35] In their ranks, whether in their 'Dalek Invasion of Earth' retro-style saucer craft or flying in Dalek army ranks through the depths of space, the Daleks had – in the space of two 2005 stories – been made over from screeching fibreglass dustbins into a force of nature. This epic-scale season ender, together with 'Dalek', crystallises the essence of the evil of the Daleks.

Shearman's 'Dalek' retains from his original script for the audio 'Jubilee' the scenario of a lone Dalek, deprived of mobility and weaponry, kept in the dark and tortured by humans. By changing the setting from an alternate-history Britain to an eccentric billionaire's bunker underneath Utah, Shearman is able to capitalise on the perception of Americans as crude, tasteless and violent – epithets all appropriate to characterising Henry Van Statten, the billionaire antagonist, and his team. The ninth Doctor's confrontation with the 'Metaltron' in its cage presents us with a one-to-one interaction, as personal as it is disturbing, that signifies a fundamental deepening of the conflict between the Doctor and the Daleks; one that bears examining at length:

DALEK: I am waiting for orders.
DOCTOR: What does that mean?
DALEK: I am a soldier. I was bred to receive orders.
DOCTOR: Well you're never gonna get any. Not ever.
DALEK: I demand orders!
DOCTOR: *(voice rising)* They're never gonna come! Your race is dead! You all burnt, all of you. Ten million ships on fire – the entire Dalek race wiped out in one second.
DALEK: You lie!
DOCTOR: I watched it happen. I MADE it happen!
DALEK: You destroyed us?
(The Doctor's expression changes. He walks away, his back turned on the Dalek.)
DOCTOR: *(quietly)* I had no choice.
DALEK: And what of the Time Lords?
DOCTOR: Dead. They burnt with you. The end of the Last Great Time War. Everyone lost.

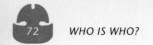

DALEK: And the coward survived.

DOCTOR: *(mockingly)* Oh – and I caught your little signal … help me … poor little thing … *(resumes normal tone)* But there's no one else coming 'cos there's no one else left.

DALEK: *(lowers eyepiece)* I am alone in the Universe.

DOCTOR: *(smiles)* Yep.

DALEK: So are you.[36]

'Dalek', like the earlier 'Resurrection of the Daleks', is a story with no happy ending for anyone, and both underwrite a theme that the misdeeds of the Daleks are so widespread and vile that they defy our attempts to rationalise them (as the Doctor attempts to do in 'Genesis'). Initially powerless – except for its formidable persuasive powers, which it uses on companion Rose Tyler to secure its release from bondage – the lone Dalek exhibits evil primarily in its desire for, and unquestioned obedience to, orders. This demonstrates a deficit of conscience similar to that demonstrated in Stanley Milgram's infamous 'Experiment 18' at Yale University, in which Milgram's associates tested participants' fidelity to instructions from authority figures by making them think they were administering increasingly painful electric shocks to their fellows. Of course, episodes such as 'Power of the Daleks' and 'Victory of the Daleks' (2010) showed that the ability to *appear* servile often masked Dalek plans to infiltrate and take over by exploiting human desires to use Dalek force for partisan ends. Yet the lone Dalek intransigently refuses to take orders from just anyone, and this tempers the megalomania of Van Statten by refusing to even acknowledge his existence.

In the context of Christopher Eccleston's portrayal of the Time Lord as a guilt-wracked 'traumatised war veteran',[37] the Dalek and the Doctor triangulate their pain on an even greater evil: the Time War itself. 'Dalek' also gives us a glimpse of the carnage that even one member of this race is capable of inflicting as it electrocutes nearly every security guard and scientist in Van Statten's bunker. Yet, Shearman tells us, 'As destructive as the Dalek is, it reaches out to the Doctor: his enemy is the one creature in the universe who might understand him, and is worthy of talking to him, or of giving him orders.'[38] The Dalek's repeated request for orders keenly illustrates a disconnect between the creature's understanding of means and of its ends – it cannot help seeing itself merely as a means to be used to any end, despite its development of an individual personality and its human DNA, absorbed from Rose. It also successfully obtains orders to self-destruct from Rose, the only person in 'Dalek' to show it kindness, and carries them out in the end. The Dalek has begun to experience feelings different from hatred and aggression, which it has been hard-wired to view as 'sickness'. Its last, pathetic conversation with Rose appropriately resembles the final rationalisations of a terminally ill patient asking for assistance with ending their life.

The episode sends a powerful message about evil and conscience, one that Rose delivers to the Doctor, who is armed and about to 'exterminate' the Dalek, when she plaintively tells him, 'It couldn't kill Van Statten – it couldn't kill me – it's changing. What about you, Doctor? What the hell are you changing into?' Rose is insisting that the Doctor adhere to one of Hannah Arendt's preconditions for avoiding evil: the ability to think for oneself. According to Arendt, 'the one common denominator uniting opponents of Nazi rule in Germany was a capacity to ask, at all times, what kind of person one was or wished to be'.[39] It seems wise to concur with Chapman's conclusion that 'it is an indication of the ideological differences between American (utopian) and British (usually more pessimistic) SF that "Dalek" does not offer the possibility of humanising the creature'.[40] Yet, by effectively asking Rose for permission to kill itself rather than suffer any more racial pollution, the Dalek has both shown a glimmer of an ability to make a fundamentally free choice and, ironically, in doing so, also stayed true to its most basic prejudice at the same time.

The explosive two-part conclusion to the 2005 series, which promised an answer to the year's story arc puzzle, 'Who or what is Bad Wolf?', brought the Daleks back in full force. In many respects, 'Bad Wolf' and 'The Parting of the Ways' present a mirror-image of the quite unorthodox episode, 'Dalek'. Hidden in space, a huge fleet of the creatures has been playing a long game (literally, as they have been behind the manipulation of humans in the 'Fourth Great and Bountiful Human Empire' since the events of 'The Long Game' of the same series), keeping Earth placid and sedentary while also obtaining 'the waste of humanity' to become Daleks themselves. We have often seen this common Dalek strategy of disguising their true intentions, whether by operating through cloned duplicates ('The Chase', 1965) or human infiltrators like Lytton and Stien ('Resurrection of the Daleks'), or by shamelessly pretending to be benefactors to other races, as they have done in some of the best BBC Radio and Big Finish audio adventures, such as 'Blood of the Daleks', written by Nicholas Briggs.

Like the ninth Doctor's initial face-off with the lone Dalek, his confrontation with those holding Rose Tyler prisoner – with considerably better odds on their side – shows a new side of both the Doctor and, by implication, the Daleks:

> **DALEK:** We have your associate. You will obey or she will be exterminated.
> *(Rose, shaking, looks up at the Doctor on the screen.)*
> **DOCTOR:** No.
> **DALEK:** *(clearly not having anticipated this answer)* Explain yourself.
> **DOCTOR:** I said 'no'.
> **DALEK:** What is the meaning of this negative?
> **DOCTOR:** It means 'no'.
> **DALEK:** But she will be destroyed.
> **DOCTOR:** No! 'Cos this is what I'm gonna do – I'm gonna rescue her. *(true hero, fiery)* I'm gonna save Rose Tyler from the middle of the Dalek Fleet, and then I'm gonna save the Earth, and then just to finish off, I'm gonna wipe every last STINKING Dalek outta the sky!
> **DALEK:** But you have no weapons! No defences! No plan!
> **DOCTOR:** *(grinning)* Yeah. And doesn't that scare you to death?[41]

The closeness of his relationship with Rose, together with the events of the Time War, have, apparently, made the Doctor into a hyper-confident hero, a saviour figure willing to challenge all odds. This is in stark contrast to the fear of the Daleks he has demonstrated in the past, as well as to the 'team effort' that was typically required to face down a platoon of Daleks.

Earlier, I mentioned that this series promised an apotheosis for the Daleks. This episode may also be the first time that the Doctor has been cast in a position of divinity, willing to sacrifice himself to save us all. 'The Parting of the Ways' is full of religious motifs, not least of which is the sweeping score by Murray Gold as the Time Lord fulfils his promise and miraculously materialises the TARDIS around Rose in the Dalek base ship; soon after, the Doctor identifies himself as 'the Oncoming Storm' from Dalek legend. The Doctor's divine opposite, the Emperor of the Daleks, explicitly claims to be a god. When Rose infers that the Emperor's plan of turning dead Earthlings into Daleks makes the monstrous creatures half human, she is accused of 'blasphemy', demonstrating that the Daleks have turned a programmed ideology of racial purity into a dogmatic religion. 'I cultivated pure and blessed DALEK,' the Emperor replies. 'I am the god of all Daleks.'

Why then does the Doctor find it so hard to believe that the Daleks have 'found religion', to the point of suggesting instead that they have been driven mad during years of isolation by 'the stink of humanity', i.e. their own tainted bloodline? How can the Doctor claim that creatures that have played such a long game to survive actually 'hate their own existence'? Certainly this may be a metaphor for the Doctor's deep guilt as the destroyer of his own people. Equally, the Daleks are as psychologically crippled by their obsessions as the insipid citizens of Earth, who have had to suffer through an isolated century of recycled reality programmes. Even so, the Doctor hesitates before employing his Delta-wave transmitter lash-up, which will kill not only the Daleks but also all living things on Earth. The Doctor's decision not to use the device parallels the refusal of his earlier incarnation to detonate the Dalek embryos on Skaro, but the ninth Doctor admits he would rather be seen as a coward than as a killer. As Ignatieff warned about justifying a lesser evil to ourselves, the influence of others is highly significant here. Rose's presence is crucial, particularly when we recognise how likely it was that the Doctor rode out the Time War alone. In asking the Time Lord, 'What the hell are you changing into?' Rose reminds the Doctor that doing evil alienates us, not only from others, but also from ourselves. She channels the Danish philosopher Kierkegaard, who wrote: 'The biggest danger, that of losing oneself, can pass off in the world as quietly as if it were nothing.'[42] While it is likely that the Doctor's primary reason for including others in his travels is companionship, he increasingly finds himself in situations in which close friends like Rose, Donna Noble or Amy Pond are called upon to remind him that he should not be above standing on his principles, even if he has no equal to make him give an accounting for himself.

3

WE ALL DEPEND ON THE BEAST BELOW

The Monstrous Other

In one of the most remarkable of the early episodes of the new iteration of *Doctor Who* in 2006, 'The Girl in the Fireplace', a young woman whom the Doctor becomes protective of named Reinette, the future Madame de Pompadour, makes an observation that is wise beyond her years: 'The monsters and the Doctor. It seems you cannot have one without the other.' In a few compelling episodes, it's difficult to tell the Doctor from the monsters.

Philosophers have, from time to time, likewise meditated on monstrosity. In *City of God*, St Augustine takes a brief break from theologising and tackles the stories, brought from distant shores by explorers and traders, of 'whole nations of monsters', not least of which are the left-side-female-, right-side-male-bodied of the 'Pygmies', the dog-headed Cynocephalae, and the race of Sciopodes, who 'have but one leg with two feet' and, since the feet are large enough, they 'lie on their backs in the summer and they keep the sun off with their feet'.[1] A problem that vexed Augustine was posed by the reported existence of creatures intelligent and social enough to be called human, yet which God had clearly not created in his own image. Could God have offered these quasi-humans a special revelation unknown to the Christian world of the fifth century CE? This question turns out to be a version of the problem of evil, with ignorance of the whole of God's explicit revelation taking the place of suffering from natural or moral evil. How could God have established separate revelations, excluding knowledge fundamental to being saved, much as the humans working for the Morpeth/Jetsan Company keep their Flesh-constructed 'Ganger' duplicates ignorant of their own Xeroxed nature ('The Rebel Flesh'/'The Almost People', 2011)? Augustine's reply takes aim at our aspirations to attain even a *basic* knowledge of God's ways:

> The trouble with a person who does not see the whole is that he is offended by the ugliness of a part because he does not know its context or relation to the whole [...] Either the accounts of the whole nations of monsters are valueless; or if there are such monsters, they are not human; or, if they are human, then they have sprung from Adam.[2]

One of the greatest sparks of conflict in a pluralistic universe like the Doctor's is how the protagonists in a given story react to Others. Alien biology, cultures, religions and even humour often conflict with that of the human companions or the audience at home, and this conflict may become intractable. Pluralism implies that at least some beliefs or practices central to the cultures in question are incommensurable, that is, incapable of being reconciled. Whether this incommensurability is genuine or merely perceived is usually not the point, for, as Colin McGinn writes,

> The evil intention has built into its very content the idea that the other is fully other. Anything that qualifies or weakens this otherness reduces the evil of the act; any conception that unifies agent and victim tends to undermine the possibility of evil.[3]

Base Under Siege

It's unlikely that there would be such a discourse of Otherness today if Georg W.F. Hegel had not spent time considering the hidden role of conflict in the history of human self-consciousness in his 1807 *Phenomenology of Spirit*. In situating the individual and social importance of mutual recognition of equals – a concept we have already encountered – Hegel argues for the existence of phases in individuals' striving for full realisation of their mental capacities, such as understanding and reason. Postulating that humans are first self-interested, desiring machines that scour their environment for life-sustaining natural resources – much as Thomas Hobbes does with his idea of the 'state of nature' – Hegel claims that something changes when one individual meets another. 'Self-consciousness has before it another self-consciousness; it has come outside itself.' In the encounter of two desiring, active subjects – call them D and M – each becomes a mirror to the other, enabling D to see himself in new ways through M's reactions to him, and vice versa. However, how D interprets the implications of this mirroring is also profoundly confusing to him: Hegel claims that, in the encounter, D, like M, 'has lost its own self'.[4] D has, through the mere confrontation with M, an Other, become alienated from himself. As a result, Hegel says, conflict erupts: 'It must cancel this its other.'[5] To re-establish his equilibrium with his environment and achieve what Hegel calls 'the truth of self-certainty', a self confronted by an Other will try to subdue that Other, and will face the threat of being subdued himself. D and M engage in this conflict not only to 'neutralise' the Other – the opaque, resisting subject standing against each other's desires – but also to stem the tide of their own confused self-consciousness: what am I, if not this Other?

As mentioned above, Hegel treats this process as a necessary condition for the development of humanity's full rational powers, both as individuals and as a species. As a result, the broader philosophical and historical significance of wars and genocides can be spelled out by mapping them onto the dialectic of self and Other. But Hegel is not concerned about the pathologies that can irrupt from the process. He ignores what is truly evil in the *Phenomenology of Spirit*'s 'recognition dynamic'. McGinn, however, recognises this evil in the possibility of the conflicted self becoming pathologically focused on the moral and metaphysical distance between the two subjects: 'Evil feeds off the notion of otherness', he writes. 'The pleasure of evil has the idea of the victim's sharp distinctness from me built into it: what I relish is that it is *not me* that is suffering.'[6]

The *Doctor Who* metaphor for the evil that results is the 'base under siege' scenario that was pioneered in Hartnell's 'The Tenth Planet', which also introduced the Cybermen. It took off in the late 1960s, with no less than a third of Patrick Troughton's serials employing this basic premise, and was refined and questioned to raise new problems of alien–human interaction in Jon Pertwee's first year as the third Doctor (1970). Two recurring themes that Tulloch and Alvarado view as characterising much of *Doctor Who* are the central hinges of 'base under siege' stories, namely 'the threat of human defilement which is opposed by the liberation of the oppressed', in service of the writer's and director's project of 'the naming of what it means to be human'.[7] 'Base under siege' stories only work because of the operation of the dialectic of familiar and strange, self and Other, in the mind of the characters and the audiences, and they are only resolved by examining the role of alienation and conflict in a wider whole of which we are a part.

To treat them as a subgenre of *Doctor Who* (and indeed, science fiction in general) that affords philosophical understanding, it is probably necessary to go well beyond the discussion of Hegel into the continental tradition of ethics and the Other represented by Sartre, de Beauvoir, Heidegger and Emmanuel Lévinas. Space does not permit a full extension of this theme, but it is helpful to point out the finessing of the 'recognition dynamic' that, for example, Simone de Beauvoir accomplishes when treating it in the context of concrete, lived experiences of modern human beings. The struggle for recognition reminds us, in de Beauvoir's thinking, that being 'responsible for one's own freedom brings into view the need for connection to others'; that 'others are both obstacles to freedom and liberators'[8]; in short, 'there is nothing in human ontology to preclude reciprocal relations, although such relations will be held "sometimes in enmity, sometimes in amity, always in a state of tension"'.[9]

In the rest of this section, I examine the way in which monsters are considered the Other, and how humans see themselves in reference to those Others, in four 'base under siege' stories, a venerable subgenre of *Doctor Who* tales:

- Patrick Troughton's 'The Moonbase';
- Jon Pertwee's 'Doctor Who and the Silurians';
- David Tennant's 'The Waters of Mars';
- Matt Smith's 'The Hungry Earth'/'Cold Blood' (2010).

Similarities exist between the Troughton and Tennant stories in that their bases under siege represent late twenty-first-century efforts in humankind's move beyond national divisions into a new era of cooperation on the Earth's moon and Mars, respectively. The monsters invading 'The Moonbase' are the blank-faced Cybermen, the most persistent of the Doctor's recurring nemeses after the Daleks, and their primary tactic in the story is to spread a virus among the small crew of a weather control base on Luna. The Flood, an intelligent, virus-like creature that spreads through humans who are touched by 'The Waters of Mars', is an original and fairly horrific creation of Russell T. Davies. The Pertwee and Smith stories, meanwhile, are set on Earth in near-contemporary times and feature another iconic *Doctor Who* race, the primordial Earth reptiles erroneously called 'Silurians'.[10]

The Cybermen of 'The Tenth Planet' and 'The Moonbase' were deliberately crafted in 1966 to serve as Others for the entire human race. The premise by which co-creator Gerry Davis interested Kit Pedler – a medical researcher at London University – in contributing to *Doctor Who* became the framework for Hartnell's swansong as the Doctor, 'The Tenth Planet'. Pedler's greatest science fiction-flavoured fear, 'dehumanising medicine', was taken to a degree whereby the very survival of another human race from this rogue twin planet – named Mondas – would depend upon the replacement of all or nearly all of their human flesh by cybernetic parts. Davis believed that the natural consequence of this would be the loss of 'human feelings of love, pity, mercy, fear, compassion', replaced by the need for power and the raw desire to survive at any cost.[11] In 'The Tenth Planet', the leader of the Cybermen asserts that their only organic part is the brain, and although it is in 'Moonbase', rather than in this story, that the cyborgs become interested in 'altering' humans, the value they place on the human cerebrum becomes the basis of the rather gruesome, Auschwitz-like scenes of mass conversions in 'The Age of Steel'.

The weather control base on the moon that contains the Gravitron – the Cybermen's objective in 'Moonbase' – is a model of international (or at least European) cooperation. Its staff of 'British, French, Italian, German and Dutch' scientists and engineers is headed by Director Hobson, a 'large, thick-set Yorkshireman of forty-five'.[12] Hierarchies of scientific and political authority and the carrying out of technological procedures dominate the interactions of the non-TARDIS crew, as with other 'base under siege' adventures from the 1960s. Although these scenes appear quaint and padded today, they were modelled on footage of control rooms monitoring space shots such as the American Gemini and Soviet Vostok missions. The Russians are absent from the story, probably because they are the Cybermen's real-world analogue. Their absence acts as a warning message to Western nations that they must safeguard valuable technology (here, the Gravitron) from co-option by enemy agents. It is not primarily their flat and expressionless aspect and tonelessly electronic voices that make iconic Others of the Cybermen, but above all their view of human beings. Cybermen see themselves as superior to humans because they've left behind all emotions of mercy and sympathy. While this stance, when screen-written effectively (as in 'Earthshock' [1982]) seems quite alien to how we view ourselves, it is actually a chilling reflection on humanity's inhumanity to itself. At best, subjects of the Cybermen are pure instrumentalities for carrying out plans (as when they strap cyberbombs to Stevenson, Lester and the Doctor to use them as mobile detonators in 'Revenge of the Cybermen' [1975]); at worst, they are simply 'Human Resources' (the title of a 2007 audio drama starring Paul McGann). The Cybermen thus serve to illustrate a key elaboration of the 'recognition dynamic' by Jean-Paul Sartre in his *Being and Nothingness*: the Other exists as something opaque to us. In our day-to-day relations with many of the people we meet, these Others exist only as 'facticity', something that impresses itself upon us without our consent and that we cannot change to suit our desires. What we do have to work with, however, is 'the look' (interpreted very broadly as any sort of perceptual exchange) that the Others transfix us with, and our interpretation of the meaning of that look when we realise that we are the object of other people's attention. When we are scrutinised in this way, Sartre says, 'The Other's freedom is revealed to me across the uneasy determination of the being which I am for him.'[13] While the Cybermen can hardly be said to be free, the root of their evil can be found not merely in how they callously act on their colourless threat, 'You will become like us.' They are also the former inhabitants of a rogue planet precisely like Earth that grew proportionally colder even as its people's desperation grew.[14] They present humanity with one logical outcome of the success of the instinct to survive, an outcome that allows no common ground between freedom and survival.

Characterisations of Others as having nothing in common with 'us' – particularly when class, race and gender are concerned – have historically been often cast in terms of infection versus purity. In 'The Moonbase', the Cybermen use a virus called 'neurotrope X' to disable the crew before they can be snatched for conversion (a tactic they replicate in 'Revenge of the Cybermen'). Infection is also a crucial part of 'The Waters of Mars', in which the tenth Doctor arrives, unaccompanied, on the red planet in 2059 and quickly finds himself in the middle of a crisis at Bowie Base One, the first human colony there. While the leader of the colony, Captain Adelaide Brooke, is again British, the team is more widely representative of national cultures, mirroring the increased cultural pluralism of British society in the twenty-first century. Mars has nothing particularly important about it that would draw an alien invasion; here, the threat comes from the planet itself. The Doctor theorises that its original reptilian inhabitants, the Ice Warriors, encountered a strain of invasive, microscopic entities with a collective intelligence before they left their native planet. For some reason, they froze these creatures, 'the Flood'. The colonists on Bowie Base One took advantage of the native ice field, seemingly a bit of good luck, but the seemingly insignificant failure of a water filter unleashes the Flood in the colony's biodome. It is the insidious, faceless nature of the menace here that distinguishes it from the Cybermen. As mentioned in the previous chapter, *Doctor Who* has always excelled at taking the familiar and making it uncanny. Here, water itself – the giver of life – is made the enemy.

Because it was known well in advance that Tennant was leaving the programme, in the five hour-long specials of his last year there is a deliberately ominous mood. 'Waters' contributes to this in a memorable way by placing the Doctor into what he perceives as a 'fixed point in time' from which there seems no escape. Immediately upon his arrival at the base, he recognises the famous faces around him, only to realise that Bowie Base One and its entire team were annihilated in a nuclear blast 17 months after landing on Mars. When the Flood comes on the scene after infecting two agronomists, the theme of impurity and infection is introduced into a 'race-against-time' scenario to evacuate the base. With the choice of intervening or leaving, the Doctor chooses the latter, sighing, 'It's one of those very rare times when I've got no choice.'

'Waters' is remarkable for the Doctor's early resignation to Bowie Base One's fate. If the Time Lord civilisation exists in the distant future – as some writers and fans of the series have suggested – then every human event is history to them. Thus, the events of 'Moonbase', no less than of 'Waters', are, from the Doctor's point of view, a matter of record. In the first case, the Doctor takes the viral infection of the crew and other quirks as anomalies to be investigated. In the latter case, the scheme of history is already set, with the only missing piece being the mysterious reason for the self-destruct order that will destroy the base. In the script, water provides the metaphor for the Doctor's resignation: 'Water is patient, Adelaide. Water just waits. It wears down the cliff-tops, the mountains, the whole of the world. Water always wins.' While the Doctor ultimately reassumes the mantle of hero by resisting fate, the end of the tale is one in which fate wins, because the courageous Brooke is convinced she must sacrifice her own life. Does she do this to preserve the continuity of the 'fixed point in time'? Or does Brooke do it to spite the Doctor, the self-proclaimed 'Time Lord Victorious' who saves Kerenski and Bennett, yet who also seems like a menace potentially equal to the Flood?

The themes of infection and wholesale cyber-conversion make the human body as the nexus of invasion an important part of 'The Moonbase', but this is even more noteworthy in 'The Waters of Mars', where the total reduction of the base crew to siege engines occurs. Any good 'base under siege' story presents us with well-defined secondary characters, each of which has achieved professional recognition by being excellent at some speciality. The Doctor's intoxicated introduction of the characters early in 'Waters' serves the purpose of justifying his admiration for their accomplishment. The Flood, however, merely needs the Bowie team as transportation so that it can seed itself in the oceans of Earth. The makeup and staring grey eyes of those who are infected by it, as well as the horrific effect of their sinuous, coordinated movements, leave no doubt that there is nothing left of their original human personality in their husks. Their resemblance to the original crew – especially in the case of Margaret Cain, whom the audience knows is affected but who doesn't manifest the symptoms until she is quarantined – adds to the colony's and the audience's distress. Because the Flood's infection can be spread by water, this simplest of substances, the small comfort of the skin-barrier's bodily separation between alien enemy and self that was established in 'The Moonbase' is not available to the Bowie colonists.

The menace of the Flood heightens the colony team's awareness of their own bodies situated in space: the

Doctor's admonishment that 'just one drop' is enough for the Flood to perpetuate itself creates dramatic possibilities for the infection of Roman Groom and Steffi Ehrlich. The absolute distinction between self and Other is quickly broken down. This conflict is possible just insofar as one can offer resistance to the other. Because the self/Other distinction is philosophically inviolable in Sartre, resistance is always possible. While the same distinction is bridged by the social value of freedom in de Beauvoir's philosophy, she too assumes that conflict is an eventuality. This is ultimately the path that the Doctor takes as the 'Time Lord Victorious', since he is unable to face the human costs of allowing the Other to fully annihilate the self. What is curious, though, is how he 'Others' himself to Brooke in the intensity of his desire to change history on Mars:

> **ADELAIDE:** But you said we die. For the future, for the human race.
> **DOCTOR:** Yes, because there are laws. There are Laws of Time. Once upon a time there were people in charge of those laws, but they died. They all died. Do you know who that leaves? Me! It's taken me all these years to realise the Laws of Time are mine, and they will obey me!
> **ADELAIDE:** Environment controls are down. Sorry, Doctor, it looks like history's got other ideas.
> **DOCTOR:** I'm not beaten yet. I'll go outside, find the heat regulator.
> *(His spacesuit helmet is damaged.)*
> **DOCTOR:** Not beaten. Not beaten! You've got spacesuits in the next section.
> *(Water is pouring through the ceiling.)*
> **DOCTOR:** We're not just fighting the Flood, we're fighting time itself. AND I'M GONNA WIN![15]

Can there be resistance to evil that is worse than the original evil itself? Brooke's ultimate message to the Doctor affirms her belief that this can be the case, and this colours the Time Lord's view of his own death in 'The End of Time' (2009).

No, They're Scared of Me

Classic *Doctor Who*'s serialised structure had to attract audiences over weeks and months by giving them a reason to tune in next week: hence, the cliff-hanger. One reliable tactic in carrying this strategy out is the 'partial monster reveal' used as a bridge between the crucial episodes one and two of many stories. As the episode fades to black with the series' eerie signature theme, the viewer 'can only imagine the dreadful spectacle of the monster' – the limits of monstrosity are only those of the audience member's imagination. When the serial returns the next week, these traces of monstrosity resolve into the creature as a definite object in a world we co-occupy by suspending our disbelief in the narrative. As is all-too-true for *Doctor Who*, in sight 'the monster must always fail to be monstrous enough'.[16]

The 'monsters' that inhabit the Doctor's universe are thus aptly named, the etymology of the word (*monstrum*) entailing 'that which reveals or warns'.[17] Genuine medieval monster-hunters like witch-smellers, and fictive ones like Van Helsing in Stoker's *Dracula*, claimed to have expert knowledge in telling which signs indicated for their prey: there is always a detectable trace of evil to be found. Footprints, spoor, symbols are vital indicators for the monster-hunter because the monster is essentially defined in terms of the grotesque bodies, which 'often give them away at once—as giants, centaurs, gnomes, dwarfs, golems, cyborgs, aliens, or as sphinxes, chimeras, witches, satyrs, and fauns'.[18] In classic *Who*, the cliché for a monster's presence is green skin and/or livid green goo (which is typically oozing out of a dead creature's carcass). *Who* routinely offers a veritable bestiary of freakish monsters representing the result of unhappy amalgamations, in which 'the monster's appearance may combine (exaggerated) human and animal features and include other elements, for instance, parts of machines or plants'.[19]

Despite appearances, monsters in *Doctor Who* are frequently treated not as the embodiment of evil, but as a part of a larger whole that the trigger-happy chaps of UNIT, for example, don't fully comprehend. In some cases, they are treated as characters in their own right; as Colin McGinn remarks: 'For the monster must not merely be a physical expression of *our* inner life, but must also have an inner life of its own. And what is this to be like, aesthetically speaking?'[20] The third Doctor serial 'Doctor Who and the Silurians' and the two-part story 'The Hungry Earth/Cold Blood', featuring the eleventh Doctor, are episodes that combine the suspense of humans discovering warning traces of the *monstrum* with an aesthetically and morally well-developed race of creatures who share the Earth. The irony of both these stories is that humanity discovers that 'we have met the aliens, and they are us'. They are not stories of alien invasion as much as they are experiments in cultural compatibility between Earth reptiles and humans.

Besides 'Doctor Who and the Silurians', two of the four serials in Jon Pertwee's first year as the Doctor ('The Ambassadors of Death' and 'Inferno', 1970) revolve around humanity's penetration of new frontiers – both off and under the Earth – and the forces that are unleashed on the unprepared scientists who head these efforts. Although unscrupulous or obsessed researchers drive the plot in each case, these serials send a message about the deficiencies of man's ability to live up to his own hubris. In the case of 'Silurians', a 'new kind of nuclear reactor, one that will convert nuclear energy directly to electrical power', has been installed under Wenley Moor in Derbyshire.[21] When the reactor continually fails, the station security officer, Major Barker, suspects sabotage; the theme of Eastern bloc infiltration runs throughout the story. The Doctor is summoned to join UNIT's Brigadier Lethbridge-Stewart and restore the reactor to full operational efficiency. Like in 'The Moonbase', the supporting cast is made up of competent professionals, albeit with varying agendas. In 2020, according to 'The Hungry Earth'/'Cold Blood', the Discovery Drilling Project in Cwmtaff, Wales, has a correspondingly crucial goal: to discover new, renewable sources of energy by 'drilling further than anyone's ever drilled into the Earth', more than 21 kilometres. Upon arrival, the Doctor is instantly interested in the 'big mining thing' over the rise. True to post-2005 *Who*, the emphasis in the writing for the supporting cast de-emphasises on their roles as scientists and engineers and instead stresses relationships of family and love. The goal of brave Elliot Northover, grandson of one of the project's leaders, is to find his father Mo, who has disappeared down the mysterious 'mole-holes' that appear in the drill complex.

Both tales explore the evils of colonialism and the limits of community through inverting the normal dynamic of invasion *from without*. Malcolm Hulke, who created the Silurians, claimed, 'In science-fiction there are only two stories. They come to us, or we go to them.'[22] In 'Silurians', our first encounter with the reptilian race is mediated through the delusions of Spencer, who has suffered a nervous breakdown while in the caves underneath the nuclear centre and attempts to throttle the Doctor. 'Some kind of fear,' the Doctor muses after examining the monstrous images from Spencer's marker on the walls of the centre's sickbay. 'It's absolutely incredible. It's thrown his mind back millions of years.' A primordial terror of the Silurians, passed down from proto-ape to modern humans, remains a race memory in Spencer's mind; this basal and irresistible horror prepares the way for a more direct experience of what Spencer encountered.

The notion of racial memory is an element of Carl Jung's psychology of archetypes and the 'collective unconscious', which, like von Däniken's *Chariots of the Gods*, figured in a good deal of popular SF of the late 1960s and 70s. Spencer's breakdown and race-memory-inspired fear implies that the reptilian creatures represented in his wall paintings have power over humans that is ineliminably part of our psychology. Widespread knowledge of the very existence of the Silurians as primeval analogues to modern humankind would probably cause a more serious crisis of species identity for humans than even the revelation of intelligent, extra-terrestrial life. This is because much of our implicit self-concept is historical in nature, as emphasised by not only Hegel and Marx, but also (in very different ways) Michel Foucault and Charles Taylor. Phenomenologist Emmanuel Lévinas (1906–95) relates the importance of history in this way:

> The existence of the ego takes place as an identification of
> the diverse. So many events happen to it, so many years age
> it, and yet the ego remains the same! The ego, the oneself
> [...] does not remain invariable in the midst of change like
> a rock assailed by the waves [...]; the ego remains the same
> by making of disparate and diverse events a history – its
> history.[23]

If some of human history is merely a recapitulation (or worse,
a pale shadow) of Silurian achievements, then the implications
of this make it unsurprising – even if still ethically troubling –
that UNIT's final action against the creatures is to seal off the
exits from their caverns to the rest of the world.

The direct experience of the monstrous follows closely
along in 'Silurians'. Self and Other, familiar and strange, are
juxtaposed using the technique of filming from the monster's
point of view – specifically, Morka, an injured Silurian, dragging
itself across the moor in episode two, complete with laboured
breathing piped in and use of a triangular red filter over the
top portion of the camera field to replicate the Silurian's third
eye. Morka's journey to a farm leaves one person dead and
leads to a cliff-hanger in which Morka attacks the Doctor's
assistant Liz Shaw. This point-of-view technique is unusually
well deployed and paints the Silurians as genuine, monstrous
threats (only later will we find that Morka, referred to only
as the 'Young Silurian' in the script, is unusually hostile to
humans). In the novelisation of the episode, Hulke writes
about these events from the perspective of Morka. His alien
characterisation of Morka takes into account the facts that
the Silurians have only recently had their slumber disturbed,
and that they would only be familiar with the now-dominant
mammals of contemporary Earth from experience of early,
primitive primates:

> Cautiously he uncoiled and went up the ladder step by step.
> He put the top of his head against the hatch and pushed
> gently upwards until there was a thin slit of light. He adjusted
> his eyes and looked into the barn. Although the faces of the
> creatures all looked the same to him, helpfully they all wore

different clothes. There was a male creature in a long black frock coat, and he was kneeling by the body of the creature that Morka had killed. Standing close was a female creature with blonde fur on her head – long fur that hung to her shoulders.[24]

Contrasting images of the 'normal' body of a person fuel much of the discord in both 'Silurians' and its 2011 sequel. When Dr Quinn, a power-hungry nuclear scientist, makes contact with Okdel (the scripted 'Old Silurian'), Hulke writes the scene in a way that emphasises a visceral reaction to an intelligent creature of another species:

> Quinn looked at the reptile face in front of him. It was impossible to tell whether Okdel was angry or forgiving. It was the first time he had really looked closely into Okdel's scaly green face because the sight of it made him want to be sick.[25]

Correspondingly, much of the Silurian dialogue is peppered with derisive comments about the 'apes'. Even the Doctor's reactions to the Silurians were toned down between Hulke's treatment and the writing of the shooting script. In the former, the Time Lord refers to them as 'an entirely alien form of intelligent life' that is 'highly dangerous',[26] but he also attempts repeatedly to broker peace between the two races, as he does in the televised version. The Silurians' primary weapon against the humans is a highly contagious virus that 'causes a surge of energy which burns up the body's resources'. If death does not follow immediately, 'the afflicted ones wander mindlessly over great distances, infecting all others'.[27] It is with perhaps unintended irony that the primary vector for the Silurian virus, the person who 'wander[s] mindlessly' from Wenley Moor to London, is the bureaucrat, Masters, a pompous and thoroughly ineffective civil servant.

The Silurians awakening from hibernation under Cwmtaff have also been provoked by human interventions, and, like them, they utilise the tactic of sending young and aggressive members to the surface, where they successfully capture both

Mo and his son Elliot. These Silurians are also clearly divided into scientific and military contingents. Their defence force in 'The Hungry Earth'/'Cold Blood' is entirely female, and they present a forbidding façade with their reptilian masks that hide far more humanoid features than those of the earlier breed of Silurians. The lizard-like denizens of the deep also demonstrate advanced scientific and engineering capacities and have a semi-prehensile tongue as a venomous, built-in defence mechanism that substitutes for the more conventional virus in 'Silurians'. When Alaya, one of the advance guards, incapacitates Tony Mack, one of the heads of the Discovery Project, the situation quickly deteriorates, and the Doctor has to scramble once again to prevent all-out war between humans and Silurians.

Years of experience at mediating conflicts in the dialectic of strangeness and familiarity have left the Doctor more eloquent in defending the awakened aggressors. 'They're not aliens,' he instructs Mack and his daughter, Ambrose.

> They're Earth-liens. Once known as the Silurian race, or, some would argue, Eocenes, or Homo Reptilia. Not monsters, not evil. Well, only as evil as you are. The previous owners of the planet, that's all. Look, from their point of view, you're the invaders. Your drill was threatening their settlement.[28]

Charged with 'being the best that she can be' and keeping Alaya safe as the Doctor's 'bargaining chip', Ambrose's nerve weakens in the face of Alaya's taunts and threats, and Ambrose kills her.

The eleventh Doctor's diplomatic approach to the Silurians is an attempt to defuse a potential escalation of the conflict by the use of humour. His response is wisely based upon a philosophical insight into the unavoidably *agonistic* or struggle-based process of forging mutual recognition. As Lévinas writes:

> War is not a pure confrontation of forces; it can perhaps be defined as a relationship in which force does not alone enter into account, for the unforeseeable contingencies of

freedom – skill, courage, and invention – count too. But in war the free will may fail without being put into question [...] Freedom is put into question by the other, and is revealed to be unjustified, only when it knows itself to be unjust.[29]

In the human/Silurian interactions of the second part of the story, 'Cold Blood', the Doctor puts the freedom of both sides into question in an effort to stave off war. The Silurians can choose to leave their hibernation in vast numbers, without first discussing terms with humanity, and, to them, there is no injustice in this. The humans can choose, as Brigadier Lethbridge-Stewart did in 'Doctor Who and the Silurians', to pre-emptively eliminate the Silurian problem by force. Because of sheer anathema to the Other, or simply the familiar 'it's us or them' rationalisation, the tendency for each race will be to treat their own actions as self-defence, and thus no injustice is done.

Here, only the direct confrontation of selves and Others can begin the process of the development of cultural and moral self-consciousness on both sides that Hegel described in the *Phenomenology of Spirit*. There, the possible outcomes of the struggle for recognition between persons like our 'D' and 'M' are the death or enslavement of one by another, not *mutual* recognition. The Doctor clearly believes, like contemporary thinkers Paul Ricoeur and Axel Honneth, that Hegel got this last bit wrong. While we might question the wisdom of his choice of human diplomats – Amy Pond and Discovery Project head Nasreen Chaudhry – to essay such a momentous task, it is not often that the Doctor gives such a stirring call to change history:

There are fixed points through time where things must always stay the way they are. This is not one of them. This is an opportunity. A temporal tipping point. Whatever happens today, will change future events, create its own timeline, its own reality. The future pivots around you, here, now. So do good, for humanity, and for Earth.[30]

This diplomacy, like that which an earlier Doctor offered personally in 'Silurians', fails. Thanks to the SF orientation of the episode, the Cwmtaff Silurians are able to voluntarily withdraw and re-enter hibernation, becoming invisible again to humans through another resolution that Hegel did not predict for D and M.

In the final section of this chapter, we look closely at how D and M both confront and, paradoxically, identify with each other.

Dark Doctor, Light Master

The most memorable villains of *Doctor Who* are *human* monsters – megalomaniacal, devious, dishonourable, unscrupulous, perhaps classically flawed. Their list must include at the very least:

- 'The Celestial Toymaker', a game-playing miscreant;
- Tobias Vaughn, a cyber-quisling;
- Professor Stahlmann (both of him);
- Omega, a lost Time Lord stellar engineer;
- Davros, creator of the Daleks;
- Magnus Greel, the 'Butcher of Brisbane';
- the Black Guardian;
- the Rani, a devious Time Lady chemist;
- the Family of Blood;
- Madame Kovarian;
- and, of course, the Master.[31]

Plus, perhaps surprisingly, we should count the Doctor himself.

We have already seen how a number of philosophers have interpreted the possible relations of self and Other, particularly through the 'recognition dynamic', to give evidence for a hidden logic behind conflicts. Such struggles, understood in the grand sweep of history as Hegel had intended them to be, are part of a larger process by which freedom evolves, and the very limits of human self-consciousness develop with it. That makes the wailing, gnashing of teeth, and inevitable demise of *Doctor Who*'s equivalent of 'redshirts' – from Katerina to Adric to Astrid Peth – rather insignificant by comparison. Andrew Blair, in the Blog *Den of Geek*, writes:

> *Doctor Who*'s total death toll must surely be the highest of any television science-fiction series, which is all the more impressive when you consider the show's family audience. From the death of Old Mother in *The Forest of Fear* to the presumed demise of Madame Kovarian in *The Wedding of River Song*, thousands have died on screen, and trillions off it.[32]

Popular ideas about 'fate' play into narrative conceits about certain characters being 'destined to die'. But many philosophers, sceptical of such a force, interpret the worst of human evils in terms of deliberate injustice and wilful cruelty.[33] Alternatively, we might return to one of the key themes of the last chapter: the creation of theodicies to reinterpret the appearance of evil in terms of a greater good, specifically a god or gods.

What might be called the 'secular theodicy' of Benedict Spinoza (1632–77), a Dutch Jew, initiates a promising new modern trend for dealing with the ethico-metaphysical concept of evil. Spinoza was a highly systematic thinker in an age of scientific ferment, and his unorthodoxy makes it possible for later, secular readers to disentangle certain crucial and innovative philosophical ideas from their conceptual dependence on the existence of a god. One feature of nearly every theodicy is the attempt to show the reader that while the perception of chaos, evil or anomie gains firm support at the level of convention or common sense, there is another vantage point from which we can, if we make the effort, see the world in a completely different light. This perspective not only demonstrates the systematic place that misery, death and decay occupy in a rational universe, but also explains the displacement of groups, genocides, and the dying out of entire cultures. In the twentieth century, and specifically after Auschwitz, thinkers such as Theodor Adorno and Hannah

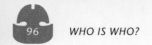

Arendt have, in their own way, affirmed the end of theodicies. Emmanuel Lévinas believes that, nonetheless, theodicy persists

> in a watered-down form at the core of atheist progressivism which was confident, nonetheless, in the efficacy of the Good which is immanent to being, called to visible triumph by the simple play of natural and historical laws of injustice, war, misery, and illness.[34]

Spinoza's secular theodicy is compatible with a certain kind of theism, but doesn't require belief in an omnipotent creator or divine providence. This, unfortunately, was only one of the many serious concerns that the Dutch and Jewish authorities had with Spinoza's fundamental ideas. As a result, for nearly a century and a half on the continent, 'Spinozism' would be the worst charge that could be laid against an intellectual. Spinoza's 'one substance', examined in geometrically organised, almost absurdly minute detail, is the subject of the first part of the *Ethics*, 'Of God'. There, Spinoza shows that what he will later call the 'intellectual love of God' begins with faith in an axiom that Spinoza though was self-evident: the principle of sufficient reason. It reads:

> To each thing must be ascribed a cause or reason both for its existence and for its non-existence. For example, if a triangle exists, a reason or cause of its existence must exist. But if it does not exist, there must also be a reason or cause which hinders it from existing, or, which negates its existence.[35]

While mainstream theological thinking of the time had it that God is both the cause and reason for the existence of creation, but that the two are substantially separate, Spinoza denied this. God must be another name for creation, or 'Nature' – as the sum of all essences. God and Nature are, if we consistently observe the principle of sufficient reason, different names for the same thing. 'His philosophy', Matthew Stewart writes,

> is at a deep level a declaration of confidence that there is nothing ultimately mysterious in the world; there are no

inscrutable deities making arbitrary decisions, and no phenomena that will not submit to reasoned inquiry—even if that inquiry is inherently without end; in short, that there is nothing that can't be known—even if we do not necessarily know everything.[36]

Although Spinoza was starting out from precisely the same point as other philosophical 'rationalists' of the seventeenth century, he was also frankly attempting to show in his *Ethics* how a rigid adherence to this principle puts much of Western thought's metaphysical and epistemological wisdom into jeopardy. For example:

> I hold that the human body is a part of Nature. As regards the human mind, I maintain that it, too, is a part of Nature; for I hold that in Nature there also exists an infinite power of thinking which, insofar as it is infinite, contains within itself the whole of Nature ideally, and whose thoughts proceed in the same manner as does Nature, which is in fact the object of its thought.[37]

Given this, it is not difficult to see how many of Spinoza's contemporaries would have seen him as the source for threatening claims, and, by extension, as an evil heretic.

The Doctor's occasional clashes with the Master often revolve around similar arguments, albeit ones elevated to the cosmic level, about whether there is transformative meaning or merely brute power in a cosmos devoid of 'inscrutable deities'. The characters represent two differing stances on these arguments, although the positions they occupy over the history of the programme are dynamic. Programme historian John Peel summarises the Master's career as follows:

> The Master is a skilled mathematician, and a graduate of the Prydon Academy [on Gallifrey]. He has a degree in Cosmic Science that is better than the Doctor's own. His one failing, according to [fellow Time Lord] the Rani and others, is a thirst for revenge that knows no rational boundaries. 'Vanity is his weakness,' the Doctor claims.[38]

Since *Doctor Who* left the air in 1989, the Master was less well developed away from the television screen than both the Daleks and the Cybermen, despite his retaining a position in viewer consciousness as the Doctor's 'best enemy'. The neglect was due to editorial decisions at Virgin's 'Doctor Who' and, later, to the BBC's book lines that emphasised development of original storylines and the recycling of fewer old monsters and villains. Also to blame was the fact that the two longest-running actors in the role, Roger Delgado and Anthony Ainley, were unwilling or unable (Delgado died in a car crash in Turkey in 1973; Ainley died in 2004) to return to record Big Finish audio adventures or the new series.

'You'll never understand,' the third Doctor tells the Master in one of their earliest meetings. 'I want to see the universe, not rule it' ('Colony in Space'). The Doctor is right, at least in part: more often than not, the Master is interested in utilising his own strength of will to bend the will of others. Viewers often see this symbolically in the Master's favourite tactic (after disguises): hypnosis. The Doctor is also only half right about himself: it is true that anyone robbed of the power of free travel, as he is in his exile, would again want to 'see the universe'. The Doctor, however, also wants to change it for what he sees as the better, and finds tragedy where he cannot. Hegel's struggle for recognition, remember, begins with *eros* or desire, and this never leaves the picture. Spinoza, whom Hegel learned much from, claimed that evils 'arise from this, that all happiness or unhappiness depends solely on the quality of the object to which we are bound by love. For strife will never arise on account of what which is not loved.'[39] As far back as 430 BCE, love and strife had been identified by Empedocles, a Sicilian thinker influential to Pythagoras, as the two basal forces that make change in the universe. As causes, love and strife are forces that unite things or divide things, and so unity and multiplicity are both derivative from their action; as reasons, love is the motivation that strives for harmonious relations, while strife – inevitable conflict – rationalises discord.

The Doctor and Master may represent love and strife, respectively, but they don't always represent them comfortably. When introduced in 1971, the Master formed the third point of a triadic relationship that already included the Doctor and the Time Lords. Doctor and Master both serve as prodigal sons to their civilisation on Gallifrey. In classic *Who*, the Doctor can be 'managed' by subtle Time Lord manipulation ('The Brain of Morbius'; 'Attack of the Cybermen', 1985). In the reboot, the story arc of the Master's resurrection and rehabilitation (as a combatant in the Time War) is also a Time Lord plot, although it takes the form of a long, long game. Combats between them are often on the cosmic scale represented by *Doctor Who: The Movie* (1996). Here, as the Master opens the 'Eye of Harmony' in the Doctor's TARDIS to renew himself at the end of his regeneration cycle, the stability of the Earth itself is at stake. Unlike in previous attempts to achieve this same goal ('The Deadly Assassin'; 'The Keeper of Traken', 1981), the Master is singularly focused on taking over the Doctor's body and, with it, all his remaining regenerations. What is common to all three stories is the Master's malicious resolve to use any means, even destroying worlds – Gallifrey, Traken or Earth – to prolong his own life.

There is almost no heroic quality to the Doctor that has not been 'doubled' in some dark way by the Master, which prompted Tulloch and Alvarado to cast the two into the role of Romantic Gothic hero and villain, respectively. With Gallifrey left behind (or destroyed), 'who was to say that the creative revolt against social masks and hypocrisy was authentic? Who was to know at what point the anti-institutional thrust became solipsistic, or turned to paranoia and madness?'[40] The time they spent together in youth on Gallifrey, together with the mutuality of their rejection of Time Lord hypocrisy and insularity, established equality between them that provided the basis for their need for mutual recognition from each other, and the desire to struggle for it. In 'The Sea Devils' (1972), the third Doctor's sympathy in the face of the Master's imprisonment is palpable, and by the time of 'The Five Doctors', the Master agrees to visit the aptly named Death Zone on Gallifrey to attempt a rescue of his foe, because 'a cosmos without the Doctor scarcely bears thinking about'.

If we look at the last two televised years of the original series, we can see that the Master may have been overly optimistic.

In what some refer to as the 'Dark Doctor' development of Sylvester McCoy's seventh Doctor in 1988 and 1989, the Doctor's origins, the extent of his powers, his motivations and trustworthiness, were suddenly made mysterious again, returning the character to his murky origins.[41] The comic depiction of the character in McCoy's first season was toned down considerably, with the Doctor being recast as a kind of chess grandmaster, playing out complex strategies and defeating ancient evils throughout space and time. Andrew Cartmel, the motive force behind this change, said, 'It all goes back to "Doctor who?" The mysterious, scary, powerful Doctor [...] It struck me this was the most interesting way to do the show.'[42] Cartmel was interested in inverting the normal course of the Doctor's adventures; instead of having the TARDIS materialise somewhere randomly, only to have the Doctor and Dorothy 'Ace' McShane fall into another set of escapades, they would be venturing onto game-boards on which the Doctor had been playing for some time. In direct opposition to the rather haphazard wandering of previous incarnations, the seventh Doctor is 'frequently shown to have a degree of foreknowledge about the situations into which he arrives, as in 'Remembrance of the Daleks', 'Silver Nemesis', 'The Greatest Show in the Galaxy', 'Battlefield', 'Ghost Light' and 'The Curse of Fenric'.[43] The Doctor often describes himself as 'more than just a Time Lord', and frequently gets into hot water with Ace when he refuses to reveal what he knows. This conflict, and the intensity of McCoy's portrayal, comes to a head in 'The Curse of Fenric' in which the Doctor plays a game of chess for prodigious stakes on an extensive chessboard: the northern English coast during World War II. As was often the case during the McCoy years, the script references previous off-screen encounters of cosmic significance, in this case with Fenric, an archaic creature that requires a host body to act in the world. In tales from previous series, including 'Remembrance of the Daleks' and 'Silver Nemesis', the Doctor has already alluded to the fact that he may be far older and more influential, cosmically speaking, than he has let on. Now, with the immaterial Fenric occupying the body of a former love interest of Ace's, the Russian Captain Sorin, the Doctor reveals Ace's true significance in events, shaking her faith in him to its foundations:

> **CAPTAIN SORIN:** The choice is yours, Time Lord. I shall kill you anyway, but if you would like the girl to live, kneel before me.
>
> **ACE:** I believe in you, Professor.
>
> **CAPTAIN SORIN:** Kneel, if you want the girl to live!
>
> **DOCTOR:** Kill her.
>
> *(Sorin laughs.)*
>
> **CAPTAIN SORIN:** The Time Lord finally understands.
>
> **DOCTOR:** Do you think I didn't know? The chess set in Lady Peinforte's study. I knew.
>
> **CAPTAIN SORIN:** Earlier than that, Time Lord. Before Cybermen, ever since Ice World. Where you first met the girl.
>
> **DOCTOR:** I knew. I knew she carried the evil inside her. Do you think I'd have chosen a social misfit if I hadn't known? She couldn't even pass her chemistry exams at school, and yet she manages to create a time storm in her bedroom. I saw your hand in it from the very beginning.
>
> *(Sorin laughs.)*
>
> **ACE:** No.
>
> **DOCTOR:** You're an emotional cripple. I wouldn't waste my time on her, unless I had to use her somehow.
>
> **ACE:** No![44]

Cartmel and *Doctor Who* producer John Nathan-Turner were playing a very dangerous game themselves with the 'Dark Doctor' concept, straining the limits of the audience's sympathy and identification with their hero while at the same time enriching the depiction of companions as characters in their own right and stressing the fragility and emotive content of the Doctor's relationships to travelling companions and strangers alike. They were, at least in this second respect, breaking new ground that would pave the way for post-2005 *Who* to reframe its central characters. After the cancellation of the classic programme in 1989, the Virgin and BBC books series were able to take the darker side of McCoy's characterisation even further: in 1996, Lance Parkin published *Cold Fusion*, in which the fifth and seventh Doctors – without meeting until the end of the book – seem to be working at cross-purposes, with survivors and artefacts from deep in Gallifrey's past at stake. To prevent his earlier self from remembering what occurred on the barren ice world in the future where the story takes place, the seventh Doctor has his rough-and-tumble companions Roz and Chris nobble the fifth Doctor on the back of the head so that a selective memory extraction can be accomplished! In BBC Books' *Bullet Time*, the popular travelling companion of the fourth Doctor, Sarah Jane Smith, is on her own in Hong Kong in 1997. Investigating gangs and cronyism there, Smith discovers that the seventh Doctor has been dealing drugs with aliens and holds high rank in the Chinese mafia. As the back cover blurb puts it when they meet: '"You're not the Doctor I knew." "Perhaps you never knew the Doctor."'

The circumstances of the regeneration from the seventh to the eighth Doctor in *Doctor Who: The Movie* is therefore quite ironic. McCoy's seventh Doctor steps out of the TARDIS in Chinatown, San Francisco, only to be riddled with bullets in the middle of a gangland fight. This is surely one of the most ignominious causes for regeneration in the Doctor's history. With Paul McGann's interpretation, the 'Dark Doctor' aspect disappears, forgotten.

Were we to contrast Spinoza's *Ethics* with the manipulation and other evils that can be laid at the doorstep of the Doctor, particularly in his seventh incarnation when he essentially assumed the form of a natural force – 'Time's Champion' – we would find a great disparity. Just as 'God' is the same thing as 'Nature' in Spinoza's metaphysics, everything that we might consider to be a substantial individual – whether an idea, a tree, a person or a whole solar system – is, from the perspective he calls *sub specie aeternitatis*,[45] a part (or 'modification') of the rational whole. Since the whole is necessary, so is each part (and both of these because of the principle of sufficient reason, mentioned above). According to Spinoza, most people are guilty of *playing god*, albeit not on the scale that the Doctor plays. By this he means that we anthropomorphise natural forces, especially those that are hidden to us; examples are rife, from primitive animism to today's evangelicals who blame droughts and hurricanes on the sins of whole populations.

> After human beings had persuaded themselves that all the things that happen occur on account of them, they were bound to consider as most important in each thing that which was most useful to them, and to reckon as most excellent those things by which they were best affected.

Such, Spinoza says, is the origin of a dizzying array of conceptions: 'good, bad, order, confusion, hot, cold, beauty, and ugliness'.[46] While Spinoza doesn't counsel resignation or quietism in the face of the necessities of life, he does claim that 'whatever we endeavour to do in accordance with reason is simply to understand',[47] and that conceptions of the understanding, rather than those of the imagination, are of the highest value. In this regard, the Dark Doctor's efforts to impose order on the chaotic system of galactic history smack of a kind of *hubris*; rather than simply 'seeing' the universe, he is engineering its outcomes out of a 'dangerous illusion of omnipotence'.[48]

It may be a surprising discovery, then, that the Master's efforts fit rather better with Spinoza's system. The will to accumulate power to survive (the *conatus* in Spinoza's word), a concept that exercised significant later influence on Arthur Schopenhauer, Nietzsche and Freud, is most probably the Master's driving motivation. 'Each person exists by the highest right of Nature, and consequently each person, by the highest right of Nature, does what follows with necessity from his own nature.'[49] While Spinoza would never condone the depths to which the Master sinks in trying to persist past his natural death(s), there is a certain Spinozistic honesty in him that the Doctor doesn't possess. F.W.J. Schelling, a contemporary of Hegel's, appreciated Spinoza's holism but thought that theodicy was a vain task: 'all attempts to deny the reality of evil are unsatisfactory evasions'.[50] It is Schelling who makes us fully able to understand why the Master's *conatus* is so disastrous for the rest of the world. One Schelling scholar explains, 'The will to self-disclosure is wrought with negativity, fused with drives that are blind and impulsive, sometimes erupting with the raging force of mania.'[51]

In the 2007 and 2009 David Tennant stories that revive the Master with the face of actor John Simm, this theme is particularly prominent. Things start with the story of the amnesiac Professor Yana, introduced in 'Utopia' (2007), a Time Lord who, like the Doctor in 'Human Nature' (2007), has had his essence hidden in a decorative pocket-watch by chameleon arch technology. The likable, eccentric Yana (played by Sir Derek Jacobi), doesn't realise he is the Master, and has been put in the ironic position of saving humankind as the only expert left alive who is fit to finish the Utopia Project. This is essentially a massive spacecraft whose intended purpose is to 'find a way of surviving past the collapse of reality itself' at the end of the universe. With the hindsight of knowing Yana's true identity, much of the dialogue of mutual admiration between the Doctor and Yana can be appreciated on several levels:

> **DOCTOR:** You've built this system out of food and string and staples? Professor Yana, you're a genius.
> **YANA:** Says the man who made it work.
> **DOCTOR:** Oh, it's easy coming in at the end, but you're stellar. This is, this is magnificent. And I don't often say that because, well, because of me.
> **YANA:** Well, even my title is an affectation. There hasn't been such a thing as a university for over a thousand years. I've spent my life going from one refugee ship to another.
> **DOCTOR:** If you'd been born in a different time, you'd be revered. I mean it. Throughout the galaxies.
> **YANA:** Oh, those damned galaxies. They had to go and collapse. Some admiration would have been nice. Yes, just a little, just once.[52]

Soon after this, the Master regains his memory and regenerates into the Simm incarnation. The reversal of major character traits of Doctor and Master in these stories, together with the tenth Doctor's propensity to wrath (noted already in 'Waters of Mars' but also in 'The Runaway Bride' [2006]), illustrates ways in which the Romantic Gothic opposition of hero and villain as 'doubles' of each other can be refashioned for dramatic effect.

A Gothic villain's 'ultimate threat' to the world is, according to Tulloch and Alvarado, 'to convert the world into one's own passion for identity'.[53] Russell T. Davies's interpretation of the character emphasises this. Simm's Master is 'lighter' than previous versions, offering comic relief and pop culture references; he also seems to have gone quite mad by this point. And the Master is obsessed with 'converting the world' into an image of himself. By his putting the Doctor, Jack Harkness and Martha Jones on the run as prime minister of Great Britain ('The Sound of Drums', 2007), we are reminded of UNIT's hunt for an earlier version of the Master during the Pertwee years. As a further example, when the Master uses his 'laser screwdriver' to rapidly accelerate the Doctor's ageing process, he makes his nemesis suffer in a similar way that the Master did while he was in his burnt and broken 'final' regeneration, first seen in 'The Deadly Assassin'. The plots of both recent Master stories revolve around his dangerous attempt to harness the power of the Spinozistic whole. First, he creates a global consciousness from the minds of Earth's inhabitants with the use of the Archangel Network, satellites projecting a low-level psychic field ('The Sound of Drums'/'The Last of the Time Lords', 2007). Second, he repairs the Immortality Gate for billionaire Joshua Naismith but uses it for his own purposes: to transmit his genetic template across the world, effectively making every human a clone of himself ('The End of Time', Parts One and Two).

If the Doctor's fault is the occasional *hubris* of his seventh, tenth or eleventh selves, the Master's flaw in these stories is the attempt to erase the 'particularity' of other personalities in favour of a new 'totality' that encompasses only him. He is, in this respect, the ultimate sociopath. The Master's flaw is, however, a tragic one in 'The End of Time'. Although the Immortality Gate had given him the greatest presence and power he had ever enjoyed – the guarantee of survival, billions of times over – this all paled in comparison to the revelation that he had been manipulated, seemingly since birth, by his own race. By the Doctor's efforts, Gallifrey had become time-locked during the events of the Last Great Time War, and the Master's mind had become an anchor in the 'real' universe to which the Time Lords could cleave when they decided to emerge from stasis. This, we find out, is the meaning of the 'sound of drums' that has driven the Master mad over centuries. For Spinoza, the irony in this would be obvious: the Master's evil in dissolving the personalities of others in favour of his own erects a new whole in which the Master is in control of all the parts. There is and always will be, however, a greater whole in which the most lofty machinations of dark souls operate. Until we also reach 'the end of time', there will constantly be opportunities for reinterpreting evil in the terms of transformative, shared meanings.

4

THE ETHICS OF THE LAST OF THE TIME LORDS

A Cosmic Prometheus

Talk about the Doctor's ethics is complicated by his inhumanly archaic nature. While there had been occasional allusions to the Doctor's astonishing longevity in the 1960s, it was Jon Pertwee's Doctor who claimed, 'I'm beginning to lose confidence for the first time in my life – and that covers several thousand years.' On the other hand, extreme maturity seems to understandably bring greater confidence – Sylvester McCoy's Doctor says that it's 'easy' to rewire a piece of alien machinery 'when you've had nine hundred years' experience'. But what often appeared as a joke in classic *Doctor Who* has become an ethical leitmotif of the new iteration of the show – the Doctor's age gives him a unique, distinctively alien perspective on matters of life and death.

The Doctor's role as the ultimate outsider complicates the evaluation of his moral choices. Gary Gillatt, a cultural historian of *Doctor Who* notes, 'In many ways, the Doctor is defined by our distance from him [...] we are rarely given access to his thought-processes or motivations, which in turn only adds to the character's enigmatic appeal.'[1] To anchor its claims of justifying and explaining moral life, ethics must anchor its claims 'anthropologically' by making reference to *humans* as paradigmatic moral agents, with emotional, cognitive or logical abilities that make possible the apparently non-natural phenomena of duty, obligation, conscience and character. It may seem frivolous or highly academic to ask after the ethics of fictive characters; after all, only the creators' imagination (and standards of audience plausibility), and not anthropological facts, constrain the development of the characters. But well-developed fictional characters who have passed through the hands of a diversity of writers, critics, editors, authors, interpreters, producers or directors can lay a certain claim to having a widely acknowledged 'essence' to them, and they may serve as cases against which we can test our moral intuitions.

A familiar theme of the programme since 2005 has been the way that the consequences of the Doctor's actions affect both him and those he defends as they resound through time. The Doctor's character and values do develop, and so does the possibility for developing dramatic tensions between the slightly different ethical perspectives of his various incarnations. This was a tension that began to be seriously developed after the regeneration from fifth to sixth Doctor in 'The Twin Dilemma' and that Terrance Dicks exploits in the first novel in the BBC eighth Doctor range, *The Eight Doctors*. McGann's version of the Time Lord, the latest at that point, is swept forward through his own personal timeline, meeting his first two selves only to confront his third incarnation, who has just defeated the Master in a post-'Sea Devils' tussle and who still possesses the latter's Tissue Compression Eliminator weapon. The Third Doctor, stranded on Earth, is 'toying with' the Eliminator while 'looking longingly' at his future self's fully functioning TARDIS:

> 'I know you won't do it,' said the [eighth] Doctor. 'Because you didn't …'
>
> Even as he spoke the Doctor realised what he said wasn't necessarily true. By his very presence he was already altering time. Who knew how much more things might change, perhaps for the worse?

The Third Doctor picked up the doubt in his mind and smiled grimly. 'Exactly! Now you're here, anything can happen!'[2]

For these temporal aspects of one person to conflict, it seems as though the Doctor must also pass through phases of moral development. Through reflecting on the moral development of fictional characters, we can often profitably recall our own, similar experiences. In many ways, the Doctor resembles the questing hero of Joseph Campbell's interpretations of ancient mythology.[3] Like this hero, the Doctor's decisions and motivations can, in a number of important ways, be 'mapped' onto features of our own common moral lives, rendering a fictive character as an extended set of metaphors. His actions and their consequences become hypothetical occasions for the audience to engage in what John Dewey called 'dramatic rehearsal of possibilities'. In the end, of course, anything meaningful we can say about Gallifreyan ethics will have to be modelled on our own empirical knowledge of the human moral condition and on our own moral intuitions.

The Ethics of Exile

Although it is impossible to know how long the third Doctor's exile on Earth lasted in 'continuity years', his adventures from 1970–4 put him in close contact with our own mad species during the show's history.[4] The decision to ground the cosmic traveller on Earth in the near future and to give him backup in the form of the paramilitary intelligence organisation UNIT was made by producer Peter Bryant and script editor Derrick Sherwin in the last year of Troughton's time as the Doctor. This portended a major revolution for the show's storytelling, especially given the BBC's recent, exciting shift to colour broadcasting. The creation of the framework for the Doctor's 'UNIT years' was the first of three sea changes for the show, each of which was created as a response to mounting external pressure from audiences whose film-going and telly-watching activities redefined what the expectations were for science

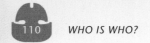

fiction and fantasy. *Doctor Who* scholars Howe, Stammers and Walker explain:

> As the sixth season of *Doctor Who* progressed, viewers appeared to forgo *Doctor Who*, preferring the regional ITV fare of *Voyage to the Bottom of the Sea*, *Land of the Giants*, *Tarzan*, and an imported series from Australia, *Woodbinda, Animal Doctor*. At the end of the sixth season, individual episodes of *The Space Pirates* and the ambitious ten-part *The War Games* received the lowest ratings so far in *Doctor Who*'s history, with the final story not even managing on average to break the five million mark, and Episode 8 managing only 3.5 million, making it the lowest-rated episode to date.[5]

A keener edge was needed, Sherwin and Bryant agreed, to infuse potent action and alien invasions with Cold War adult themes popular at the time, such as the international spy industry and the arms race.

Pertwee's first series as the Doctor is marked, not only by the new plot pivots of character development and explicitly political scripts, but by a fresh foregrounding of the ethical. The plots of three 1970, seven-part stories, 'Doctor Who and the Silurians', 'The Ambassadors of Death' and 'Inferno', are similar in that each lays blame for a catastrophe – whether the careless development of nuclear power, the loss of space exploratory missions, or the infernal end of the world itself – on one or a small group of unscrupulous scientists who care little for the victims of their quest for power. Pertwee's debut, 'Spearhead from Space' (1970), is more of a traditional romp with an alien menace at its middle, but nonetheless it shows us a newfangled Doctor more eager to *leave* Earth than to help its inhabitants, a character whose first decisive act is to steal stylish clothes for himself from a hospital![6] Although it is not incorrect to say that Pertwee played the role as 'an implacable ultra-English hero in the Bulldog Drummond mould',[7] his character, chafing under the constraint of being trapped on one world, living in Greenwich Mean Time, and forced into an unlikely alliance with United Nations military intelligence, is problematic. Representing a potential threat to the insular human race, the Doctor's alien nature as a sword of Damocles is dramatically exploited by the forces of Operation Golden Age in 'Invasion of the Dinosaurs' (1974), in which the Doctor's loyalty to his human allies is questioned not once but twice.

If we set aside appeals to virtue and character for a moment and restrict ourselves to the two dominant, modern wings of reflection about morality, there are two broad paths to take for judging the Doctor's moral behaviour. *Consequentialist* views about ethics state that what matter in morality are the consequences of our actions, and these views are marked by our attempt to see that those actions are motivated by the intent to maximise some good. The 'good' may be pleasure or happiness for the individual, the group or the community, or indeed some other secular or theological consequence, like glorifying the state or gazing at the City of God. It's tempting to say that consequentialist ethical attitudes and theories are all united by the slogan, 'The ends justifies the means', but the tremendous diversity of views about how ends and means are to be conceived and related proves this slogan is merely a cliché. In contrast, *deontological* views (from *deon*, Greek for 'duty' or 'obligation') claim that moral behaviour is to be judged by how it adheres to a rule or set of rules. Although the best-known deontologist is the Prussian thinker Immanuel Kant (1724–1804), more recently the late John Rawls (1921–2002) and his student Thomas Nagel (1937–) have championed formalist ethical theories that aim to justify moral rules or principles and explain how they are rationally derived. For Nagel, a careful process of thought reveals that there are two types of reasons for acting: personal or subjective ones and timeless and intrinsic reasons that would be reasons for *anyone* in a similar position to ours. What this implies is that altruistic actions – as examples of objectively morally correct actions – are morally justified by their *impersonal* nature. Therefore, they transcend place, time, culture and the contingencies of circumstance. While a consequentialist might reason that in many circumstances, making a false promise to others would result in more good than refraining from doing so, Nagel urges us to put ourselves in the position of the person being lied to. The basis for our negative reaction at being lied to, for Nagel, is *resentment,* and our resentment means that we think that others have a reason not to hurt us in such a way. 'But if it's a reason anyone would have not to hurt anyone else in this way, then it's a reason *you* have not to hurt someone else in this way (since *anyone* means *everyone*).'[8] There are at least some principles – whether warning against bringing about some bad consequences or enjoining us to pursue some objective good – that have an impersonal, non-subjective authority, the deontologist claims.

Deontological ethics grow more robust when they incorporate the view that good judgement is key to *applying* principles to complex situations. After all, no two moral situations can be precisely alike, so the question becomes: what are the morally significant differences between a past and a current scenario? A good judgement requires at least the capacities to assess the weight of relevant facts and the creativity to envision what principle(s) fit the situation, and how they fit. While some situations can be addressed by mechanical application of principles, many of the problems that the Doctor and his companions face are not so simple. In 'School Reunion' (2006), the tenth Doctor is presented with a tempting offer from Brother Lassar (Anthony Head) of the Krillitanes. If the Doctor addresses himself to the problem of the Skasis Paradigm, 'reality will become clay' in the hands of its solver. 'Imagine what you could do – think of the civilisations you could save. Perganon, Assinta ... your own people, Doctor. Standing tall. The Time Lords ... reborn', Lassar tells him.[9]

This would be an easier choice for the Doctor if the judgement were merely one of 'inclination' or self-interest (to save the Time Lords) as opposed to duty (to stop the evil Krillitanes). This is often how Immanuel Kant's rule-guided deontology frames moral choices, but it's not obvious that alliances with evil for the sake of the greater good (like the brief Doctor–Master alliances in 'Logopolis' and 'The End of Time', Part Two) or that using the creative powers unlocked by the Skasis Paradigm with benevolent intent are absolutely and automatically morally wrong. In fact, it is primarily the complex nature of the moral judgements put upon the Doctor that make it difficult to apply traditional ethical theories like deontology to judge his conduct. Not only are the Doctor's intentions both complex and usually private, but also they often relate to unique situations in which conventional rules don't apply.

Similarly, consequentialist views on moral justification are presented with difficulties by the Doctor's unique relationship to *time*. There is already an ambiguity in consequentialism about the grounds on which our conduct should be judged: should it be based on our *intention* to bring about the greatest balance of happiness or pleasure? Or on the good or bad consequences that our actions *do in fact* produce? So, in 'Attack of the Cybermen', the sixth Doctor's involvement on Telos undoubtedly produces the best results for everyone on Earth when the Cybermen are robbed of the power of time travel and Halley's Comet is deflected from crashing into the Earth in 1986. But both the Doctor's *intention* to bring about these results, and his morose reflection on the death of the mercenary Lytton (Maurice Colbourne), indicate that he recognises an important discrepancy between intent and actual consequences.

The case of a time traveller with the potential for changing a historically finished chain of consequences or diverting future trains of repercussions provides additional difficulties ('The Fires of Pompeii', 2008). Assessing the decisions or administering praise and blame in terms of consequences assumes a linear, cause-and-effect notion of how the universe works. But *Doctor Who* often demonstrates that thinking in terms of linear cause and effect is merely a convenient fiction – for example, in the cases of the TARDIS jumping a time dimension in 'The Space Museum' (1965), or the insight into our timeline provided by alternate universes of 'Inferno' (1970), 'Rise of the Cybermen' (2006) and the Master's Paradox Machine in 'The Sound of Drums'. The conundrums resulting from trying to apply consequentialist or deontological tests arise whenever we attempt to make assessments of whether our hero (were he a real person) is generally blameworthy or praiseworthy. This is one of the reasons the original run of the programme was less explicitly moralistic than *Star Trek* or even *The Twilight Zone*. In many respects, the Doctor's morality is an 'ethics of ambiguity'; I will try to explain this view and its attractions in the rest of this chapter.

The Romance of Time

Aside from deontology and consequentialism, there is another approach that better captures the *ethos* (from the same Greek root as *ethical*) of *Doctor Who* as a whole, and capitalises on the humanistic dimension of the Doctor's character that we explored in the first chapter. Simone de Beauvoir sees the very possibility of ethics as entrenched in the ambiguities of human nature, and the Doctor's character shares many of these ambiguities. De Beauvoir's existentialist ethic is thoroughly modernist, tempered by crises such as war and depression and reflecting a fundamental intellectual insecurity about the difference between good and bad and how these relate to human nature. She is suspicious of reducing the richness of ethical life to a moral code, and calls rigid adherence to moral theories the attribute of the 'serious man', who 'take[s] refuge in the ready-made values of the serious world', transforming conventional moral views into unconditioned values.[10] 'Ambiguity' typically refers to the fact that a sentence can have more than one literal meaning, but de Beauvoir extends its use to assert the truth of multiple meaningful self-images for persons, claiming that there is no *single* ground in human nature making morality possible and necessary. 'Ambiguity signals the tension between seemingly opposing experiences of the self as both a free subject and an object for others.'[11] We face multiple and competing self-descriptions, equally valid and equally coherent: we take on roles that are incommensurable with each other; we are free, yet bound by commitments and by our 'facticity', or the theories that describe and delimit us. We are both body and mind, both frail and capable of transcending our mundane nature; it is these *tensions* between a person's conflicting natures that make ethics possible and necessary. The roots of existentialist ethics, though, spring from the fertile ground of the European Enlightenment and the reaction to it in the form of the Romantic movement. In particular, we can look to the Romantic development – in art, poetry and other forms of culture – of the aesthetic and moral values of *the sublime* and the diversity and power of *sensibility*. These two ideas can work well together – Romantic sensibility urging us to pay attention to the evidence of the sense and emotions and to refrain from over-intellectualising life, with sublimity, or surpassing and transcending boundaries, achieving new heights, as the ideal goal of life. There is also a dramatic tension between them, a tension that sheds light on the major transformation of *Doctor Who* germane to its ethics, the genesis of which was in 1996.

This is because bold decisions were made in re-imagining *Doctor Who* in the years prior to 1996's *Doctor Who: The Movie*, and later for the new series begun in 2005. An explicit stress was to be laid on the emotions and the relationship dynamics between characters, especially between Doctor and companions, and these changes seemed justified in light of a general mainstreaming of SF characterisation reinforced in popular programmes such as *Buffy the Vampire Slayer*, *Heroes* and *Lost*. Kim Newman detects a seismic shift starting with the design of the character of the eighth Doctor, who is 'impulsive, open (if the heart is the centre of feeling, this would explain why [Paul] McGann has emotion enough for two), eager to share knowledge even if he knows he should keep it to himself'.[12] Lance Parkin could not have helped contrasting McGann's characterisation with the calculating, always-one-step-ahead seventh Doctor when he wrote, 'The Eighth Doctor [...] lacks arrogance, instead demonstrating child-like qualities of wonder and boundless energy. Everything is done in earnest, with a passion. He fixes on things and is capable of brilliant improvisation.'[13] Christopher Eccleston and David Tennant have also injected significantly more pathos into the role since 2005 as well as multiplying the number of times the Doctor has kissed (or been kissed by) companions and other fellow travellers – an ironic turn given the negative fan reaction to the eighth Doctor's snogging with Grace Holloway in the TV movie.

The portrayal of the ethically ambiguous and the passionate in *Doctor Who* converges with the ideals of Romanticism, less a philosophical system than a temperament and worldview born in Britain and Germany out of the collapse of the Enlightenment adulation of reason. Its spark was the French Revolution, in many ways the logical outcome of agitations of the French Enlightenment thinkers such as Denis Diderot and Voltaire. The overthrow of the French regime inflamed the continent, conveying an 'intoxicating sense that now everything was possible', and led many intellectuals to believe that human nature, rather than being doomed to sin and redemption, was actually perfectible.[14] The dark side of the Enlightenment, though, was found in the revolution 'eating its own children' in terms of the irrationality and excess of its 1793–4 Reign of Terror (which, as we know, the first Doctor was helpless to prevent). The Marquis de Condorcet, one advocate of the perfectibility of man and ironically a victim of the Terror himself, nonetheless held out hope for the species in general in his *Outline of the Progress of the Human Spirit*, crying, 'May I live! for after this there is nothing which I am not daring enough to hope.'[15] In a parallel construction to this movement in history, *Doctor Who* has the Doctor's character evolve from his initial 'enlightened' alienation from sterile Gallifreyan society towards more positive relationships with his (mostly) human companions, to whom he frequently preaches perfectibility through diverse experiences and moral development. In post-2005 *Doctor Who*, blatantly Romanticist themes emerge from the utter destruction of Gallifrey. It is notable that the very first time we see the Doctor openly weep is in 'The End of the World' when Jabe confronts him about the destruction of the Time Lords; similarly, a poignant welcome to a New Year's dinner, at the end of 2011's 'The Doctor, the Widow and the Wardrobe', coaxes a rare tear from the eleventh Doctor when Amy and Rory Williams tell him that they always set a place for him.

If a single ideal could be found to represent Romanticist ethics, it would have to be an ideal that has indefinite potential for richness and depth. This ideal is found in the quest for what it means to become more fully human. In face of the Reign of

Terror and the collapse of the goal of a society organised by principles of reason, historian of ethics Warren Ashby tells us,

> there arose the ideal and reality of the individual in his or her uniqueness, with potential and realised richness and depth [...] Each of these individuals broke previous rational limits and discovered new ways of feeling and thinking. In each there emerged new perceptions of what life essentially was and might be.[16]

The Romantics share with later existentialists the idea that human nature is not a given, but that its shaping is essentially in the hands of each person as expressive and free. So begins a fascination with the *quality* of experience as well as with the social conditions that made this quality better or worse.

The problem with Romanticism – the core 'philosophy' of which emerges from the literary and historical examination of poets and writers such as Wordsworth, Blake, Keats, the Shelleys, Byron, and especially Coleridge – is that (like the existentialists) it presents us with metaphors, images and narratives rather than theories. Nonetheless, a theory does not need to be *explicitly* held by those to whom it is attributed in order to do work for future generations. As I mentioned earlier, the post-Enlightenment focus on the intoxicating power of human sensibility and the sublime potential of experience are enough to begin framing a Romantic theory of the good life. The sublime, on this view, is aesthetic code for the 'transcendent', or whatever falls beyond or above the normal range of human knowledge or experience. While Romantics like Wordsworth and Byron would hearken back to Milton as the master of transcendent imagery, the Doctor seems to have the view that humans, at their best, are diligent pursuers of the sublime. While the fourth Doctor lauds the cryogenically frozen denizens of 'The Ark in Space' (1974) as indomitably 'ready to outsit eternity', the eighth chuckles that we are 'always finding patterns in things that aren't there'.

These two sides of the Romantic, his commitment as well as his 'starry eyes', are both equally important. The characteristic 'longing' of the Romantic was not for any *particular* experience, but for the 'infinite' itself, 'a feeling and a yearning that had to be realised through finite, small things'.[17] Wordsworth's 1805 poem *The Prelude* rejects an ideal of setting moderate and piecemeal goals, finding infinite longings intrinsic to the human spirit:

> Our destiny, our being's heart and home,
> Is with infinitude, and only there;
> With hope it is, hope that can never die,
> Effort, and expectation, and desire,
> And something evermore about to be.[18]

It is by exploring our feelings about the experience in question, as well as focusing on the indefinite and ambiguous qualities of the experience, that we begin to catch a fleeting glimpse of the infinite. Romantics like poet Percy Bysshe Shelley would disagree with traditional moral philosophers who hold that principled appeals to reason or consequences are enough to tell us how to live a flourishing life. Instead, as Shelley declares in his poem *The Sensitive Plant*:

> For love, and beauty, and delight,
> There is no death or change: their might
> Exceeds our organs, which endure
> No light, being themselves obscure.[19]

The human faculty of *imagination* is underappreciated, Shelley thinks. 'Reason is the enumeration of quantities already known', he writes, '[while] imagination is the perception of the value of those qualities [...] Reason is to Imagination as the instrument to the agent, as the body to the spirit, as the shadow to the substance.'[20] It is clear that this ideal is operative in *Doctor Who*'s more subtle characterisations. That is, it is more work for the audience of *Doctor Who* to have to look carefully at a character or a race and to be willing to revise judgements about them. American audiences are likely to have a different attitude towards Captain Jack's open bisexuality than British ones, for instance, and sensitively fabricated 'monsters' like Malcolm Hulke's Silurians may require real labour from audiences in order to make a sound moral judgement about them. The attitude common to both existentialism and Romanticism – in the face of the limitations of our all-too-human perspective – is a stance of *openness to surprise* in face of the unique experiences of others.

The Doctor-as-Romantic exemplifies this attitude perfectly, and it is when he wears it on his sleeve that he provides the most penetrating example of how to think about the worth of life for the rest of us. In his connection with vast and alien cosmic forces, the Doctor often pronounces how different he is from his (mostly) human companions: 'I'm a Time Lord [...] I walk in eternity' ('Pyramids of Mars'); 'The ground beneath our feet is spinning at a thousand miles an hour, and the entire planet is hurtling around the Sun at sixty-seven thousand miles an hour, and *I can feel it*' ('Rose', 2005). What is beyond the limits of current knowledge for humanity is the Doctor's normality, and what he takes as the sublime – the Eye of Orion or the Fifteenth Broken Moon of the Medusa Cascade – often surpasses his travelling companions' ability to take in. Nonetheless, the Doctor's challenge to have companions fully engage their sensibilities on their shared travels is a reflection of the rehabilitation of the power of sense experience that began in the sixteenth and seventeenth centuries with Michel Montaigne's essays and John Locke's epistemology and that flourished with the Romantics. Works such as Johann Wolfgang von Goethe's *The Sorrows of Young Werther* (1774) and Jean-Jacques Rousseau's *Émile* (1762) led readers to question the social status quo while at the same time leading them into the 'labryinths of human consciousness', as Jane Stabler writes:

> Goethe's hero [Werther] and Rousseau's natural man question the ties which bind individuals into civil society and assert a natural democracy of feeling. Spontaneous responses such as sighing, blushing, weeping, and fainting were revered as physical embodiments of this innate moral sense [...] While virtuous sensitivity was often perceived as a feminine trait, [Samuel] Richardson's *Sir Charles Grandison* (1753–4), Oliver Goldsmith's *The Vicar of Wakefield* (1766), and [Henry]

MacKenzie's *The Man of Feeling* (1771) all portrayed male characters vibrating with sympathetic impulses.[21]

Much as the Doctor's sympathies function as the mainspring for his cosmic rescue operations, the 'Sensibility Movement', beginning in the late eighteenth century, 'played a crucial role in humanitarian movements on behalf of the poor, on behalf of native peoples around the globe, as well as on behalf of the abolition of slavery'.[22] To play this role, Romantics had to first develop a new 'cosmopolitanism of the senses', in which each human is seen as united with every other through the universality not of our rational faculties, but of our feelings. 'Courts of law, theatre, church, court, government, public assemblies, academies, colleges etc. are as it were the specialised inner organs of the mystical individual, the state', wrote the epigrammatic critic Novalis.[23] With its fresh outlook on communities as organic wholes, as fragmentary societies united through ideal identities, Romanticism would also provide a framing ideology for nationalism in the nineteenth century and, ironically, for the individual-swallowing European fascism and totalitarianism of the twentieth. One of the great failings of Romanticism's weakening of the power of rational criticism (at which Enlightenment *philosophes* had so excelled) is the opening that it provides for the strong to exploit the sensitive, whether ideologically or through pure force. In Wordsworth's poetry for example,

> there was a deep tension between attitude and conceit, for the essence of the right attitude was 'wise passiveness', resignation in the face of human transience and receptivity toward nature's eternal Being, while the conceit ultimately meant poetry's triumph over fate. Poetry, in a word, could accomplish what social arrangements could not.[24]

The Doctor does not often engage in this 'wise passiveness' (one notable exception being the ninth Doctor's repeated assertion that 'Everything has its time and everything dies') but *Doctor Who* in the twenty-first century often emphasises two Wordsworthian themes – the inevitability of tragedy and the salvific power of human feeling and empathy in the face of the failures of even our most assured projects and plans.

It should be noted that the Doctor's many peccadilloes – his anachronistic and sometimes tasteless dress style being only the most prominent of these – have surprisingly exceptional status within the 'philosophy' of Romanticism as well. Romantic poetry – especially pastoral works – frequently exercises the imagination by revealing new dimensions of seemingly inconsequential things. Part of the attraction of the Doctor's eccentricity is how he immerses himself in 'finite small things', like a cup of tea, flowers, exotic hats, home cooking ('Battlefield', 1989) and, of course, little shops. 'For some people, small, beautiful events are what life is all about!' the fifth Doctor reminds us in 'Earthshock'. In some respects, the discovery of the Romantics that attentive and focused sensibilities point to transcendent natures of even ordinary things presaged the development of continental phenomenology that we examined briefly in the first chapter.

Pariahs and Existentialists

The American novelist James Baldwin observed that 'nothing is more unbearable, once one has it, than freedom'.[25] In our examination of the Doctor's adventures in time and space, we have spent little time on the notion of *freedom*, a theme of exceptional significance in both Romanticism and existentialism. The TARDIS is emblematic of this freedom: from the very first episode in 1963, we see that the Doctor's time and space machine gives him limitless opportunities to travel everywhere and everywhen – a freedom most of us would love to possess.[26] Freedom may be fathomed either in terms of what it is an escape *from*, or as an *enhancement of powers* to decide or accomplish, or both. In the Doctor's case, the significant obstacle to the freedom afforded by the TARDIS (at least in his first three incarnations) is his spotty knowledge of how to work his ship. While companion Jamie McCrimmon makes a running joke of the second Doctor's inability to pilot the craft accurately, the knowledge of 'time travel law' is actively and coercively suppressed from the third Doctor's mind by the Time Lords during his exile on Earth.

This theme of liberty as freedom from obstacles and from coercion sits well with certain strains of Enlightenment thought inspired by the work of Sir Francis Bacon, who sees 'the dignity of man in his assuming control of an objectified universe through instrumental reason'.[27] Kant would later hint in his work that liberty implied for us the possibility of a spontaneous sort of action – something sublime that is reducible to neither habit nor behaviour, but that is, rather, a '"something" that is left over when I have excluded from the determining grounds of my will everything belonging to the world of sense'.[28] According to Kant, all praiseworthy moral acts are unquestionably of this stripe, since their source is reason. Quite unfortunately, however, Kant's account leaves us without a naturalistic framework on which to hang our explanations of freedom and morality; in short, it sunders freedom and nature in order to protect the purity of both.

However, there is also a discourse that runs through Romantic thought claiming this picture of human dignity is achieved only through an artificial and ultimately harmful split in thinking between nature and freedom. What Charles Taylor calls the 'expressivist turn' begins with a very un-Enlightenment thought that is well expressed by Friedrich Schiller, who along with Goethe is a patron saint of German letters. 'Reason does indeed demand unity; but Nature demands multiplicity; and both these kinds of law make their claim upon man', Schiller writes. 'Hence it will always argue a still defective education if the moral character is able to assert itself only by sacrificing the natural.'[29] For Schiller, as for the poet Hölderlin and philosopher G.W.F. Hegel after him, if there were to be no way to reconcile the opposite sides of the human condition – freedom and duty on the one hand and nature, feeling and desire on the other – then we would have to content ourselves with the possibility of a permanent 'underclass' of the ignorant and incapable. This is the undesirable outcome when 'not merely individuals, but whole classes of men, [are] developing but one part of their potentialities, while [in] the rest, as in stunted growths, only vestigial traces remain'.[30] It is an unacceptable cost, even if we accept the dualistic basis for the struggle between freedom and nature.

Furthermore, Schiller seizes on an important point when he claims that 'freedom' as 'freedom from obstacles' is an oversimplified sense of the concept. He claims:

> Civilisation, far from setting us free, in fact creates some new need with every new power it develops in us. The fetters of the physical tighten ever more alarmingly, so that fear of losing what we have stifles even the most burning impulse toward improvement, and the maxim of passive obedience passes for the supreme wisdom of life. Thus do we see the spirit of the age wavering between perversity and brutality, between unnaturalness and mere nature, between superstition and moral unbelief; and it is only through an equilibrium of evils that it is sometimes kept within bounds.[31]

We should read Schiller here as suggesting that ethics properly balances a view of the freedom and rights of the individual with empirical theories of the human good to find a way to structure society to maximise both. That is, ethics leads towards the perfectibility of individuals and the species.

When we consider the importance of having both the opportunity and the audience to express one's own unique solution to Schiller's dilemma of morality versus nature, we find the link between the Romantics and the twentieth-century existentialists. Perhaps the best known of these latter, Jean-Paul Sartre (1905–80), has pointed out that freedom not only means having choices between a range of options for acting, but also refers to a *positive ability* to make one's own choices. Sartre's widening of the concept of freedom calls attention to the ways in which a traditional moral sense constricts available notions of what 'ethics' is all about: are we simply to *avoid* forbidden actions, as rule systems such as the ancient Egyptian code of Ma'at or the Ten Commandments require? But then, what should we *do*? The content of a *flourishing* life is not something gleaned from a set of rules, even if one concedes that it must work within it. Must we focus on performing our absolute duties, as Kant recommends?

This ignores the possibility that we might have insoluble *conflicts* of duties, but also fails to deal with the possibility that we might be simultaneously commanded to both do and refrain from doing an action – surely a deep problem![32] Are we simply to act in favour of the greatest pleasure for the greatest number, as hedonistic consequentialists would have it? This exposes us to the possibility that the happiness of the many may consistently depend upon the oppression of the few, a situation that the Doctor encounters far too often as evidenced by 'The Mutants' (1972), 'The Sun Makers', 'The Happiness Patrol' (1988), 'The Rebel Flesh'/'The Almost People' and many other adventures. Rejecting the very idea that moral theory might be helpful in grappling with our own 'dreadful freedom', Sartre instead offers a compelling story of a young French student who came to him for advice during World War II:

> The boy was faced with the choice of leaving for England and joining the Free French Forces—that is, leaving his mother behind—or remaining with his mother and helping her to carry on. He was fully aware that the woman lived only for him and that his going-off—and perhaps his death—would plunge her into despair. He was also aware that every act that he did for his mother's sake was a sure thing, in the sense that it was helping her to carry on, whereas every effort he made toward going off and fighting was an uncertain move which might run aground and prove completely useless.[33]

What choice did Sartre advise his troubled student to make? The answer may be surprising; to understand it, we must make a short hop in the TARDIS to other existentialist views. Without seeming obtuse, I want to explain these views through answering what could be the most decisive question in *Doctor Who* (besides, of course, 'Who is the Doctor?'), namely, 'Why did the Doctor leave Gallifrey?'

More than forty years after the show's première, we still know little about the Doctor's reasons for his lifestyle choice of 'wandering through space and time in a rackety old TARDIS' ('The Five Doctors'). At first, both the Doctor and his granddaughter Susan speak longingly of one day returning to their unnamed homeworld, from which they have been exiled. The Doctor's confessed inability to control the TARDIS suggests that he left home in less than ideal circumstances. In this role, the Doctor clearly represents a forlorn individual like Sartre's student: both must face up to both the opportunities and the dreadful responsibilities of being free.

But things are not so clear! In 'The War Games', the second Doctor is seized by the Time Lords and put on trial for interference in the course of established history. He claims to his companions that he left Gallifrey *voluntarily*, because he was bored. What are we to make of the inconsistency of the Doctor's motives and, indeed, his entire history? Existentialism will weigh in that inconsistency and ambiguity are to be treasured because they are close reminders of our own freedom to revise our identity and our future. Dostoevsky – not a philosopher but nonetheless a keen observer of the complex web of reason and subjectivity – has his 'underground man' tell us,

> Reason knows only what it has managed to learn (some things, perhaps, it will never learn; this is no consolation, but why not say it anyways?), while human nature acts as an entire whole, with everything that is in it, consciously and unconsciously, and though it lies, still it lives.[34]

Both Dostoevsky and de Beauvoir, albeit in very different ways, acknowledge that the pursuit of human wholeness requires not only a recognition of the ambiguities of our nature but also our efforts towards 'impossible possessions', like Sartre's injunction about man attempting to *be* God. All three highlight our struggles towards making ourselves a 'lack of being', that is, wresting ourselves from whatever is mechanical and uninflected in our lives in order to continuously reaffirm our freedom.[35] Consistency of character, and perhaps even of self-description, is often the casualty of meeting this challenge. And, as James Chapman writes in his cultural history of *Doctor Who*, 'The cultural politics and narrative ideologies of *Doctor Who* [...] serve to encourage difference and non-conformity.

This is evident [...] in the characterisation of the Doctor himself as an eccentric and a social outsider.'[36]

This is important because existentialists, like the Romantics, put a premium on the unique character of subjective, concrete experience as well as on passion. They take a page from the phenomenologist's notebook in affirming that an individual consciously 'renounces its possibilities only by acquiring others. It can *freely make itself* akin to things, but it cannot *be* a thing.'[37] The self, though, is confronted by an indifferent universe, in which 'planets come and go. Stars perish. Matter disperses, coalesces, forms into other patterns, other worlds. Nothing can be eternal', as the sixth Doctor tells Peri in 'The Trial of a Time Lord'. Like the multiverse of parallel worlds, diminished when the Time Lords' influence died away, 'the walls of reality closed, the worlds were sealed. Everything became that bit less kind' ('Rise of the Cybermen'). Sartre gives the name 'facticity' to the world of social probabilities and physical constants, since its possibilities are similarly 'sealed'. In such a sphere for human expression, it seems that values must gain their action-guiding form by the fact that they are possibilities, not actualities. If the good pre-existed our achieving it, there would be no reason for acting at all. As a result, existentialists see that it is *our choices themselves* that confer value on a situation. The opposite perspective, embraced by most traditional ethical theories including deontology and consequentialism, is that value is a pre-existing good that we reach for (and hopefully, achieve) when we act correctly.

Against this seemingly common-sense approach, Sartre tells his student to avoid relying on religious doctrines or philosophical theories for advice: not only do they lead us to different outcomes based on arbitrary presuppositions, but they are a way of transferring the ultimate responsibility for value and choice onto something *other than us*. Never one to claim ideal relationships with his companions, the fifth Doctor is nonetheless a shining example of Sartre's advice in his treatment of Vislor Turlough, an exiled noble from the advanced planet Trion 'imprisoned' at a boy's school in contemporary England. After a car accident that left him hanging between life and death, Turlough made a bargain with the Black Guardian to assassinate the Time Lord; he makes several attempts, yet it is unlikely that the Doctor is so naïve as to be ignorant of his goal. Perhaps wanting to redeem himself for the death of Adric, another troubled young man under his care, the Doctor supports Turlough in making difficult choices, even when he disagrees with them. When Turlough is rewarded with an enormous diamond at the end of the Eternals' space-yacht race ('Enlightenment', 1983), he refuses the prize and at the same time betrays the Black Guardian, prompting the Doctor to intone, 'Enlightenment wasn't the diamond. Enlightenment was the choice.' Sartre would have approved of the contrast between the Enlightenment crystal (as a metaphor for reified value), and, on the other hand, Turlough's authentic choice. To accept wholesale the advice of others when making a choice, or to avoid the full responsibility for that choice, is to engage in what Sartre calls 'bad faith', the act of denying the aching truth of our freedom. Sartre's advice is simple but troubling: make *some* choice and *assume responsibility* for the choice. Hiding behind pretended absolutes or allowing others to make the decision for us is equally inauthentic – again, bad faith!

A final benefit to examining the Doctor's exploits through the lens of existentialism is the affirmation that tragedies will always occur. Given the contingency of both human choices and life in general, there lies the constant possibility of the eruption of irremediable evil that destroys the warp and woof of the values and goods we treat as our safety net. Sartre integrates the ethics of tragedy into his ethics by affirming that anyone who genuinely acknowledges her freedom will inevitably feel anguish, forlornness and despair, thus rehearsing key parts of the emotive regimen of the victim of contemporary horrors. Typically not one to wear such negative (if cathartic) emotions on his sleeve, the Doctor has also demonstrated anguish, forlornness and despair, not only in the face of his own actions, but also in the face of those of his companions and allies. It's difficult, for example, to suppress one's sympathy for the third Doctor when he motors off into the twilight in Bessie after Jo Grant takes her leave from the role of assistant ('The Green Death'). While Tom Baker and Peter Davison dramatically underplayed their farewells to companions, the post-Gallifreyan-apocalypse Doctor – especially the Eccleston and Tennant versions – often display 'cosmic angst' corresponding to his utter 'abandonment' (another Sartrean concept) in being the last of his kind.

Perhaps the best indicator of each Doctor's success in striving for existential authenticity, however, is how he engages with situations in which his travelling companions avoid or abuse their own freedom. It is with little sense of remorse that the angry ninth Doctor leaves Adam Mitchell behind after only one trip in the TARDIS, during which time Rose's would-be boyfriend attempted to exploit future technology for gain in his present ('The Long Game'). It is with more remorse, and perhaps more authenticity, that the tenth Doctor betrays his preference for Rose after Mickey Smith joins the TARDIS crew on a trip to a parallel-universe Earth. Forced to choose between following Rose or Mickey into inevitable danger,

> *(The Doctor turns from Rose to Mickey. They're both walking away from him and he doesn't know which way to turn.)*
> **MICKEY:** *(gesturing to Rose)* Go on then. No choice, is there? You can only chase after one of us, and it's never gonna be me, is it?
> **DOCTOR:** *(to Mickey)* Back here in twenty-four hours! *(And he runs after Rose. Mickey watches his retreating back.)*
> **MICKEY:** *(to himself)* Yeah. If I haven't found something better.[38]

Mickey does find something better, taking over the role of Rickey Smith, the slain parallel-Earth leader of the anti-Cybus forces. That he had to travel so far to find an authentic role to play as the leader of people who genuinely depend upon him (unlike Rose) is perhaps ironic. This subplot of 'Rise of the Cybermen'/'The Age of Steel' underscores the important fact that although the Doctor's unspoken ethics are based on mediating his own existentialist despair by placing his companions in situations in which they can grow and flourish in ways conducive to the Romantic ethos, he also puts them at extreme risks in doing so. Whether we see this wager as acceptable or not will largely depend on where our own attitude towards tragedy and the importance of human perfectibility falls in our hierarchy of values.

Prometheus is a Fast Bowler

The Doctor's morality is not algorithmic. Particularly when one incarnation of him is judged against another, he is less predictable than other protagonists of long tenure in SF such as Doc Savage, Isaac Asimov's detective Lije Bailey, or Captain James T. Kirk of the USS *Enterprise*. In his existentialist leanings, the Doctor acknowledges both his ultimate freedom *and* responsibility for his choices by largely rejecting Time Lord culture and defining himself through his wandering and his relationships with those of others species. As a Romantic, the Doctor seeks the infinite in small events – whether in the joy of running through corridors, or in the tragic loss of Shakespeare's 'Love's Labour's Found' – and recognises that, since his own path to self-actualisation must be idiosyncratic, everyone else's must be as well. But in what sense does this lead us to an ethics that is transmissible and action-guiding for the audience?

To reiterate a theme from the beginning of this chapter, we face a problem when we try to gauge the Doctor's morality, realising that he is different to human moral agents in many significant ways. In 'The Twin Dilemma', an episode introducing the sixth incarnation of a Doctor who seemed increasingly at odds with himself, the Doctor reminds us, 'I'm not only from another culture, but another *planet*. I am in your terms an alien. I am therefore bound to have different values and customs.' I would argue that the Doctor resembles a figure in Greek mythology, Prometheus, because both are valorised by our culture in roughly the same ways.[39]

A Titan, and thus a member of a society that the Greek gods proper overthrew and destroyed, Prometheus challenged the all-powerful, all-knowing Zeus by stealing fire from Olympus to give it to humans to use as they pleased. Zeus (never known for his mercy) chained the most metaphorically important thief in history to a rock, where an eagle ate his liver, over and over again, for eternity. This was a painful process carried out daily, as Prometheus, being immortal, regenerated after each attack. The punishment was not *quite* eternal, however, as Hercules was later to kill the eagle and free Prometheus from his chains.

The Prometheus myth resonates today as a humanistic reversal of the biblical myth of the Fall: the theft of enlightenment, whether Zeus's fire or the fruit of the tree of knowledge, may be seen as merely a temptation to self-destruction. Certainly Rose's and Donna's mothers are worried about this as their daughters go off with the Doctor. Besides reinforcing the bonds of a friendship, the invitation to travel in the TARDIS expresses the Doctor's desire to *liberate* humans, giving us a degree of control over our identities that is at times delightful, at others dreadful. The gift of fire from a Gallifreyan Prometheus – in the Doctor's words, 'a whole galaxy to explore, millions of planets, aeons of time, countless civilisations to meet!' ('The War Games') – is an existentialist allegory for escaping from the provincialism of life on one planet and, further, from the mediocrity of much of contemporary mass culture. It is also a Romantic's metaphor for cultivating our imagination and creating provocations against bias and narrowness, whether our own or that of others.

These reflections disclose the latent content in discussions of popular culture in philosophical contexts. Fictive scenarios, properly contextualised within the 'field' of a programme's 'universe', video-game scenarios or other narrative continuities, provide accessible ways for nearly anyone to challenge dominant paradigms of thinking. The Doctor's proclivity for seeing his companions and adventures through the lenses of Romanticism and existentialism is itself challenging to the dominant ways of talking about ethics in schools, universities and the professions because, all too often, morality is treated as something distinct from the social, biological and cultural conditions from which it emerges. When we talk about what is valuable, the difference between good versus evil, or what a flourishing life would look like, we're best aided by not only reflections from popular culture, but also facts from other, non-philosophical disciplines such as anthropology, social psychology, game theory and cognitive science. These bodies of knowledge help put flesh on the all-too-thin bones of ethical rules and standards. They make our exploration of morality *concrete*. Perhaps this seems to conflict with *Doctor Who*'s unique, recurring narrative twist of the juxtaposition of the familiar and the otherworldly that stories such as 'The Mind Robber' (1968) and 'The God Complex' (2011) excel at executing. After all, Jon Pertwee himself was famous for saying that Daleks aren't scary, but finding a Yeti on your loo in Tooting Beck *would* be. We shouldn't overlook the likelihood that such juxtapositions may be hidden in the most unassuming of guises, even in ethical life. The Doctor's ethics are inspiring to us primarily because they present fictive examples of the all-too-human demand that we assume risk in order to improve ourselves, that we expand the very notion of freedom in the ways in which we act, and that we let ourselves be inspired by the surprising and the novel.

5

NOT THE MAN HE WAS

Regenerating the Doctor

'Is this death?' 'It's the end, but the moment has been prepared for.' 'I don't want to go.' 'Carrot juice, carrot juice, carrot juice!'

These are some of the most memorable pre-mortem lines from the Doctor, one of very few fictional characters who has had the distinction of uttering multiple sets of final words.[1] Such words are usually delivered under grave circumstances to tearful travelling companions, and, within the ongoing narrative of the programme, signify the 'end of an era'. While it remains a matter of faith and not of empirical evidence whether any human can be assured of a life after death, the Doctor has enjoyed just such an assurance – so far, 11 times over. The transformation of the Doctor that we now call 'regeneration' first occurred on 29 October 1966. 'When the fourth season got under way', write programme historians Howe and Walker, 'viewers could scarcely have supposed that in just a few weeks' time *Doctor Who* would have a new lead actor.'[2] The decision to write out William Hartnell as the Doctor and introduce a successor was one of exigency: producer Innes Lloyd claimed that Hartnell, though only 58 years old, 'was getting on and getting tired. I thought that the tiredness and the irascibility were not going to be good for the show, or for him.'[3] Hartnell apparently strongly approved of his successor, 40-year-old Patrick Troughton, who would transform the role primarily through injecting more comedy into the characterisation. Meanwhile, the production team reasoned that viewers, who already understood that the mysterious Doctor wasn't human, would follow along with the idea that

> he might well possess some extraordinary and hitherto unsuspected powers – including the ability, when his old body wore out, to rejuvenate himself. In other words, he might undergo a process of physical renewal in which his appearance, and even his personality, would be bound to change drastically.[4]

By 1974, with Jon Pertwee leaving the role, producer Barry Letts and script editor Terrance Dicks had given considerably more thought to the Doctor's transformations as part of an evolving 'Time Lord' mythology. Dicks had co-written with Malcolm Hulke's 'The War Games', the story that first featured the Time Lords themselves. In 'Planet of the Spiders' (1974), Pertwee's swansong, 'regeneration' is finally named and explained. This unusual narrative tactic of changing actors playing the same character within the course of a series, justified with in-continuity explanations, has become so closely identified with *Doctor Who* that the trope has been named 'the Nth Doctor'.[5]

Doctor Who raises questions about the nature and continuity of personal identity by its very title. In our own mundane experience, the clearest examples of 'persons' are embodied creatures with a type of consciousness demonstrating particular traits. Is the body primary in this relationship? Or is consciousness primary, or some other non-physical factor, such as an immaterial soul or the role played by an individual in the system of the universe, as perhaps Spinoza would have it? Establishing criteria for identity in general – what makes a thing what it is, and not something else – is important for classifying things into natural kinds. The periodic table of the elements and Linnaean zoological classification both rely on established theories of identity. Because personal identity has been an important, if controversial concept in legal theory, medicine, moral and political life, theology and metaphysics, it is worth asking if the depiction of persons in the Doctor's universe sheds any light on these questions. It might seem that because the Doctor is not human, this must make any inquiry into the basis of his personal identity merely academic. But, as Harry Frankfurt notes, theories of personal identity need not be species-specific, since they 'are designed to capture those attributes which are the subject of our most humane concern with ourselves and the source of what we regard as most important and most problematic in our lives'.[6]

It's Far From Being All Over

In the 2005 *Children in Need* mini-episode of *Doctor Who* called 'Born Again', the newly regenerated tenth Doctor tells a puzzled and suspicious Rose Tyler, 'I was dying. To save my life, I changed my body [...] every single cell. But [it's] still me.' When Rose asks him if he can 'change back', he looks surprised – as if he had never considered the idea – then says he can't. What convinces Rose that two completely different-looking men are in fact the same is the Doctor's ability to remember the first word he said to her: 'Run!' But he is soon stricken by post-regenerative instability (a frequent occurrence for him), and sends the out-of-control TARDIS careering towards Earth.

Rose does well to disbelieve the Doctor, at least at first. Like the rest of us, she has the psychological trait of being epistemically conservative: she prefers to stick with her established beliefs rather than change them, even in the face of contrary evidence. Philosophically, this reliance on established experience may be the main reason why we take persons we meet on Monday to be the same person on Friday, or the next week, or the next year. Intriguingly, Time Lords seem to be able to recognise each other despite their complete change of appearance. Nonetheless, problems with personal identity frequently crop up in the Doctor's universe, and not just for regenerating Time Lords. It's interesting to compare Rose's reaction to that of Ben Jackson and Polly Wright, who were present at the historic change from first Doctor to second. Their early scenes together in the TARDIS reveal not only the trepidation that any of us would feel in witnessing such an event, but also the new Doctor's wiliness:

> **BEN:** Now what's the game?
> *(The man turns, cheerfully brandishing an ornamental dagger.)*
> **DOCTOR:** Ah! The Crusades, from Saladin. The Doctor was a great collector, wasn't he?
> **POLLY:** But you're the Doctor.
> **DOCTOR:** Oh, I don't look like him.
> **BEN:** Who are we?
> **DOCTOR:** Don't you know?
> *(The man rummages further and pulls out a piece of dull silver metal. His look of mischief fades as the object triggers a very clear memory.)*
> **DOCTOR:** Extermination.
> *(The man stuffs the metal into his pocket. His concern turns to delight as he unearths a magnifying glass. He begins a careful study of his hands.)*
> **DOCTOR:** Ah. Very good. Nails need growing.
> *(Ben takes the Doctor's ring from Polly.)*
> **BEN:** Now look, the Doctor always wore this. So if you're him, it should fit now, shouldn't it?
> *(And slips it on the man's finger. It's far too big.)*
> **BEN:** There. That settles it.
> **DOCTOR:** I'd like to see a butterfly fit into a chrysalis case after it's spread its wings.[7]

Of course, healing a cut or growing fur or hair shows that every species is capable of some kind of *biological* regeneration. The Doctor might have relayed more insight if he had referenced the planarian flatworm or the freshwater hydra rather than a butterfly. Hydras have the capacity to fully regenerate tissue and organs after massive cellular dispersal, through a process called 'morphallaxis'.[8] Regeneration stories in *Doctor Who* have often implied that a new Doctor's mental instability can be attributed to incomplete renewal of the brain cells, as when the fifth Doctor tells Tegan and Nyssa that he'll stay in the TARDIS Zero Room 'until my dendrites heal. The nervous system's a very delicate network of logic junctions' ('Castrovalva', 1982). But whether we are dealing with brain cells or a whole being, some clarity is required about what makes a thing the same over time – particularly when that thing is a Time Lord, capable of having multiple iterations of himself or herself existing at the same time, in more or less the same place. Each iteration is called an 'incarnation' in the lore of the programme.

Questions about identity usually start from the basic logical principle of identity, 'A = A', which implies that 'there is no such thing as two individuals indiscernible from each other'.[9] Things are discernible from each other by their properties: so the eleventh Doctor has a faint scar on his forehead, but the tenth Doctor does not. The property of 'having a forehead scar' applies to Smith's character, but not to Tennant's. If two different things were *genuinely* indiscernible, they would both have exactly the same properties – and this would have to include properties regarding spatial and temporal location. So in 'The Almost People', the eleventh Doctor and the Ganger Doctor are (qualitatively) nearly identical and exist (for a while, at least) during the same time, but they don't occupy the same space. Just look at them complimenting each other on their inspiring plan to save the humans and the Gangers alike (is this a case of vanity or politeness?). While the Doctor and his double in this case seem *qualitatively* identical, they're not *numerically* identical, sharing exactly the same properties. We can all tell the Ganger Doctor from the Gallifreyan Doctor (check the shoes!) but the thorny problem of how to define numerical identity has exercised some of the most brilliant philosophers, not the least of whom was Gottfried Wilhelm Leibniz.

Leibniz (1646–1716), like Spinoza, lived during a particularly prolific period of the European scientific revolution, and was obsessed with integrating new discoveries in physics with the Aristotelian-influenced Scholasticism that had dominated the Middle Ages. Leibniz was dissatisfied with the Aristotelian answer to the question, 'What makes an individual different from any other individual, no matter how similar?' Leibniz used the same term as Aristotle had, that is, 'substance', to refer to genuine individuals; however, he did not find compelling the Aristotelian definition of a substance as a particular combination of matter and form. Throughout the early modern period in which Leibniz's influence was felt, 'substantial' individuals would be seen as what 'support' qualities, and what stay the same despite the inevitable change of those attributes.

Although rejecting the Aristotelian idea of essences, Leibniz was convinced that differences between similar things had to be due to some property or properties that were not shared between the two. Hence Leibniz's Law: 'if individual x is distinct from individual y then there is some intrinsic, non-relational property F that x has and y lacks, or vice versa'.[10] For reasons having to do with his own elaborate metaphysics, Leibniz excluded position in space and time from the catalogue of 'intrinsic' properties, since place and time are 'relational' properties between things, not of things themselves. In the case of persons, Leibniz thought that the key intrinsic property was the soul:

> Few theologians would be bold enough to decide straight away and without qualification to baptize an animal of human shape, lacking the appearance of reason, which had been found as an infant in the woods [...] For it would not be known whether it belonged to the human race and whether there was a rational soul in it; it might be an orang-outang [...] It is certain, I admit, that a man can become as stupid as an orang-outang; but the inner being of the rational soul would remain despite the suspending of the exercise of reason [...] So that is the essential point, and it cannot be settled by appearances.[11]

If 'hard cases' such as feral children and talking cabbages can't be 'settled by appearances', then there must be some property that is both necessary and immediately given to us that separates Leibnizian persons from non-persons. The property is the soul or 'self', which plays an important part in the complex metaphysical system Leibniz sets forth in his *Monadology*. The self is immediately given to us – we don't perceive it as we perceive things external to us, or even to our own body – as 'appearance of self', or consciousness. Leibniz acknowledges that because the state of consciousness has occasional lapses – from deep sleep to being zapped by Crozier's mind-transference device in 'Trial of a Time Lord' – we rely on society to provide information where we have memory gaps. But Leibniz cannot stress enough that the principle of sufficient reason demands there be reasons for why society reacts to us in the ways it does *and* for why we are immediately aware of certain appearances as of 'ourself'. Both can be traced back to the soul as a creation of God, but this need not be taken merely as an article of faith. In the *Monadology*, Leibniz employs other rationalist principles to explain the part the soul plays as a simple substance that is nonetheless capable of infinite changes over time.

In these musings about souls and orang-utans, Leibniz was also engaging in a philosophical duel of wits with John Locke (1632–1704), the founder of both philosophical empiricism and political liberalism. Locke's *Essay Concerning Human Understanding* represents a bold attempt to synthesise a number of dominant intellectual positions competing for the hearts and minds of Europeans as the Enlightenment dawned. As a physician, Locke would have been attracted by the mechanism of Thomas Hobbes and the corpuscularianism of Robert Boyle. Both of these views enriched the model of the human body that was emerging from scientific investigation of the brain, heart and nervous system, a model that saw our physical frame as a 'subtle machine'. Although Locke conceded, 'Whether Matter may not be made by God to think is more than man can know', he was no materialist.[12] There was, to his way of thinking, an explanatory gap between the effects of matter-in-motion, on the one hand, and the experience of 'what it is like' to be conscious of oneself and a world, on the other. This made wholehearted acceptance of materialism an unwise move.[13] As both a religious man and a philosopher who believed that experience is the test for meaning and truth, and that our experience is cashed out in terms of simple and complex ideas, Locke was attracted to the idea that a vital component of the human being is an 'immaterial Spirit'. Like Plato and Descartes before him, Locke is correctly identified as a dualist in his metaphysics; there are two basic substances: mind and body.

Locke's empiricist view of personal identity takes full advantage of the possible concatenations of these two substances. He discusses mind-swaps and body-swaps, and as a result makes himself the philosophical patron saint of SF fans everywhere. While Leibniz had seen identity as a logical and necessary relation, Locke treats the same concept as being the outcome of a particular type of experience: the experience of comparison. 'When we see anything to be in any place in any instant of time,' he explains, 'we are sure (be it what it will) that it is that very thing, and not another which at that same time exists in another place, how like and undistinguishable soever it may be in all other respects: and in this consists identity.'[14] This is an important move that puts philosophy more squarely in line with common sense, for while Leibniz shows that reflection and deduction are capable of convincing anyone that *they* persist over time, our problems about identity (like those of Rose, Ben and Polly) more often centre on others than on ourselves. Our enquiries of comparison establishing something as the same at an earlier and a later time, Locke says, actually reveal that there are three senses or 'levels' at which identity can be established: that of material objects, of organisms and of persons.

Material objects (such as rocks and sonic screwdrivers) are comprised of a multiplicity of 'atoms', or simple parts that cannot be further broken down, Locke theorised. So

> whilst they exist united together, the mass, consisting of the same atoms, must be the same mass, or the same body, let the parts be ever so differently jumbled. But if one of these atoms be taken away, or one new one added, it is no longer the same mass or the same body.[15]

In the strictest sense of 'identical', a simple 'atom' or particle remains the same, but the composite of which such 'atoms' are made does not if only one particle is taken away. Locke would have held, much as his later British empiricist counterparts Bishop Joseph Butler and David Hume did, that, 'strictly speaking, there do not exist any objects that persist through a change of material composition'.[16] This rather shocking discovery, however, didn't faze Locke, Butler or Hume, all of whom treated empiricism as a system for generalising observations of particular, non-recurrent things. The situation becomes slightly more complex when dealing with living organisms, or 'an organization of parts in one coherent body, partaking of one common life'.[17] The 'one common life' here refers to a principle or function by which 'organized parts [are] repaired, increased, or diminished by a constant addition or separation of insensible parts' according to a pattern. This is more or less the role that we know DNA plays today, or the equivalent for Time Lords (as listed on their biodata extracts on Gallifrey). An organism is the same organism (human beings as biological creatures included) just in case the principle of its 'inner motion' stays the same, making birth, life, reproduction and death possible according to set biological parameters. The actual material of the organism's body need not remain the same, and, indeed, is constantly interchanged with its environment. The 'organism' level of identity introduces a level of flexibility that did not exist at the stricter level of material objects. It is at this level that we begin to see how the tenth Doctor could be the same as the ninth, even if 'every single cell' of his body (most notably his teeth!) had been changed.

But it is Locke's discussion of the identity of 'conscious, thinking persons' that has become the touchstone for all discussions of personal identity in the Western tradition. Locke's use of 'person' is distinctive in its time because it avoids metaphysical baggage, and so makes fewer metaphysical commitments. For him, as an empiricist, it was enough to gesture at the way the word is actually used in observable practices, that is, as 'a forensic term, appropriating actions and their merit; and so [it] belongs only to intelligent agents, capable of a law, and happiness, and misery'.[18] It is important to note that the meaning of the Latin *forensis* is 'in open court', or *public* – and therefore Locke's understanding of what personal identity is has an ineliminable social character to it. Regardless of what bit of bodily matter or immaterial substance might be the underlying basis for personal identity, Locke claims that what we take to be a person is something that stands within a particular network of moral and legal commitments. But rather than claiming that 'person' is *merely* a convention or term of art, he also says that persons commit to and are held responsible for moral and legal obligations because of their capacities for intelligent action towards the ends of avoiding misery and seeking happiness. For this, Locke says, we require consciousness and memory. A creature that has intelligence and memory (and perhaps the ability to anticipate the future in some degree), he observes, 'can consider itself as itself, the same thinking thing in different times and places; which it does only by that consciousness, which is inseparable from thinking'.[19] For Locke, then, I am the same person as someone in the past just in case I can remember being that past individual. I could lose a hand to the Sycorax, be in a different body, or have changed metaphysical substances, but I am the same person if I can nonetheless 'repeat the idea of any past action with the same consciousness [I] had of it at first'.[20]

This 'memory criterion' of personal identity seems to work well with what we have seen of the regenerative process in *Doctor Who*. Although the second Doctor, in his first moments, speaks of his former incarnation in the third person (and the sixth Doctor does the same of the fifth in 'The Twin Dilemma'), in most cases the new Doctor affirms that he remembers a past, and that although the subject of that past doesn't look like him, the subject *was* him. When we add this to the Doctor's predilection for time travel – guaranteeing that his earlier incarnations will be travelling through a later time while his later incarnations are in an earlier time – we have a recipe for botched tenses that even companions Peri Brown and Jamie McCrimmon can't sort out.[21] When, in 'The Two Doctors', the second Doctor is captured by the Sontarans, his

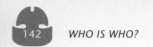

sixth incarnation tells Peri, 'If anything happens to me as a result of it I shall never forgive himself!'

You Show Me a Better Way of Surviving, and I'll Give It a Go

Even the Doctor seems to subscribe to some version of Locke's theory when, in the twentieth anniversary special 'The Five Doctors', he tells companions Tegan and Turlough, 'A man is the sum of his memories, a Time Lord even more so.' This claim, however poetic, contains a philosophical trap first pointed out by Bishop Joseph Butler in his 1736 *Analogy of Religion, Natural and Revealed*. Of all the possible memories that could sum me up, Butler asked, which are mine and which are not? While it is true that we generally only possess our own memories, what unifies a particular set of memories is that they are 'mine'. Locke *presupposes* this unifying factor (as does the Doctor when he says 'his memories'), but it is precisely this that has to be explained.

Multi-Doctor episodes like 'The Five Doctors' provide further obstacles to the easy acceptance of consciousness and memory as the primary criterion for personal identity. In 'The Five Doctors', as well as in 'The Three Doctors' and 'The Two Doctors', various scenes take place with more than one incarnation of the Time Lord present.[22] In the earliest of these episodes, for example, the third Doctor has a conversation with Omega, the lost Time Lord engineer, in which they discover that Omega has transformed into non-corporeal pure will. The second Doctor is also part of this conversation; so why doesn't the third Doctor remember it, or at least have a nagging sense of *déjà vu*? If we refrain from adding some *ad hoc* reason for why a Time Lord can't remember an experience from when he crossed his own timeline, we will be forced to conclude (on the Lockean account of personhood) that either the third Doctor isn't the same person as the second, for there is a significant discontinuity in their memories; or that, at least when the Doctor crosses his own timeline, he is not the same person in both or all of the incarnations present.

Perhaps it isn't necessary for each Doctor to have *all* the memories of his previous selves; after all, I can't remember anything before 1976. Richard Hanley suggests that the memory criterion ought to be understood as demanding mental *continuity*, not *connectedness*, which is what seems absent when the fifth Doctor fails to recall that his first self tricked Borusa in 'The Five Doctors'. Mental continuity demands 'overlapping chains of connectedness' – that is, just so long as the fifth Doctor has memories of being the fourth, and the fourth the third, and so on, the fifth Doctor's lack of memory of what his first self did in the Tower of Rassilon doesn't imply they are different people.[23]

New *Doctor Who* casts doubts on the determination of personal identity by use of Hanley's 'neo-Lockean' memory continuity as well. Of particular interest are 'The Rebel Flesh'/'The Almost People' and 'The Girl Who Waited' (both from 2011). In the two-part story set in the twenty-second century, 'the Flesh' is a living, self-replicating material that is 'the government's worst-kept secret'. It is used to create human doppelgängers (or 'Gangers') which humans can 'drive' instead of having to personally work with harmful substances. During a solar storm, while a group of Gangers are active, the Gangers don't dissolve back into Flesh when their 'drivers' disengage but instead retain their physical form, memories and other mental states; at first, they are not even aware that they are Flesh and not strictly human.

This scenario raises the difficulty that there could be two individuals who can recall the same memories. In 'The Almost People', the Ganger Jimmy Wicks struggles with his emotional connection to the human Jimmy Wicks's son. At first, he is convinced that, since he is *only* a Ganger, he is not entitled to his paternal feelings. Here is a case in which a particular set of memories are causally connected to events in the past that only occurred to the human Wicks, but that are shared by two individuals. On the memory continuity view alone, we must either be content to say that both men are the same person (which becomes difficult to uphold when the human Wicks dies), or that the continuity of memory is merely a *necessary*, but not a *sufficient*, condition for personal identity.[24]

One advantage that the human Wicks would have had over the Ganger duplicate, had the former survived, would have been the 'closest continuer' modification to the memory continuity view of identity. This modification was originally suggested by Robert Nozick, and has been employed to explain identity in the context of *Doctor Who* (especially in the ingenious 2008 Christmas special 'The Next Doctor') by Richard Hanley.[25] While it is true that the Ganger and the human Wicks may have the same sets of memories, what also counts for personal continuity are the *causes* for those memories. Jimmy Wicks gained his memories as a result of negotiating a world of objects, events and other people. The Ganger Wicks gained the same memories from Flesh being formatted into something like neurons and ganglia. This makes the human Wicks the 'closest continuer' from the pre-solar storm person called 'Jimmy Wicks'.

This is apparently the theory behind the Doctor's tragic decision at the end of 'The Girl Who Waited'. In this tale, Amy Pond, her husband Rory, and the Doctor visit the Two Streams Facility on the planet Apalapucia. The paradise world has been impacted by a fatal disease, Chen-7, and the Two Streams Facility has utilised temporal engineering to create two distinct zones: 'Red Waterfall', a compressed timestream for the infected, and 'Green Anchor', where time runs at its normal rate for family and friends of the afflicted.

Amy, having entered the Red Waterfall zone after the Doctor and Rory have already moved into Green Anchor, spends *36 years* wandering the entertainment and edification zones of Apalapucia, avoiding the 'kindnesses' of Handbots who dispense medications toxic to humans. When the TARDIS finally breaks into Red Waterfall, this older Amy doesn't want to be rescued. The Doctor has a plan to save Amy in the past, just after she entered the facility, but he requires the cooperation of older Amy, who will cease to exist once her younger self is rescued. Rory and the Doctor are faced with the dilemma of whether to save the older Amy, who has suffered but survived for nearly four decades, or to use her to retrieve the younger Amy, thus eliminating the possibility that she will experience the suffering at all. The Doctor seems to opt for the younger Amy because she is the 'closest continuer', at least in terms of time, to the Amy who walked into Red Waterfall. Her memories have the 'right' causes, while older Amy's could be seen as the effects of an aberrant loop of time that should never have happened. Furthermore, the older Amy's 36-years-worth of memories in the Two Streams Facility are *not* shared by her younger self, so on any of the interpretations of Locke so far, she is a different person. The episode does not write off the older Amy easily – one person or the other must be saved; both cannot be. Brilliant acting and scriptwriting convinces the audience that, by sacrificing the older Amy, the Doctor and Rory have clearly done wrong. They haven't killed a person, but they have made it so that an actual set of 'time-slices' of that person never existed. As to which of these might be worse, only future ethicists of the *Doctor Who* universe can tell us.

Contemporary neuropsychologists and cognitive scientists could intervene in the discussion at this juncture to point out that there is a biochemical basis for human memory that we understand fairly well, and so focusing on memory as a criterion of personal identity is like mistaking the symptom for the sickness. At the head of this chapter, we said that things are discernible from each other by their properties and that two (apparently) different things that had exactly the same properties would be identical. *Physicalism*, a term coined by the positivist Otto Neurath, is the view that philosophically proper explanations of mind, consciousness and identity need to be structured around purely physical properties – not merely matter, but also energy, physical forces and processes, and information, to name a few. In this respect, the brain rather than the soul or memory becomes the centre of attention, and Locke's and Leibniz's theories can be treated as episodes of 'folk psychology', or common-sense ruminations on mind and identity that utilise pre-scientific concepts.

The literary antecedent of physicalism is, of course, Mary Shelley's *Frankenstein, or the Modern Prometheus*, published anonymously in 1818.[26] Its *Doctor Who* correlate, 'The Brain of Morbius', was co-written by series stalwarts Terrance Dicks and Robert Holmes. Under the helm of producer Philip

Hinchcliffe, seasons 13 and 14 were effectively televisual studies in Gothic horror, so much so that they raised the ire of moralist and activist Mary Whitehouse; 'The Brain of Morbius' was undoubtedly the centrepiece of that achievement.[27] Like Frankenstein, the creature's creator in Shelley's tale, the brilliant brain surgeon Solon has shuttered himself away from society on the planet Karn in order to use techniques of dubious ethicality to revive the dead. As in the case of Solon's creation, the urge to do evil was carried in the very flesh of the deceased madmen and criminals that Frankenstein's creature was sewn from. Solon, though, has only the brain of Morbius, an executed Time Lord warlord whom the Doctor calls 'one of the most despicable criminally minded wretches that ever lived'. A member of the cult of Morbius, Solon intends to transplant the brain – which is alive, conscious and, with electronic help, capable of communicating – into 'a head that will soon command the universe'. Solon's first conversation with the brain is cleverly filmed so that the audience cannot see whom the surgeon is talking to:

SOLON: I have worked night and day in your service, Morbius. When I brought you here there was nothing! I had to build my own laboratory out of ruins. I had to invent and construct my own equipment to start experiments.

MORBIUS: Experiments? When we formed this plan to outwit the Time Lords, nothing was said of experiments! You told me it could be done.

SOLON: And it can, Morbius, it can. I've made so many discoveries. I have mastered new techniques no other man has even conceived. I can transplant limbs, organs. I can create life. And all against the most appalling difficulties.

MORBIUS: Yet I am still here! I can see nothing, feel nothing. You have locked me into hell for eternity. If this is all there is for me, I would sooner die now.

SOLON: There is so much at stake. I cannot afford to take a risk. Every step is an advance into new fields of surgery. Every step has got to be tested.

MORBIUS: Solon! You desire to be known as the creator of Morbius, rather than his servant![28]

Morbius's brain, which was the only part of him to survive Time Lord vaporisation, both does and does not carry his personal identity. Being unable to see or feel anything, but possessing memories of once having had those abilities, Morbius can think, but (apart from hearing) cannot perceive and has no mobility. Morbius, 'locked into hell for eternity', clearly feels as though his identity is diminished, raising the question of whether personal identity needs to be determined in an 'all-or-nothing' way that is more appropriate to abstract and logical entities. When Solon's plan to implant his brain in the Doctor's body fails, the surgeon supplies Morbius with a travesty of a body assembled from an amalgam of alien corpses, topped with a 'fishbowl' artificial braincase. 'You really can't go on calling yourself Morbius,' the Doctor chides him. 'There's very little of Morbius left. Why don't you think of another name? Potpourri would be appropriate.' 'How about Chop Suey?' Sarah Jane chimes in.

The later Tom Baker story 'City of Death' (1979), from an original idea by the late Douglas Adams, provides puzzles for neo-Lockeans and physicalists alike. In its opening scenes, an accident occurs on Earth, four hundred million years ago before human life graced the planet. A spacecraft piloted by Scaroth (Julian Glover), one of the cyclopean Jagaroth, is atomised. The effect of the explosion is to kill all the other Jagaroth on board, but Scaroth's being is 'splintered' through time, versions of him appearing at diverse points in the future. Together, all the versions of Scaroth nudge humanity along in its technological and cultural development so that, by 1979, Professor Kerensky can invent time travel. Scaroth, posing as the human Count Scarlioni, intends to use this power to stop himself from attempting the doomed Jagaroth ship's take-off four hundred million years earlier. The drawback to his plan is that the explosion was what originally energised the primeval soup, giving rise to life on Earth. Stopping himself means a massive historical disruption, and we all disappear.

The time-splintered alien menace of 'City of Death' presents a problem for theories of identity based on the continuity of memories: what if an individual, like Scarlioni, has multiple sets of memories? There are instances in the episode where

Scaroth's various 'splinters' seem to be communicating, or at least empathising, with each other. This device is used to great effect in the way that Scaroth/Captain Tancredi arranges for Leonardo da Vinci to paint six more *Mona Lisa*s, and then has them boarded up carefully so that Scaroth/Count Scarlioni can find and sell them almost five hundred years later. Although 'City of Death' is a fictive example, it does call attention to the fact that the processes of acquiring memories are not always accurate to the facts they purport to represent. Not only can memories be lost, but also false memories can be part of an individual's mind. For physicalists, Scaroth's splintering raises the question of whether, if a particular brain/body combination is replicated exactly, each of the fragments is identical to the others. At least when the temporal fracturing first occurs, all the Scaroths are qualitatively identical. Each one, however, lives in a different time and society, and each must have distinctly different sets of experiences as a result. Surely this kind of divergence of experience is also part of the explanation of individuation? However, the intriguing metaphysical puzzles about Scaroth's personal identity are probably the least of this episode's attractions, which include an exceptionally witty script, an extensive shoot in Paris and all manner of questions about time paradoxes.

Physicalists would do well not to focus on the brain as the seat of identity, if only because it, too, seems to be a necessary but not sufficient condition for being a person. It may not even be necessary, for a few good reasons. In new *Doctor Who*, for example, it is made clear that the only organic part of a converted Cyberman is its human brain, yet Cybermen betray no features of personal individuality.[29] Similarly, personality may be transferred – or even lost – without a net loss of the brain or body to sustain it. The sixth Doctor in the second segment of 'Trial of a Time Lord', commonly called 'Mindwarp', suffers just such a loss of his companion Peri. Having been abducted by the villainous, slug-like Sil, Peri is used as a test subject by Crozier, a brain surgeon working on the electronic transfer of minds between bodies. The pattern of the mind of Kiv, the leader of Thoros-Beta, is transferred into Peri's brain. Apparently this process produces a zero-sum result: the pattern called 'Peri' is lost forever (or so it seems given the video evidence presented by the nefarious Time Lord prosecutor, the Valeyard).

One Day, I Shall Come Back

The discussion of personal identity so far has been very abstract, producing perhaps more puzzles and problems than it solves. Existential phenomenologists like Martin Heidegger have criticised the entire tradition revolving around memory continuity, physicalism and other theories. In his view, such theories treat humans – with their unique form of relating to the world – as simply objects of scientific analysis, like black holes and rocks.[30] Certainly it is not absurd to admit that when humans study *themselves*, different measures may be necessary than when we study non-human nature or the universe. Asserting this, we can at least be confident we're in good company with Aristotle and Hegel, among many others.

One related paradoxical feature of many theories of personal identity is that, in trying to establish a way to differentiate persons from each other, they focus on commonalities that all persons are supposed to share. In fact, much of what passes for the reflective identity described by Locke has more to do with our beliefs about (and care for) ourselves and a relatively small group of others. 'A central fact about persons is that each of them has a "special concern" for his or her future well-being; and because of this, each of them also has derivative special concern for the future well-being of the persons with whom he or she identifies because of ties of love and friendship', claims Sydney Shoemaker.[31] Unlike 'maverick' Time Lords such as the Master, the Meddling Monk and Drax, the Doctor seems to be an inherently social being and partially defines himself by his relationships to his companions. As the new *Who* continues to foreground the experiences of companions against strained relationships to family and friends back on Earth, these considerations become ever more significant.

The attempt to ground a philosophy of identity on the observation that we are always already part of families, groups, societies and cultures was a feature not only of the projects of existentialists like Heidegger, but also of classical American philosophy, represented by William James (1842–1910), John Dewey (1859–1952) and George Herbert Mead (1861–1931). If there is a theme common to the 'golden age' of late nineteenth- and early twentieth-century American philosophy, it is that of *experience* – a concept developed in its richness and concreteness by American thinkers in an effort to counteract the increasingly abstract views of both philosophical idealists and neo-Kantian positivists.

The emphasis on experience implies an effort to find the basis for personal identity at the crux of experience as an ongoing transaction between individuals and the environing world. Richard J. Bernstein, don of historical studies of American pragmatism, writes:

> [T]he general temper of American philosophy has been empirical in its insistence on the vital role of experience in testing and warranting knowledge claims, in the suspicion of any philosophic appeal to a transcendent or transcendental realm of principles or entities, in its commitment to a naturalistic view of man and the universe. But at the same time there has been an on-going attempt to provide a fresh theory of experience.[32]

Criticisms of Locke, and of empiricism in general, are common in James and Dewey, who understood with historical hindsight that pairing Locke's theory of personal identity together with an outdated metaphysics of substance could only lead to the scepticism of a thinker like David Hume. Hume's 'bundle theory' of the person challenged Locke's unitary self by pointing out that although we clearly have memories, we have no direct apprehension of *what it is that has* a series of memories. A 'self' is nothing more, for Hume, than a 'long series of different mental states and events [...] unified by various kinds of causal relation, such as the relations that hold between experiences and later memories of them. Each series is thus like a bundle tied up with string.'[33] But William James pilloried the bundle theory using the same reasoning he deployed against empiricist epistemology in general, showing that we do not experience memories in abstraction from each other, but as related. The self, James writes, is not

> [an abstract] being of reason [...] cognized only in an intellectual way, and no *mere* summation of memories or *mere* sound of a word in our ears. It is something with which we also have direct sensible acquaintance, and which is as fully present at any moment of consciousness in which it *is* present, as in a whole lifetime of such moments [...] [W]hen it is found, it is *felt*; just as the body is felt, the feeling of which is also an abstraction, because never is the body felt all alone, but always together with other things.[34]

Beyond this abstraction, what I conceive myself to be at my core is, for James, a function of religion, education, personal tragedies, friendships, and many more things. To dismiss all these factors as irrelevant to an abstract metaphysical concept of identity is contrary to James's way of thinking, as well as to that of Dewey and Mead, who both emphasised the social character of the self.

Contemporary American philosophers such as the late Donald Davidson and Daniel C. Dennett have worked within the same kind of 'post-metaphysical' framework as these earlier Americans, Davidson in terms of analytic epistemology and philosophy of language, and Dennett from the perspective of cognitive science and evolutionary theory. Davidson, who is well known for his theories of mind and action, has also spent time characterising humans as interpreting animals. In characterising *intersubjectivity* as the social space in which many, if not most, of our transactions with the world occur, he writes:

> [T]his much should be clear: the basic triangle of two people and a common world is one of which we must be aware if we have any thoughts at all. If I can think, I know that there are others with minds like my own, and that we inhabit a public

time and space filled with objects and events, many of which are [...] known to others.[35]

Dennett, who is a physicalist in many respects, recognises that personhood reaches out beyond the 'skin-world' barrier to take into its constitution a number of social realities. For him, persons are rational beings, to whom states of consciousness are attributed by other conscious beings. Further, a person is a person partly because of a certain stance. This is the 'intentional stance' of attributing purposes and intentions by observing behaviours taken *towards* a person by others, which that person must be capable of reciprocating. A person is also capable of verbal communication and is conscious in a special way: not merely 'state consciousness' or awareness, but a higher level of consciousness that takes other mental states as its object.[36]

As we've seen, the original *Who* often trades on the puzzles and paradoxes of the Lockean or physicalist theories of personal identity, and new *Who* sometimes does this as well – perhaps most infamously in 'New Earth' (2006) as Lady Cassandra O'Brien, the Doctor and Rose experience successive mind/body swaps. After co-opting Rose's body, Cassandra discovers, much to her dismay, that she's a chav (well, you can't have everything when you're the 'last human'). For all this, the post-2005 programme does redress the balance in favour of views of the self that privilege relationships and social identification, sometimes even at the cost of plausibility. In 'The Empty Child'/'The Doctor Dances' (2005), the ninth Doctor orders the threatening gas-mask-faced 'empty child' away from himself, Rose and Jack Harkness by confronting the boy with something that a real child would have known well: parental authority. 'Go to your room. I mean it,' he demands. 'I'm very, very angry with you. I am very, very cross. Go to your room!' As the entire story serves as a metaphor for how the traumatic upheaval of war and other political and social catastrophes interrupt and fragment the healthy development of identities, this is entirely appropriate. The 'empty child' is nothing other than the product of highly effective Chula medical nanogenes with too little information to work from. In the triumphant ending to a story in which, finally, 'everybody lives!' the Doctor explains to Rose that the nanogenes are reversing their original work of changing a few dozen people into mindless, gas-mask-faced duplicates of the young boy, Jamie. This pseudo-scientific explanation isn't the real reason for the culmination: it is a young mother's hesitant identification with her child, believed lost forever:

> **DOCTOR:** How old were you five years ago? Fifteen? Sixteen? Old enough to give birth, anyway. He's not your brother, is he? A teenage single mother in 1941. So you hid. You lied. You even lied to him.
> *(The bomb site gate opens and Jamie stands there.)*
> **CHILD:** Are you my mummy?
> **DOCTOR:** He's going to keep asking, Nancy. He's never going to stop.
> **CHILD:** Mummy?
> **DOCTOR:** Tell him. Nancy, the future of the human race is in your hands. Trust me and tell him.
> *(Nancy and Jamie walk towards each other.)*
> **CHILD:** Are you my mummy? Are you my mummy? Are you my mummy?
> **NANCY:** Yes. Yes, I am your mummy.

Nancy's efforts to bring Jamie back to the fold of the human seem to fall on deaf ears, as he continues to repeat his question:

> **DOCTOR:** He doesn't understand. There's not enough of him left.
> **NANCY:** I am your mummy. I will always be your mummy. I'm so sorry. I am so, so sorry.
> *(Nancy hugs Jamie and a cloud of nanogenes surround them.)*
> **ROSE:** What's happening? Doctor, it's changing her, we should …
> **DOCTOR:** Shush! Come on, please. Come on, you clever little nanogenes. Figure it out! The mother, she's the mother. It's got to be enough information. Figure it out.[37]

Examples like this are rife in recent adventures in time and space, from 'Fear Her' (2006) to 'Human Nature'/'The Family of Blood' (2007), the tragedy that befalls Donna Noble in 'Journey's End' (2008), and even, in a moving and highly unusual way in 'Vincent and the Doctor' (2010). The basic trope is a loss of identity or integration of personality that needs to be repaired, but the solution adopted is always one that reintegrates the original individual by technology (as Scaroth hoped to do in 'City of Death') or by imposing a pattern of habits (the not-so-hidden colonialist/imperialist message behind the fourth Doctor's relationship to Leela). In general, new *Who* favours two pragmatist theses about personal identity. The first thesis is that selfhood is dynamic, not static, and its potentials are called out by the social milieu in which we live. What George Herbert Mead called 'taking the attitude of the other' is a process of socialisation that he claimed (as Davidson would later) was constitutive of having thoughts in the first place. The genesis of selfhood is found in the reflexive activity of attempting to see myself, or something that I intend to do, from the normative standpoint of someone else. In doing so, 'the individual experiences himself as such, not directly, but only indirectly, from the particular standpoints of other individual members of the same social group, or from the generalised standpoint of the social group as a whole to which he belongs'.[38] Subjectivity is developed, for Mead, by our becoming an object to ourselves. This happens through the act of the moral imagination that puts me, so far as I can empathise with them, in the shoes of others. It all begins with the family and echoes certain Freudian theses about the development of ego and superego through internalisation of the voices of parents.

The second pragmatist thesis declares that what's distinctive about individuals is not that they have something in common or represent certain metaphysical constants, but rather that they are sources of novelty and agents of transformation for their world. As the previous chapter on the Doctor's ethics contended, whether or not individuals can work towards perfectibility largely depends upon the environment in which they are situated. This partially explains why the Doctor appreciates having friends to share his travels with. One implication of this for John Dewey is that 'the individual is a temporal career whose future cannot be *logically* deduced from its past'.[39] Dewey reasons, if the development of new aspects of identity and new capacities do occur as emergent properties of the sort of creatures humans are, then potentiality must be a real category of existence. But this is a particularly modern view of 'potentiality' not as a fixed *telos* or goal that an individual or species might intrinsically have. Dewey's environmental-transactional perspective suggests instead that 'potentialities must be thought of in terms of consequences with interactions with other things'.[40] But, like Aristotle – that ancient theorist of actuality and potentiality – Dewey sees human flourishing or well-being as the positive way to characterise potentiality. As such, the provision of a rich, stimulating, changing yet structured environment is key to human flourishing. Many philosophers, particularly those of the analytic stripe, have objected to what they see as Dewey's overly moralistic tone, especially in his writings on ethics and politics. But this ignores the most important and most misunderstood presupposition of pragmatism. Clarence Irving Lewis gives an excellent summation:

> Pragmatism could be characterized as the doctrine that all problems are at bottom problems of conduct, that all judgments are, implicitly, judgments of value, and that, as there can be ultimately no valid distinction of theoretical and practical, so there can be no final separation of questions of truth of any kind from questions of the justifiable ends of action.[41]

This is not to claim the Doctor is a pragmatist. While his faith in science, his devotion to exploring the range of possible experiences and his romanticism also characterise pragmatists like James, Dewey and Mead, he is far too idealistic – and perhaps in some of his incarnations, like the seventh, too cynical. River Song, the Doctor's ostensible wife and Rory and Amy's daughter, is a better candidate. A human with Time Lord DNA, her hybridity serves as a symbol of the way in which American philosophy takes up classic themes from the European tradition and answers them in novel, distinctively American ways. As an archaeologist based in Luna University, she is trained in the kind of sustained inquiry and problem solving that characterises pragmatism, capacities that she demonstrates in episodes such as 'Silence in the Library'/'Forest of the Dead' (2008) and 'The Time of Angels'/'Flesh and Stone' (2010).

What makes River a student of human nature who respects the significance of the potential for dynamic individuality is found in how she deals with the fact that she and the Doctor 'keep meeting in the wrong order'. It is not merely her wicked sense of humour that moves her to chirp, 'Spoilers!' whenever the Doctor asks about something in his future that has already occurred in her past. It is out of the respect for the value of self-development (whether under good or bad circumstances) that she first learned from the Doctor ('Let's Kill Hitler', 2011). Not only does 'taking the attitude of the other' in the case of Amy and the Doctor help River discover who she really is in Hitler's Germany; the second chance she's given by them affords her a reason to affirm a Deweyan lesson in her future dealings with the last of the Time Lords.

> An individual is not original merely when he gives to the world some discovery that has never been made before. Every time he really makes a discovery, even if thousands of persons have made similar ones before, he is original. The value of a discovery in the mental life of an individual is the contribution it makes to a creatively active mind; it does not depend upon no one's ever having thought of the same idea before.[42]

6

SPEAKING TREASON FLUENTLY

Can You Hear the Sound of Empires Toppling?

Previous chapters have revealed the Doctor as a radical individualist who nonetheless cares about the fates of communities and as someone who refuses to countenance the status quo by virtue of the knowledge of a higher science and centuries of wisdom. While he admits to Madame Kovarian that good men don't need rules, he also warns, 'Today is not the day to find out why I have so many' ('A Good Man Goes to War'). Yet he also claims to be 'a citizen of the universe, and a gentleman to boot', implying that there are political principles and social values behind the way he conducts himself.

The Doctor's unique status, in all these ways, implies that he is not a particularly political animal; indeed, he mentions many times in his first eight incarnations that he left home because he wasn't comfortable alongside his people in their high, starched collars. Gallifreyan politics and culture are Byzantine in their complexity, as befits a world that has enjoyed 'ten million years of absolute power' in the universe ('The Trial of a Time Lord'). It is not so much this fact, but rather the basic hypocrisy of the Time Lords, that the Doctor rejects. The High Council of the Time Lords, comprised of their President, Chancellor, Castellan of security, and various other high-ranking officials, is most often portrayed as a bickering mess. Through their intelligence service, the Celestial Intervention Agency, they do in fact make historical adjustments while cleaving to a policy of strict neutrality in the affairs of the cosmos. In one momentous case, they put an entire planet to the sword to protect secrets in the Matrix – the repository of all Gallifreyan knowledge ('The Trial of a Time Lord') – while, in another, they fail to prevent one of their own from destroying the Daleks' home planet of Skaro ('Remembrance of the Daleks').

Gallifreyan society is divided into six 'Chapters', with the Prydonians (which the Doctor and Master hail from), the Patrexes and the Arcalians being dominant and the Dromeians, Ceruleans and Scendles being less politically active. A number of Houses subscribe to each Chapter, of which the Doctor's is called 'Lungbarrow'. Members of Houses are related to each other as cousins, but are born from genetic Looms, not parents.[1] In 'The Deadly Assassin', one of the first explicitly political of the Doctor's adventures, we find out from Castellan Spandrell that the Doctor, now in his fourth incarnation, is considered an embarrassment to the High Council and a criminal by the general populace. The situation becomes vastly worse when the Master and his puppets frame him for assassinating the Lord President of Gallifrey, and on the latter's resignation day, no less. Interrogated and tortured in the vaults deep beneath the Capitol, the Doctor is aghast to find out that Chancellor Goth (Bernard Horsfall) is eager to have him done away with in light of the upcoming election. 'What? Well, that's monstrous! Vaporisation without representation is against the constitution!' the Doctor blurts.

In extricating himself from the situation, the Doctor's knowledge of Time Lord laws and procedures – which he also demonstrates adroitly in 'Arc of Infinity' and 'The Five Doctors' – becomes key. To extricate himself from the snares of the Time Lords' arch-bureaucrats, he will 'out-bureaucrat' them. However, when it comes to defeating Goth in the bizarre virtual landscape of the Matrix and thwarting the Master's plans to gain an entirely new set of regenerations, whoever can corner the market on sheer power will be the winner. Can humans preserve justice, unaided by the wisdom of millions of years of Time Lord memories safeguarded in the Matrix, as the Doctor demands in 'The Deadly Assassin'? Or are there merely balances of power beneath shifting political allegiances, as the second Doctor's evil twin Salamander realises in 'The Enemy of the World'? In 'Ghost Light', one of the final serials of the original programme broadcast in 1989, the Doctor sadly tells us, 'I can't stand burnt toast. I loathe bus stations. Terrible places. Full of lost luggage and lost souls [...] And then there's unrequited love. And tyranny. And cruelty.' Which sorts of governments, societies and civil associations succeed and which fail in the *Doctor Who* universe? As we'll see, the programme has much to say about war, political violence, and the pathologies that result when economic reasoning trumps the moral dimensions of politics.

I Just Don't Like Nastiness and People Getting Away With It

Western philosophy typically links political philosophy very closely to ethics and to social theory. With few exceptions, political theory usually gets the worst of these alliances because of two tendencies in understanding their connections. One is to treat the study of political relationships as simply a version of ethical duties or principles writ large. The other is to classify political institutions as a subset of social institutions. Phenomenologist Alfred Schutz provides such a framework in his concept of *social reality*, which is

> the world of cultural objects and social institutions into which we are all born, within which we have to find our bearings, and with which we have to come terms. From the outset, we, the actors on the social scene, experience the world we live in as a world both of nature and of culture.[2]

Philosophers also tend, in the grand scheme of things, to subordinate projects in all three of these areas – political, social and ethical – to considerations of what might be seen as more 'foundational' problems in areas like metaphysics and epistemology. The idea is that, since claims about reality or about knowledge encompass political as well as non-political actions, categories and events, fundamental questions must be settled first. Arguably, this relative lack of autonomy has undermined the creativity and concrete problem-solving abilities of twentieth- and early twenty-first-century political philosophy. Just as in other disciplines, philosophers usually accept that the questions they ask should fit a certain well-established, traditional schema and, as a result, they have been myopic to the fact that each and every human activity, including philosophising itself, has its political dimension. In this, we have less of an excuse, because it was one of our own, Aristotle (384–322 BCE), who noted that 'man is more of a political animal than bees or any other gregarious animals' because of the power of speech, which

> is intended to set forth the expedient and the inexpedient, and therefore likewise the just and the unjust. And it is a characteristic of man that he alone has any sense of good and evil, of just and unjust, and the like, and the association of living beings who have this sense makes a family and a state.[3]

The varieties of political theory, like those of the other human sciences – including history and sociology – are numerous and diverse. The examination of states, laws, constitutions, civil associations and institutions that those theories share also differs from the physical sciences in two crucial respects. First, political theory and its humanistic correlates are *reflexive* disciplines that demand methods for how humans can inquire after *themselves*, not merely about an objectified nature of physical properties, energy or chemicals. Second, because of this, they cannot make a plausible claim to value-neutrality. The diversity of approaches in thinking about political life stems from worthwhile research programmes in the area, each of which cannot be entered into without adopting a framework or 'paradigm' that, at least, stipulates the meaning of key terms (like 'state', 'individual agent', etc.) and describes a method by which investigation will progress. So, despite what some political scientists or philosophers might claim, it cannot be true that 'they are seeking to match or test empirical claims against a political reality which is *itself* "objective" and "value-neutral"', as Richard Bernstein explains.[4] Although we needn't commit to any one particular framework of valuation to engage in political philosophy, it is clearly true that no work can be done without accepting one that 'contain[s] beliefs and expectations about what is correct, appropriate, or "rational" behaviour'.[5]

The Doctor has his own strong opinions about politics, even if the nature of political life is never the same from destination to destination. One particular piece of wisdom comes in 'The Face of Evil' when the fourth Doctor lectures Leela:

> You know, the very powerful and the very stupid have one thing in common. They don't alter their views to fit the facts. They alter the facts to fit their views. Which can be very uncomfortable if you happen to be one of the facts that needs altering.

This same episode contains a subtle illustration of the social and political problem of unintended consequences, as the Doctor slowly unravels the reason for a bizarre schism of cultures – the Sevateem and the Tesh – on a colony world in the far future. It soon becomes clear that his own efforts in the past to set the colony spaceship's computer to rights has failed, and that it has suffered from the silicon equivalent of a split personality after the Doctor forgot to wipe his own 'memory print' from it. While the programme earnestly tackled concerns about repressive taxation ('The Sun Makers') and alternate energy sources ('Planet of Evil', 1975; 'The Hand of Fear', 1976), 'Face of Evil' can be interpreted as a rare instance of the programme criticising the intrusiveness of the welfare state, symbolised by the mad computer Xoanon's experiments with eugenics among the Sevateem and Tesh.

As these and other examples will show, the 1970s were the high-water mark of clearly discernible political positions in *Doctor Who*, and, unsurprisingly, the values of socialism and welfare liberalism often provided its critical edge. In their discussion of 'The Sun Makers', the authors of *Doctor Who: The Unfolding Text* reference the Doctor's humorous pastiche of Karl Marx ('What have we got to lose?' 'Only your claims!') when elaborating the story's message against oppressive taxation. Indeed, many of the most political *Who* episodes from the 1970s are also the funniest, a coincidence explained by Tulloch and Alvarado in *Unfolding Text* as a narrative strategy in which 'capitalism and class exploitation were propounded only to be displaced by the family conflict between "inhuman" bureaucracy and "human" spontaneity'.[6]

With Tom Baker now a confident lead, the show did not shirk from employing humour and irony to throw barbs at the political and economic status quo. Like 'The Sun Makers', two other adventures of the fourth Doctor, 'The Robots of Death' and 'The Pirate Planet' (1978), use economic realities rather than moustache-twirling villains to oppose the protagonists. The latter of these was Douglas Adams' initial script contribution to *Doctor Who*, and the second adventure in the quest of the Doctor and fellow Time Lady Romana for the 'Key to Time': a fabulous artefact needed by the White Guardian to restore balance to the universe. Adams' idea for where to hide one of the six gleaming pieces to the Key was, typically, absurdly outsized: it is disguised as the planet Calufrax, which has just been swallowed by the space-hopping 'pirate planet', Zanak. The story is a thinly veiled allegory for rapacious capitalism, as Zanak's Captain – who not only swears like a genuine pirate but also allows a robotic parrot to perch on his shoulder – cares nothing for the worlds that are compressed, mined out and then discarded after each of the planet's jumps. Another target of Adams' wit is the populace of Zanak, most of whom enjoy the bounty the Captain rains down on them every so often without so much as questioning it. Precious jewels are a common sight in the gutters of Zanak, and the citizenry are close to a state of permanent ennui from the ever-more-frequent 'golden ages of prosperity' that the Captain brings about. A trope for the spiritual opposition to this languid materialism emerges in the Mentiads, citizens of Zanak whose incipient telepathic powers are boosted each time a planet is devoured:

> **DOCTOR:** You were absorbing what you would call the life force from the plundered planets.
> **PRALIX:** What is the life force?
> **DOCTOR:** Well, er, well, it's quite difficult to explain in simple terms, but basically, Romana?
> **ROMANA:** Every atom of matter in the universe has a certain amount of energy locked inside it. Now, with something the size of a planet, there's an enormous quantity.
> **DOCTOR:** Oh, enormous.
> **ROMANA:** So every time Zanak crushes a planet, it releases all that energy. Now, some of it will be on psychic wavelengths.
> **DOCTOR:** Right.[7]

The Captain is not without scruples, but those he has are sadly misplaced. When the Doctor confronts him in the midst of his gallery of super-compressed planets, of which Calufrax is only the latest (and Earth is to be the next), the Time Lord can barely control his rage: 'What, you commit mass destruction and murder on a scale that's almost inconceivable and you ask me to *appreciate* it? Just because you happen to have made a brilliantly conceived *toy* out of the mummified remains of planets?' The Captain is not ultimately in control of Zanak, however. When it is revealed that its staggeringly old queen, Xanxia, needs destroyed planets to fuel time dams that are extending the life of her withered corpse, the serial's message is hammered home about moral decadence being the outcome of unrestricted exploitation of the environment.

'The Robots of Death', a futuristic murder-mystery by Chris Boucher, who also scripted many *Blake's Seven* episodes, has been lauded as 'a fine example of a story on which everyone involved was clearly committed to achieving the best they possibly could'.[8] Through an integration of fine acting, scriptwriting and design, the story portrays a future human society that is decadent in morals and baroque in taste. A sandminer combs the deserts of an unnamed planet for traces of valuable zelanite, keefan and lucanol. It is manned, not by the sort of intransigent miners who play such an important role in activist stories like the earlier 'Curse of Peladon' (1972) and 'The Monster of Peladon' (1974) but by upper-crust citizens of Kaldor City, members of the 20 'founding families'. Bickering between the spoiled and often bored members of the crew soon turns ugly as their fellows begin to die in unpleasant ways. Their leader, Commander Uvanov, never conceals his bitterness at being from a lower social stratum than his crew, and is more interested in keeping pace with profitable sandstorms than in solving the murders. This is the situation that the Doctor and Leela walk into when the TARDIS appears on the sandminer.

'The Robots of Death' trade on worries about large-scale industrial exploitation, since the sandminer's brutally efficient processing powers and its tendency to sink beneath the sand if not in constant motion are sources of two of the three cliff-hangers. It is also an effective demonstration of how technology and the profit motive sunder social reality. The deepest message in this regard is sent through the story's eponymous robots, which fall into three classes. The 'Dums' are drones that cannot communicate; 'Vocs' speak, carry out complex functions and even take care of the human crew; and the 'SuperVoc' coordinates the efforts of all the rest. Writer Boucher utilises black humour and plays on tensions about the threat of impersonal technology in the following exchange from the witty script of 'Robots of Death'. The sandminer crew has just found that one of their number, Chub, has been killed and a red disc is spotted on his hand:

DASK: It's a corpse marker.
UVANOV: What?
DASK: Robot deactivation disc. They use them in the construction centres. If ever we used the stop circuit and turned off all our robots, they'd have to go back to a construction centre for reactivation. On arrival, each would be marked with a disc like that to show it was a deactivated

robot. The technicians call them corpse markers. It's a sort of a joke.

POUL: It seems our murderer has a sense of humour.

UVANOV: That was on the back of Chub's hand.

BORG: Not just a murderer, then. Seems like one of us is a maniac.

CASS: Use your brain, Borg. We would know, wouldn't we?

BORG: But we don't.

(Borg puts the marker on Cass.)

BORG: Do we?[9]

Sinister comments like Borg's abound in the story, emphasising how little these future humans care about each other. An ingenious invention of Boucher's here is the condition of 'robophobia', or Grimwade Syndrome. This is a debilitating mental illness that stems from spending too many of one's formative years solely around robots, and is acted out with relish by David Collings as the miner's 'Mover', Poul. The robophobic reaction Poul suffers after the initial killings aboard the sandminer is treated as a pathology by Commander Uvanov, his second, Lish Toos (Pamela Salem), and the Doctor. In a clever twist, Poul's suspicion of the robots proves to be correct, as the SuperVoc SV7 has been reprogrammed to coordinate the sandminer's mechanoids to kill every human. By an even cleverer turn of events, the human who reprogrammed SV7 was also raised by robots, with the result that he has come to believe that he 'was brought up a superior being. Brought up to realise my brothers should live as free beings, and not as slaves to human dross.'[10]

I stated earlier that political theory cannot hope to get off the ground without adopting a framework that stipulates the meaning of central concepts and uses a method for research. Like the 'base under siege' stories considered in Chapter 4, the closed environment of the sandminer provides an environment of 'micropolitics' exposing the interplay of authority, proper procedures and, in this case, the desire to get out alive. Using a detailed and powerful definition of the 'realm of politics' offered by Benjamin Barber, the situation in 'Robots' clearly qualifies as a case of the political. Barber writes,

> One can understand the realm of politics as being circumscribed by conditions that impose *a necessity for public action, and thus for reasonable public choice, in the presence of conflict and in the absence of private or independent grounds for judgment.*[11]

In this view, we have to account for the actions in the face of conflict aboard the sandminer as a frank failure; of its original human crew, only three remain alive. The fundamental elements of the social reality that fuels the sandminer's micropolitics, Barber would probably claim, lead to the breakdown of politics as public problem solving. But an atomistic sense of individualism frames most issues in Chris Boucher's 'Kaldor City' future. This casts all political concepts in terms of a 'vocabulary of materiality' that today characterises much modern political discourse in the real world. The terms of this vocabulary include

> *property* as an extension of the physical self and of physical self-ownership (the labour theory of value); [...] *boundaries* as the crucial metaphor in conflicts of rights, autonomies, and jurisdictions; *sanctions* as an extension of physical penalties, designed to control behaviour through the mechanics of hedonism; *freedom* as the absence of external impediments to motion, as liberty from 'chains, from imprisonment, from enslavement by others' (Isaiah Berlin); and *power* as brute force, physical coercion, the absence of freedom.[12]

The citizens of Zanak and the sandminer crew are *alienated* from the social values of human interdependency and community as well as from the political values of cooperation and citizenship. Similarly to the disastrous politico-economic decisions found in episodes like these, Karl Marx proposes that a theory critical of capitalist societies can begin by adopting all the presuppositions of profit-oriented political economy – 'private property, the separation of labour, capital, and land; [...] also division of labour; competition; the concept of exchange value, etc.' – and still come to revolutionary conclusions. He writes:

Using the very words of political economy we have demonstrated that the work is degraded to the most miserable sort of commodity; that the misery of the worker is in inverse proportion to the power and size of his production; that the necessary result of competition is the accumulation of capital in a few hands, and thus a more terrible restoration of monopoly.[13]

If *recognition*, a concept introduced in Chapter 2, names the ways in which we see ourselves as social beings and moral agents by taking the attitude of others towards us, Marx's *alienation*, the key to each worker's immiserisation, is its opposite. For Marx, one can be alienated in three ways: from oneself, from the products of one's labour, and from others (the social context in which production takes place). The lassitude of those living on 'The Pirate Planet' and the mutual hostility of the mining crew in 'The Robots of Death' qualify them under all three characterisations. Marx, who spoke the language of revolution (some would say treason) fluently, would have appreciated the Doctor's assessment that the events aboard the sandminer represent a focal point in that particular future history. Leela asks, 'So what happens if the strangler is a robot?' Without batting an eye, the Doctor replies, 'Oh, I should think it's the end of this civilisation.'

Well, That's Democracy For You

So should our political views fit the facts, or may we change the facts to fit our views? In 'The Face of Evil', the Doctor seems to prefer the former, since he calls those who act on the latter either 'very powerful' or 'very stupid'. Yet Barber's sketch of the conditions that must be met for action to be *political* sheds doubt on the possibility of there being non-trivial 'political' or 'social facts'. Recall that he claims that there are *'private or independent grounds for judgment'* in public problem-solving scenarios. While I may have *private* grounds for judgements in (non-political) decision making that concerns only me or those I have close relationships to, Barber is implying that there are many opportunities for public decision making that do not have 'independent' grounds for deciding one way or another. Putting it another way, regarding many first-order problems or questions (such as, 'Should abortion be outlawed?' or 'What is the effect of political contributions on free speech?'), there is no algorithmic way to apply second-order values or methods, such as 'democracy' or 'equality'. The philosopher's concern is that if these terms are fundamentally contestable, lacking an essential and universal definition, then we are stuck with one of two options.

The first is a facile political realism in which 'anything goes' given the concatenation of power relations at the time. This is very similar to the 'state of nature' of Thomas Hobbes (1588–1679) or the opportunities for gaining and holding power that the Renaissance prince finds himself in, according to Niccolò Machiavelli (1469–1527). The second option is that taken by the *radical* democrat, like Marx or Barber in their different ways, who realises that the foundation laid by political philosophy for political life today is misleading in its basic approach. Barber sums up the error when he writes:

> In a word, politics is not the application of Truth to the problem of human relations but the application of human relations to the problem of truth. Justice then appears as an approximation of principle in a world of action where absolute principles are irrelevant.[14]

European theorists of democracy such as Claude LeFort attribute attitudes like Barber's to the 'dissolution of the markers of certainty' in understandings of power, law and knowledge.[15]

What kind of models for political practices and institutions can we generate if Barber is correct? Generating such models is an endeavour as old as politics itself. It is an oversimplification to say that there are two species of such models, the ideal and the empirical. Accepting such an uncluttered ontology of political life does give us the advantage of being able to clearly trace the roots of political philosophy back to Athens and the approaches of Plato and Aristotle. Plato's *Republic*, the ancient subtitle of which was 'On Justice', is an early entry in the tradition of constructing an ideal political system: a tradition continued by Thomas More's *Utopia* in the sixteenth century and John Rawls's *A Theory of Justice* in the twentieth, among many other illustrations. Aristotle's *Politics* is an empirical study of city-states and their constitutions around the Mediterranean, and Plato's late work – the *Laws* – is a hybrid of ideal and empirical theory focusing on the pros and cons of the political institutions of Sparta and Crete. To 'consider what form of political community is the best of all for those who are most able to realise their ideal of life', Aristotle suggests we examine constitutions 'as actually exist in well-governed states, and any theoretical forms which are held in high esteem'.[16] Plato and Aristotle both thought that, given the various options for governance, democracy was one of the worst. Aristotle demarcates democracy as a state in which 'the free, who are also poor and the majority, govern'.[17] While Plato's ideal state described in the *Republic* is meritocratic and run by the *wisest* men, Aristotle's preference in his political and ethical works is for an aristocratic state guided by the *best* (that is, the most virtuous) men.

Both Athenians would have disagreed with the claims we examined earlier made by Benjamin Barber, who is not only a committed democrat, but advocates a radically participatory democracy in his very definition of politics. In particular, they would have taken issue with Barber's idea that politics is 'the application of human relations to the problem of truth', since both Plato and Aristotle thought that the truth about human nature, and in particular human moral psychology, dictates preferable political forms. In the dialogue *Laws*, one of Plato's characters, an unnamed Athenian, claims that:

> pleasure and pain, you see, flow like two springs released by nature. If a man draws the right amount from the right one at the right time, he lives a happy life; but if he draws unintelligently at the wrong time, his life will be rather different. State and individual and every living being are on the same footing here.[18]

Indeed, this is a truncated version of the argument for the ideal city-state in the *Republic*, where the economic and social separation of the 'guardian' class from the working class is made on the principle of 'the natural division of labour'. In short, this principle implies that 'more plentiful and better-quality goods are more easily produced if each person does one thing for which he is naturally suited, does it at the right time, and is released from having to do any of the others'.[19]

The goal of the leader – what Plato calls *politikos* or statesman, and who in the *Republic* is referred to as a 'philosopher-king' – is 'to make [the citizens] wise and to provide them with a share of knowledge, if it was to be the [art] that benefited them and made them happy'.[20] Democracy is a fundamental perversion of the principle of the natural division of labour because it presents the populace with two values that are illusory: freedom and equality. 'Democratic freedom presupposes, contrary to the principle of the natural division of labour', Plato scholar David Keyt explains, 'that human nature is sufficiently plastic to allow for real choices among different lives.'[21] Valuing equality, likewise, assumes that each person is just as good as anyone else at the work of governance. And, while Aristotle agrees that these two political values are fictions given the relative rigidity of human nature, he also argues that Plato

> deprives the guardians even of happiness, and says that the legislator ought to make the whole state happy. But the whole cannot be happy unless most, or all, or some of its parts enjoy happiness [...] And if the guardians are not happy, who are? Surely not the artisans, or the common people. The Republic of which Socrates discourses has all these difficulties, and others quite as great.[22]

After enumerating five different types of democracies, Aristotle concludes that this form of government is too unstable because it relies on popular deference to *laws* and to *demagogues*. Democracies are more likely to ignore the former and be misled by the latter, he claims, and so once again the theme of a well-ordered state, guided by the more restricted group of those citizens who see further, emerges as a philosopher's preference.

In contrast, the claims made on behalf of democracy have typically been based on moral claims about freedom and equality rather than on attempting to refute the ancients on the questions of efficiency and effectiveness. 'Its cardinal principle has always been that, in matters affecting their collective life and interests, the people appropriately rule themselves,' as Ian Shapiro writes.[23] *Doctor Who*'s ethos is generally pro-democratic, and it is not unusual among other sci-fi venues in expressing doubts about the viability of political utopias; in 'The Savages', the glory of the Elders' civilisation is based on their draining of the life force of the savages outside their walls, and 'The Keeper of Traken' rehearses the story of the serpent in Eden, with the Master playing the part of the tempter. The programme more often tends to plumb the social reality of *dystopias* ('Frontios'; 'Gridlock') and has received attention for its revealing – and often disturbing – disclosures of the pathologies of democratic societies in stories such as 'Vengeance on Varos' (1985) and 'The Beast Below'.

Besides emphasising the democratic values of freedom and equality, episodes such as these deploy narratives about democratic competition and deliberation to heighten drama. 'Vengeance on Varos', the third outing for Colin Baker's sixth Doctor, is a multi-layered tale which,

> at its simplest, is a tense and mildly horrific monster story that can be enjoyed as a piece of pure escapism, but at the other end of the spectrum it is an intelligent and thought-provoking discourse on such weighty issues as video nasties, torture and the responsibilities of leadership.[24]

'Vengeance', the first contribution to the programme from writer Philip Martin, is an unremittingly grim tale set under the 'Punishment Dome' of the planet Varos, where the Doctor and companion Peri Brown have set down in hopes of finding Zeiton ore to boost the power reserves of the TARDIS. 'Areas of danger lurk around every corner,' says one of the characters they meet, a woman named Areta. 'You can die in oh so many ingenious ways.'[25] The tale is edgy, to say the least, as it features not only televised torture but also a gallows scene, a reprehensibly flinch-worthy, slug-like villain named Sil (Nabil Shaban), and violent reprisals by the Doctor against his attackers. It was one of several stories that drew the wrong sort of attention to *Doctor Who* in the mid-1980s, a period of time in which the Controller of BBC 1, Michael Grade, complained that 'the show has got rather violent and lost a lot of its imagination and a lot of its wit'.[26] The criticism did not only come from the top of the BBC: the President of the Australian *Doctor Who* fan club, Tony Howe, wrote in his group's newsletter in 1985:

> The 1985 season with Colin Baker is NOT the scary, stylised horror of the mid-1970s *Doctor Who*. The new style is sick, shock violence like Andy Warhol's: the Cyberleader crushes a prisoner's hand until it oozes blood; two men die in a vat of acid in 'Vengeance on Varos'; there is an attack with a kitchen knife in 'The Two Doctors'; and in the Dalek story someone is stabbed in the chest with a hypodermic needle. These incidents occur unexpectedly, they are not part of a total atmosphere for the whole story, they do not make the story interesting.[27]

In hindsight, the effort that script editor Eric Saward had made to bring 'a sense of realism' to the show, together with what many viewers found to be a jarring, bombastic portrayal of the Doctor by Colin Baker, was a recipe for disaster. Dedicated viewers could express disappointment, but little surprise, when the show was 'rested' for 18 months after Baker's first full season. With further hindsight, though, 'Vengeance on Varos' not only emerges as a prophetic example of what would become a fascination in mainstream SF with cruelty and meaningless violence, but also stands as a well-played meditation on political violence.

Varos is a human colony on a cold and uninhabitable world. There, weary and jaded miners, descendants of the population of the criminal and insane when Varos was a prison planet, live under opaque domes in dirty and dreary apartments. Their rations are unreasonably small, their mandatory 'entertainment' – footage from the Punishment Dome – of highly questionable taste. The miners produce one of only two things of value on Varos: Zeiton-7, a mineral that allowed craft, including space-time vessels like the TARDIS, to generate orbital energy. The other export consists of videos of torture and executions from the Punishment Dome. With Varos little more than a 'third world' outpost controlled by a thin layer of lawfulness hiding naked force, the Doctor's journey through the Dome is not unlike that of Kurtz in Joseph Conrad's *The Heart of Darkness*, at the end of which lies, 'The horror! The horror!'

In many ways, Varos represents the complete inversion of Plato's ideal state. Plato emphasised the signal importance of the principle of the natural division of labour in order to make Kallipolis self-subsistent in a world in which alliances and rivalries with other *polei* or city-states could be remade quickly. Yet Varos is at the mercy of cosmic conglomerates like the Galatron Mining Corporation, whom Sil represents; its Zeiton-7 is underpriced by their monopolistic tactics. There are no philosopher-kings on Varos: the malicious Chief Officer (Forbes Collins) is in collusion with Sil and has no concept of the common good for his people. Fortunately, standing between him and complete exploitation of the planet is the Governor (Martin Jarvis). But the Governor is worn down by the rants and demands of Sil and by the very nature of his job – which reflects a direct democracy in that every citizen of Varos (save those in the Punishment Dome, of course) must vote on each of his policy proposals.

This direct democracy, however, reflects only cruelty and desperation in its design. If the Governor is successful when calling for a vote, he's bathed in rays of healing light; the opposite occurs if his proposal is voted down, which happens more than once in the episode. As Peri watches, he prepares himself in front of Varos's ever-present television cameras for a 'final vote' after unsuccessful negotiations with Sil, chronicled by Martin in the novelisation of the story:

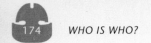

The Governor looked away. 'We haven't a hope, Peri.'

The leader's gloom deflated Peri a little but she tried to imagine what the Doctor would do and began glancing around the office, searching for a way out.

'How long have we got?' she demanded.

'Not long. Once the officer elite is assembled the twelve most senior officers must gather to witness a final vote-down [...] once the Governor is eliminated regulations insist the dozen candidates place their names in hazard. The unlucky winner is brought in here and forced to govern.'

'And to go through the same daft process you did?'

'Yes.' A mirthless smile formed on the Governor's mouth. 'The theory being that a man terrified for his life will somehow find solutions to this planet's problems. The poor unfortunate will discover, like me, that there are no popular solutions to the difficulties he will find waiting for him here.'[28]

While it is true that the Governor, unlike Sil or the Chief Officer, aspires to the Platonic ideal of ruling in favour of the advantage of his subjects rather than himself, the coercive conditions of Varos – both for him and for those unfortunates in the Punishment Dome – indicate that social harmony cannot be his goal. Each of the officer elite on Varos is unwilling to rule, meeting another criterion of good leadership for Plato, but their unwillingness stems from the wrong reason: fear. Plato writes:

> Now the greatest punishment, if one isn't willing to rule, is to be ruled by someone worse than oneself. And I think that it's fear of this that makes decent people rule when they do. They approach ruling not just as something good or something to be enjoyed, but as something necessary, since it can't be entrusted to anyone better than – or even as good as – themselves. In a city of good men, it if came into being, the citizens would fight in order *not to rule*, just as they do now in order to rule.[29]

Despite the story's happy ending, we have to wonder if political violence, such as what is taped and televised off-world for the pleasure of other planetary populations, isn't in the life-blood of Varos. Indeed, for many citizens of democracies today, the issues and common problems faced in the public sphere are of much less interest than political theatre and charged ideological exchanges. To Barber's necessary conditions for politics of *'a necessity for public action, and thus for reasonable public choice, in the presence of conflict and in the absence of private or independent grounds for judgment'*,[30] I suggest we also need to add a reflexive understanding of the nature of the political in the minds of agents of change within such a social reality. This is obviously what is lacking when, at the end of 'Vengeance on Varos', the public entertainment terminals are all unplugged as the 'video nasties' are ended. 'It's all changed,' says Etta, the wife of the miner Arak. 'We're free.' 'What shall we do?' Arak asks. 'Dunno,' she replies.

The citizens of *Starship UK* in 'The Beast Below' also pride themselves on their democratic ways. 'Twenty-ninth century', the eleventh Doctor explains as he and Amy Pond prepare to materialise on Amy's first spaceship:

> Solar flares roast the Earth, and the entire human race packs its bags and moves out till the weather improves. Whole nations. I've found us a spaceship. This is the United Kingdom of Britain and Northern Ireland. All of it, bolted together and floating in the sky. *Starship UK*. It's Britain, but metal. That's not just a ship, that's an idea. That's a whole country, living and laughing and shopping. Searching the stars for a new home.[31]

Despite the Doctor's enthusiasm, the moment he steps out of the TARDIS he seems to have another of his intellectual intuitions about the social reality of *Starship UK*. After speaking briefly with a crying girl, he tells Amy:

> Hundreds of parents walking past who spot her and not one of them is asking her what's wrong, which means they already know, and it's something they don't talk about. *Secrets.* They're not helping her, so it's something they're afraid of.

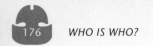

Shadows. Whatever they're afraid of, it's nowhere to be seen, which means it's everywhere. Police state.

The Doctor is correct: the people of *Starship UK are* living in a police state, tended by cowled 'Winders' who tend the creepy 'Smiler' machines (and, sometimes, turn into them!). But they, and their queen, Liz X, only understand the gravity of their situation at an implicit level. This is because the appearance of democratic consensus and civil accord on the ship is kept up by a mutual agreement – a social contract, as it were – of the citizens in order to keep themselves mutually ignorant of the great secret at the heart of their migration to the stars: the 'beast below'. Comparing this adventure to 'Vengeance on Varos', it seems that the citizens of *Starship UK* have a degree of conscience that the Varosians lack, since they don't want to be reminded of the violence that makes their political system possible. When Amy Pond enters Voting Cubicle 33C soon after arriving on *Starship UK*, she is presented with two buttons – 'PROTEST' and 'FORGET' – and the following video message:

> You are here because you want to know the truth about this starship, and I am talking to you because you're entitled to know. When this presentation has finished, you will have a choice. You may either protest, or forget. If you choose to protest, understand this. If just one per cent of the population of this ship do likewise, the programme will be discontinued with consequences for you all. If you choose to accept the situation, and we hope that you will, then press the Forget button. All the information I'm about to give you will be erased from your memory. You will continue to enjoy the safety and amenities of *Starship UK*, unburdened by the knowledge of what has been done to save you. Here then, is the truth about *Starship UK*, and the price that has been paid for the safety of the British people. May God have mercy on our souls.[32]

A fleeting series of images of war, poverty, environmental disasters and (presumably) the secret behind the ship's mysteriously non-mechanical propulsion system are then presented to dizzying effect, and Amy chooses to 'FORGET' what she's seen. It seems that those leaving the UK (excepting, of course, Scotland) for a home in space have accepted the 'reflexivity' amendment to Barber's definition of the political suggested above, only to realise that they cannot live with the implications of their predecessors' actions.

As the Doctor and Amy unearth the truth, and as Queen Liz finds that she is responsible for her own mystification through past orders that she's had erased from her memory, it becomes clear that if *Starship UK* is a totalitarian state, it is a curious and perhaps unique one. The real-life anonymous bureaucracy of fascist or Stalinist totalitarianism worked to ensure that 'the people it dominates never really know why something is happening, and a rational interpretation of the laws does not exist', so, according to Hannah Arendt, 'there remains only one thing that counts, the brutal naked event itself'.[33] In 'The Beast Below', the *Starship UK* citizens have utilised democratic means to pinpoint their own collective best interest (survival) as well as the best means to that interest (their own ignorance of their complicity in harnessing and torturing the 'beast'). Their self-inflicted plight reflects a paradox about democracy that progressive or social democrats often do not want to face up to. It is of course true that the norms of 'equality' and 'freedom' may be actualised, potentially without end, to broaden and deepen opportunities for participation for the citizens of a democratic state. In the end, however, the deliberation and voting on which democratic participation is based will always leave a dissenting minority. This isn't true merely of politics, but about *any* broad consensus in a democratic social reality, like the working of effective markets and practices of social trust. While these need not historically be the same groups over time, there is nothing in the concept of 'democracy' that says that all must be satisfied with it as their primary vehicle for self-governance.

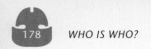

Nobody in the Universe Can Do What We're Doing!

This chapter has resolved around a debate that drives, not only political theory, but all the human sciences: structure or agency? Are political decisions the causal result of interplays of structural power and influence, such as institutionalised racism or the belief, best put by Immanuel Kant, that 'out of the crooked timber of humanity, no straight thing was ever made'? Or are individual political actors the agents of public change, with 'civil society' simply being the aggregate of all such actors? While Marx's historical materialism might have opted for the first type of explanation, and participatory democrats like Benjamin Barber engage more frequently with the second, we have recently begun to distrust the dichotomy itself. In what must surely be the most peculiar of *Doctor Who*'s politically incisive serials – 'The Happiness Patrol' – the seventh Doctor plays the spoons, is chased through sewers by an alien hunter named 'Fifi', and immobilises the seven-foot-tall confectionary killer, the Kandyman, all in the service of bringing down an oppressive regime on the planet Terra Alpha. A thinly disguised critique of Thatcherism, the Doctor takes aim at those who – like some naïve crew members aboard the sandminer and the misguided citizens of *Starship UK* – would see only stability, progress and happiness despite human misery. With some help and a few well-aimed prison breaks, an alliance with the 'Killjoys', and the decoction of the Kandyman, the Doctor and Ace successfully overthrow the regime and ensure that the blues can once again be heard on Terra Alpha. 'I can hear the sound of empires toppling,' the seventh Doctor announces as their plans come to fruition. The entire episode is a lively parody that conceals an intriguing use of the fantastic imagination to deconstruct the separation between structure and agency in the midst of a revolution.

And while it is true that *Doctor Who* is less explicitly political than SF programmes like *Firefly* and *Battlestar Galactica*, we're always on solid ground in seeing any given adventure of the Doctor as an experiment in what structures of a particular social reality can survive when a freewheeling agent arrives in his tall blue box. Like any good SF or science fantasy that entertains political dimensions, the most valuable contribution that *Doctor Who* can make to thinking about political philosophy in the twenty-first century will be to spur the human political imagination. Henry Farrell explains:

> [W]hile the fantastic imagination—the ability to imagine that things are different than they are in the world we live in—plays a crucial role for politics, it is an indirect one. It does not substitute for political activity, or even necessarily guide it, but it expands the space of political possibilities, making people aware of the contingency of existing social arrangements and the possibility of changing them.[34]

In its explorations of alterity, some of which we examined in Chapters 3 and 4, and in its willingness to present characters that defy expectations and social norms such as Vislor Turlough, Jack Harkness and Donna Noble, *Doctor Who* also makes an important contribution to the fantastic political imagination. As we have seen, the mutability of its basic premises and the chance that the Doctor could always re-engage with his own society back on Gallifrey in the future indicate that its own political possibilities are far from exhausted.

7

DID I MENTION IT ALSO TRAVELS IN TIME?

Rewriting History, Line by Line

As *Doctor Who*'s first story editor David Whitaker tells us,

> Everyone expects [...] to see large, gleaming spaceships orbiting planets. But what if the spaceships were here already, disguised as ordinary artifacts? And what if their occupants were already walking among us, keeping cautiously in the background to avoid notice and suspicion [...]?[1]

We know the TARDIS can reach any planet in space, but have I mentioned that it also travels in time?

Doctor Who confirms its status as science fantasy, and as distinct from hard SF, with every time-travel paradox, conundrum or parallel universe it presents. That is, it avoids relying on a particular theory about the *nature* of time itself, and in this regard it ducks many thorny conceptual questions about cosmology. 'In spite of the fact that travel to the past flies in the face of all common sense', claims the author of one study of the literature of time travel, 'we find it throughout the literature. Indeed, it is one of the most common fantasies we have.'[2]

What is time travel? The late David Lewis (1941–2001) satisfies the philosopher's need for precision when he explains:

> Inevitably, it involves a discrepancy between time and time. Any traveler departs and then arrives at his destination; the time elapsed from departure to arrival [...] is the duration of the journey. But if he is a time traveler, the separation in time between departure and arrival does not equal the duration of his journey. He departs; he travels for an hour, let us say; then he arrives. The time he reaches is not the time one hour after his departure. It is later, if he has traveled toward the future; earlier, if he has traveled toward the past.[3]

The discrepancy Lewis describes is between, on the one hand, the 'personal time' that elapses for the traveller from start to finish of his journey and, on the other, the 'external time' that defines the continuity of all other (non-time-travel-related) events. In the 25th-anniversary episode 'Silver Nemesis', the seventh Doctor provides an excellent example of this discrepancy in answering Ace's question, 'How can a statue destroy the world?' 'I'll tell you 350 years ago,' he replies. Moments later, the TARDIS materialises in Lady Peinforte's house in 1638.

Despite the fact that time travel violates principles of common sense and produces absurdities of personal time detached from external time, it does demand from its central premise of travel through the time vortex a certain coherency, even if the scientific standards upon which that coherency are (loosely) based have changed radically over the history of the programme. Early in its history, the first Doctor admits, 'Even after all this time [...] I dare not change the course of history' ('The Massacre of St Bartholomew's Eve'), while more recently we have been treated to the 'riddle, wrapped in a mystery, inside an enigma' of the 2011 season, in which the eleventh Doctor is killed eight minutes into the première episode, 'The Impossible Astronaut'. There is a logic to how one could gallivant through time shown to us by *Doctor Who*, which in the history of SF or science fantasy must be the most sustained meditation on time travel.

The first aired episode of *Doctor Who*, 'An Unearthly Child', introduces us to the science fantasy elements of the show gradually, using a narrative structure unusual for the programme: flashbacks to the uncanny classroom experiences of Ian Chesterton and Barbara Wright regarding their student Susan Foreman. Speaking with Barbara about one of these incidents, Ian says that, the other day, he'd 'set the class a problem with A, B and C as the three dimensions'. The flashback begins with Susan clearly upset at the assignment:

> **SUSAN:** It's impossible unless you use D and E!
>
> **IAN:** D and E? Whatever for? Do the problem that's set, Susan.
>
> **SUSAN:** I can't, Mr. Chesterton! You can't simply work on three of the dimensions!
>
> **IAN:** Three of them? Oh. Time being the fourth, I suppose. Then what do you need E for? What do you make the fifth dimension?
>
> **SUSAN:** (*quietly, mysteriously*) Space ...[4]

As quaint as Susan's own theory of time as the Fourth Dimension appears, it is at least an improvement over the naïve view that time is linear and analogous to a stream or river. Treating time as another dimension that interpenetrates and can vary with space is the same thing as accepting that there is no 'space' and no 'time', but only *space-time*, that is, 'reality consists of a single unified space-time, which contains all of the past, present and future [...] Time does not flow; time is like space.'[5] The Einsteinian unification of space and time, however, raises just as many questions as it solves and the wrinkles of quantum indeterminacy make the question, 'Is time travel possible?' a particularly knotty one. As we shall see, even if it were possible, it might not be desirable to head to the past or the future in one's own personal TARDIS. The outcome could be, as the fifth Doctor's companion Tegan Jovanka liked to say, 'ZAP!'

Change, My Dear ... and It Seems Not a Moment Too Soon

The roots of the metaphysical questions about time and, by extension, the philosopher's take on the possibility and limits of time travel go back all the way to the beginning. That is, to the beginning of Western thought before Socrates in the Eleatic school of what would become Italy. In the Greek colony of Elea, Parmenides (early fifth century BCE) and his student Zeno (c.490–c.430 BCE) were to set the terms under which Plato, Aristotle, and many others after them would think about the fundamental nature of reality. Parmenides, unlike his fellow pre-Socratics and Socrates himself, wrote down his work, but in verse. This was often the case with the Greeks; for Parmenides the ability to poetise and to reason in flawlessly logical ways were not mutually exclusive abilities. His central insight about the nature of being and the meaning of change has structured the Western view of language and reality for more than two thousand years.

In 'The Way of Opinion', the third part of the poem for which he is known, he writes:

> Thus, according to opinion, were these things born and now are,
> And from now on will grow, and will later perish.
> And for each of these human beings proposed a distinguishing name.[6]

According to Parmenides, we all have a basic understanding of change, and it seems that changes really occur, because our experience is not of a static world or an undifferentiated mental life. In order for change to occur, a particular thing – no matter whether a blue whale or an isotope (or a sense impression or idea, for that matter) – must change its state at least fractionally. A stone split in half suffers a major change, and we can no longer say 'that (whole) stone is still there'; an atom that gives up an electron becomes a 'cation', and becomes positively charged. Whatever the changed thing is, it is not what it was before (note that Parmenides is using 'is' in the strict sense of numerical identity, not mere qualitative identity, both of which were discussed in Chapter 5). Change requires that 'what is' – at least one property of the changing thing – revert to 'what is not', and this for Parmenides is an intolerable suggestion. He says, 'It is necessary to say and to think What-Is, for to-be *is* / And nothing is *not*. These things I command you to consider.'[7] Something that is 'X' cannot become 'not-X', but the transformation from 'X' into something else (even if that thing is qualitatively similar, like a stone that loses but one atom) is the most basic logical formula for change. Therefore, Parmenides concludes, change itself is an illusion, and the senses that inform us of myriad 'changes' are fundamentally defective for gaining knowledge. 'Coming-into-being' or 'going-out-of-existence' are non-sequiturs. Famously, his student Zeno would show through his 'paradoxes' that motion and other forms of change were rationally unsupportable. We cannot aim for rational coherency in our explanations and accept change at the same time. They were quite serious about all this.

Any future metaphysical explanation of the basics of change would have to engage with Parmenides. Aristotle understood there to be a *subject of change* that contained the potential for transformation. This subject remained the same despite qualitative change, moving *from* a state of privation of a particular quality in the case of 'coming-into-being' or *to* a state of privation in the case of 'going-out-of-existence'.[8] So, for instance, when Martha Jones is trying to help the crew of the SS *Pentalian* prevent their ship from falling into the living sun in '42', she needs the answer to the question, 'Who had more pre-download Number Ones, Elvis Presley or The Beatles?' She doesn't know the answer, so she goes from a state of 'privation', or lack of this information, to a state of 'being-Martha-knowing-the-answer' after calling her mother and getting the answer (it's Elvis, by the way). Knowing this trivia doesn't fundamentally change what she is, for Aristotle, so it seems that both 'what is' (Martha as a subject of change) and 'what is not' (Martha's knowledge of pre-download pop hits) are needed to explain genuine change.

Aristotle does seem to concede this to Parmenides: once a change has occurred and is in the past, it is unalterable.

'What was' and 'what was not' in the past were, and were not, *necessarily*. For Aristotle, this is more a truth from logic and language than from metaphysics. 'With regard to what is and what has been it is necessary for the affirmation or the negation [of a claim about what happened] to be true or false', he writes. 'For if every affirmation or negation is true or false it is necessary for everything either to be the case or not to be the case.'[9] Suppose we say, from the vantage point of today, that 'Rose Tyler's dad, Pete Tyler, died on 7 November 1987'. This claim is either true or false. If it's true (which, despite the events of 'Father's Day' [2005], it still is), then its contradiction, 'It's not the case that Rose Tyler's dad, Pete Tyler, died on 7 November 1987', is false. Note that if Pete were only hurt instead of being killed by the speeding car (or had escaped unscathed), the contradiction would be true and the original statement false. We could extend this sort of reasoning to any claim about anything that has happened in the past: 'Napoleon died on the island of St Helena in 1821' (true); or 'The extended news coverage of JFK's assassination delayed the broadcast of the first episode of "An Unearthly Child"' (false). For any statement the truth of which is undetermined, we must, on Aristotle's view, assume that either it or its contradiction is true.

Now, that's true of what's past, but what about the future? We know that Pete Tyler had dreams about his future and he must have made certain statements about things that hadn't yet happened. Suppose Pete, in early 1987, had said, 'One day I'll make millions from my Vitex Lite sales.' This claim doesn't seem to be classifiable as true or false, but it could prove to be one or the other years later. In 2006, on 'Pete's World' – the alternate-universe Earth that the tenth Doctor, Mickey Smith and Rose arrive on in 'Rise of the Cybermen' – this statement is true. Of course, for alternate Pete, that's all in the past. But the only reason we can give for why the statement is unclassifiable as true or false in 1987 is Pete Tyler's own ignorance of the future. In fact, Aristotle makes a very strong claim regarding statements about the future: they are true or false *now*, but we're simply not aware of which it is. In fact, these statements were *always* true or false, whether they were uttered in the past or present, or will be uttered in the future. 'Again if [a thing] is white now it was true to say earlier that it would be white', Aristotle tells us,

> so that it was always true to say of anything that has happened that it would be so. But if it was always true to say that it was so, or would be so, it could not not be so, or not be going to be so.[10]

In Aristotle's defence, it seems to make sense to say that if a statement is worded precisely enough, then it cannot be true at one time and false at another. Precision is key here. If we say 'At 5.02 p.m. GMT on 22 April 2011, a woman wearing an astronaut's flight suit on the shore of Lake Silencio, Utah, fires on a person wearing a tweed coat and bow tie', we would happily say that if all these conditions are met, then the sentence becomes true at 5.02 p.m. GMT on 22 April 2011. Because the statement is precisely indexed in time and space, however, it doesn't make sense to say that it's *false* before 5.02 p.m. on that date. Rather, like Aristotle's white object, either it *must* be true or it *must* be false, no matter when it is uttered. 'Hence, if in the whole of time the state of things was such that one or the other was true, it was necessary for this to happen, and for the state of things always to be such that everything that happens happens of necessity.'[11] Call this the *logical necessity* of past and future events (or non-events), which stems from the basic roles that truth and falsity play in language and beliefs. Aristotle's view of logical necessity means that although we may see 'possibilities' for a thing to change in more than one way, such possibilities are only apparent, not genuine – one change or the other *will* occur, and this has always been the case.

Nonetheless, Aristotle thought that the 'action and deliberation' of people like us demonstrated that there was genuine 'possibility' in the world rather than the 'necessity' that characterised the rest of nature. One reason for treating humans as a special case stems from the fact that Aristotle didn't have access to physical sciences of power and precision as we do today. This caused him to refrain from understanding the human mind or soul as operating according to the same basic principles of nature as those of the body, and so to disagree with later materialists such as Julien Offray de La Mettrie (1709–51), who proclaimed, 'Let us then conclude boldly that man is a machine, and that in the whole universe there is but a single substance differently modified.'[12] La Mettrie, like many other Enlightenment thinkers, found the hypothesis of a 'single substance', matter, producing all the changes of nature by its motion and the interaction of its parts, a particularly powerful one. Our talents and moral dispositions, for example, can be understood better as products of nature, he claimed:

> Man's preeminent advantage is his organism. In vain all writers of books on morals fail to regard as praiseworthy those qualities that come by nature, esteeming only the talents gained by dint of reflection and industry. For whence come, I ask, skill, learning, and virtue, if not from a disposition that makes us fit to become skilful, wise, and virtuous? And whence again, comes this disposition, if not from nature? Only through nature do we have any good qualities; to her we owe all that we are.[13]

On this view, there is nothing mysterious or occult about human action or deliberation; we need only know of the necessary and sufficient conditions that motivate or restrain our decisions and behaviours in order to bring them, too, into the domain of scientific prediction and control. Richard Taylor explains:

> [I]t is not hard to suppose [...] that everything that happens is wholly determined by what went before it, and hence that whatever happens at any future time is the only thing that can then happen given what precedes it. Or even disregarding that, it seems natural to suppose that there is a body of truth concerning what the future holds, just as there is such truth concerning what is contained in the past, whether or not it is known to any person or even to God, and hence, that everything asserted in that body of truth will assuredly happen, in the fullness of time, precisely as it is described therein.[14]

Call this *causal* or *physical necessity*, what philosophers often discuss under the heading of 'determinism'. Determinism isn't just a metaphysical theory; it can be applied, at least in classical Newtonian physics, with this principle: *'Classical determinism is a logical equivalence between two propositions of Newtonian dynamics with respect to two different instants of time.'*[15]

If this hypothesis about causes and effects is true, then it's easy to understand why the first Doctor was constantly warning his companions about interference in history. As a history teacher, 1960s companion Barbara Wright finds it compelling not only to participate in history, but also to think about changing it. The Doctor explodes in frustration at Barbara's attempt to make the Aztecs a kinder, gentler civilisation, telling her, 'You can't rewrite history! Not one line!' ('The Aztecs'). She's not only up against the physical necessity of causal chains of influence that deterministically produce both Aztec beauty and tragedy. She's also colliding with the logically necessary truth of past statements about the Aztecs' cruelty to their sacrificial victims and the equally logically necessary *falsity* of statements such as, 'In 1454, schoolteacher Barbara Wright, posing as the reincarnated priest Yetaxa, put an end to bloody sacrifices among the Aztecs.'[16] Barbara's situation, then, is not that different from the time traveller in the infamous 'grandfather paradox', in which a person is displaced into the past fifty or so years with the intention of killing her grandfather, and all before her grandfather has had any children.

Only two pointed questions then remain: from Barbara's perspective, nothing is physically or logically preventing her from using her power for this end, so *why* must the evil simply be lived with?[17] And if it is genuinely impossible, logically and physically, for her to make a change in history, why is the Doctor so terribly upset?

The Past is Another Country – 1987's Just the Isle of Wight

One possible explanation is that there's no impossibility to changing the past, but that the Doctor fears drawing the attention of the as-yet-unnamed Time Lords. This is his motivation in 'Frontios' when he uncharacteristically refuses to land near one of the last human settlements in the far future, citing the Laws of Time. 'Now, we mustn't interfere. Colony's too new, one generation at the most. The future hangs in the balance.'

The more interesting answer, philosophically speaking, is that the TARDIS repeatedly materialises at the 'Jonbar Hinges' of time, a term taken from Jack Williamson's 1952 collection of time-travel stories *The Legion of Time*. Jonbar Hinges, as the name suggests, are linchpins of possible change in the sea of temporal necessity; points that are particularly crucial in the grand scheme of things. The fifth Doctor seems to suggest that the human colony in the Veruna system represents one such 'Hinge', and it may be that the Aztec capital Tenochtitlan in 1454 is another one. On the other hand, the tenth Doctor adopts quite a different view in 'The Waters of Mars': 'I mean, it's only a theory, what do I know, but I think certain moments in time are fixed. Tiny, precious moments. Everything else is in flux, anything can happen, but those certain moments, they have to stand.' If this is correct (and he admits it's only a theory), then there are apparently 'Jonbar Struts' as well as 'Hinges', with the vast majority of events in space-time 'in flux, anything can happen', implying that they are causally or historically less significant than 'Jonbar' events.

We'll return to the Doctor's pet theory about time, but another reason we might share Barbara's confusion about the possibility of changing history has to do with her autonomy to act as she sees fit in 1454. While Aristotle might claim that the statement, 'In 1454, schoolteacher Barbara Wright, posing as the reincarnated priest Yetaxa, put an end to bloody sacrifices among the Aztecs' is just as false in 1454 as it is in Barbara's 'home time' of 1963, it seems puzzling that this statement would be necessarily false before Barbara acts. In physics, the 'autonomy principle' states that 'it is possible to create in our immediate environment any configuration of matter that the laws of physics permit locally, without reference to what the rest of the universe may be doing'.[18] This means that if Barbara is able to convince key Aztec leaders that sacrifices should be stopped, only the local causal laws could prevent her from doing so; something like 'historical inertia', a force that keeps chains of causes and effects from being disturbed, as Barbara intends to do, is ruled out.

Surprisingly, however, classical physics says that historical inertia would prevent Barbara from changing history, because the autonomy principle cannot conflict with the 'consistency principle', which states that 'the only configurations of matter that can occur locally are those that are self-consistent globally'.[19] There is only one history, one staggeringly complex network of causes and effects linked by ironclad chains of physical necessity, so the Doctor is correct to admonish Barbara, even if his tone seems overzealous. This is similar to Aristotle's view of the unchanging truth or falsity of any claim about the past. In 'Father's Day', Rose and the ninth Doctor unwisely travel, not once but twice, to the spot in 1987 where her father Pete was killed. Upon their second arrival, Rose rushes past her earlier self to actually save her father's life. This demonstrates a (brief) triumph of autonomy over consistency, but since her earlier self and the earlier Doctor didn't experience her rushing into the road to pull Pete away from the speeding car, they vanish, cancelled out by something like the effect of the consistency principle. What is worse, of course, is that Rose's benevolent intervention in her own history brings a particular nasty manifestation of the consistency principle: the Reapers. 'Time's been damaged,' the Doctor explains, 'and they've come to sterilize the wound.' Of course, the Reapers are a metaphorical representation of the unusual and perhaps absurd effect that consistency can have in limiting our autonomy to act in what appears to be a determined past (or future). Paul Horwich comments on this, saying:

> Time travel would allow one to influence the past but not to change it. Changing the past is indeed logically impossible. However, no such contradictions are involved in the idea of influencing the past [...] The same considerations apply to the future [...] we can bring about future events, but we cannot bring about an event that will not occur.[20]

It has been mentioned above that in classical physics, the autonomy principle and the consistency principle couldn't come into conflict with each other. The fact that only one history exists – and presumably, just one present and one future – rules out interventions in time. If we discover, for example, that it was the escapades of the fifth Doctor in Pudding Lane ('The Visitation', 1982) that led to the Great Fire of London in 1666, then that has always been the reason for the fire. The fact that the two principles accord with each other doesn't rule out time travel, but it does imply that the actions of time travellers would be constrained by what has already occurred – or perhaps that any chrononauts could only be ghostly observers of history, not participants in it, much as the first Doctor and company experience at the beginning of 'The Space Museum' when the TARDIS has 'jumped a time track'.

The possibility of 'Closed Timelike Curves' (CTCs), however, changes all this. If we briefly revert to thinking in terms of the naïve view that time is linear, like a stream, our own lives and the course of history seem to unfold in one direction: from past to present to future, from earlier to later ('time's arrow'). In Einstein's description of the universe as a unified 'space-time', as mentioned earlier, space and time are one four-dimensional entity in which each point represents a place and time – an *event*. While the lives of non-time travellers appear to be a straight line burrowed through the block of space-time like a worm's path through an apple, the 'worldline' of their life history cannot simply be an arbitrary path chiselled out through space-time. According to Einstein, the speed of light is a constraining factor on travel throughout space-time, which is the same thing as saying that my path through space-time can be shown to increase in duration along one direction of a possible worldline. Anything that obeys this constraining factor is called 'timelike'. But space-time could, through the influence of massively gravitational attractors (such as black holes), be distorted in such a way that a worldline could curve back on itself, producing a CTC and effective travel to the past. While it's not entirely clear whether or not the TARDIS might take advantage of CTCs, it is true that the basis for

Gallifrey's time-travel technology is the 'Eye of Harmony', a black hole engineered by the pioneer Omega from a star in the Sector of Forgotten Souls ('The Three Doctors'; 'Omega', Big Finish Audio Production, 2003; 'Journey to the Centre of the TARDIS', 2013).

It's helpful to think of multi-Doctor stories in *Doctor Who* in terms of worldlines and CTCs. The Doctor's own 'personal time' worldline zigzags through space-time, only coalescing into 'external time' at his destination for the length of each adventure. When his worldline doubles backwards (or forwards) on itself so that his location in both space *and* time are roughly the same in more than one segment of his personal time, he is capable of meeting himself. While this typically occurs as a pretext for having several different incarnations meet each other (as discussed in Chapter 5), every so often the Doctor does literally meet himself in the same incarnation ('Day of the Daleks'; 'The Big Bang'; 'Last Night', a short included in the 2011 sixth series set on DVD and Blu-Ray). The physics of the *Doctor Who* universe seem to either rule out this kind of meeting for non-Time Lords, or predict disastrous effects should it occur. This fictive physical law, the 'Blinovitch Limitation Effect', was first mentioned in 'Day of the Daleks' and attributed to Aaron Blinovitch from his book *Temporal Mechanics* of 1928, but it is not entirely clear what the law specifies. In 'Mawdryn Undead' (1983), two versions of Brigadier Lethbridge-Stewart meet each other aboard a spacecraft trapped in a warp ellipse, triggering an enormous and potentially deadly release of temporal energy. The pseudo-scientific explanation for what occurs when this happens is a 'shorting out of the time differential'. The way in which Time Lords get around this is rather cleverly explained in the 2007 *Children in Need* special 'Time Crash', scripted by Stephen Moffat, in which the fifth Doctor appears in front of the tenth Doctor after their versions of the TARDIS suffer a temporal collision in the time vortex:

FIFTH DOCTOR: Is there something wrong with you?
TENTH DOCTOR: Oh there it goes! The frowny face, I remember that one!

(He grabs FIVE's face in both his hands and squishes his cheeks around.) Mind you, bit saggier than it ought to be, hair's a bit grayer. That's because of me, though, the two of us together has shorted out the time differential, should all snap back in place when we get you back home. Be able to close that coat again. But never mind that! Look at you! The hat, the coat, the crickety cricket stuff the … stick of celery, yeah. Brave choice celery, but fair play to you – not a lot of men can carry off a decorative vegetable.[21]

So now we know why each incarnation of the Doctor looks older when he bumps into his future selves. Despite the effectiveness of Blinovitch's principle as a mechanism of historical inertia – keeping any substantial changes from occurring to history by travelling back in time via CTC or otherwise – in the new version of *Doctor Who* since 2005, violations of the Limitation Effect seem fairly common. River Song, Amy Pond and Kazran Sardick ('A Christmas Carol', 2010) have all met themselves without batting an eye.

'Time Crash' is also paradigmatic of another apparent paradox of time travel. What is known as the 'knowledge paradox' results when knowledge is gained by something other than typical problem-solving processes; it can also extend to any literature or art carried from the future into the past, where it is 'created'. The *deus ex machina* solution to the big problem in 'Time Crash' involves just such a paradox:

FIFTH DOCTOR: Supernova and black hole at the exact same instant.
TENTH DOCTOR: Explosion cancels out implosion.
FIFTH: Matter stays constant.
TENTH: Brilliant!
FIFTH: Far too brilliant. I've never met anyone else who could fly the TARDIS like that.
TENTH: Sorry, mate, you still haven't.
FIFTH: You didn't have time to work all that out; even I couldn't do it.
TENTH: I didn't work it out, I didn't have to.
FIFTH: You remembered.

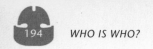

TENTH: Because you will remember.
FIFTH: You remembered being me, watching you, doing that. You already knew what to do because I watched you do it.
TENTH: Wibbley-wobbley ...
FIFTH and TENTH together: Timey-wimey![22]

As fascinating as they are, knowledge paradoxes compound the puzzles of time travel with their implications that many pieces of 'new' knowledge were never discovered or created at all, but exist because of the looping effects of something like a CTC. In their examination of knowledge paradoxes, Deutsch and Lockwood spell out the problem like this: 'What is philosophically objectionable here is not that knowledge-bearing artifacts are carried into the past – it is the "free lunch" element. The knowledge required to invent the artifacts must not be supplied by the artifacts themselves.'[23]

Of course, this is only a paradox if the fifth Doctor's observations are carried forward, to be used by the tenth Doctor within his own universe; if more than one universe is involved, we have quite a different story entirely.

So Free Will Is Not an Illusion After All

Multi-world theories (MWTs) are a mainstay of both SF and philosophy. While the term 'multiverse' was coined by American philosopher and psychologist William James, the idea's most famous philosophical proponent was Gottfried Wilhelm Leibniz, whose law of identity we discussed in Chapter 5. In trying to buttress the idea that God freely chose to create the actual world, Leibniz was forced to confront the requirements for a real choice; for him, this implied that God must have had other worlds in mind that could have been created, but were not. 'Thus was born the concept of the infinite set of logically possible worlds.'[24] Leibniz viewed ours as 'the best of all possible worlds', as it displays the greatest degree of harmony (the norm most prized by God) between unity and multiplicity in its design and providential course of events. Of course, 'parallel-world plots are much beloved of science fiction writers, who use the scheme to ask questions about worlds like our own, except that particular possibilities turned out differently'.[25] Actual travel to a parallel universe – what I'll call the phenomenon of 'paratime', following SF author H. Beam Piper – requires that worlds very much like our own be not merely logically possible, but also actual.

In this important respect, the final serial of *Doctor Who*'s seventh season in 1970, 'Inferno', is ahead of its time. Ostensibly a cautionary tale about breaching the Earth's crust in search of alternative fuels, 'Inferno' works in both a MWT-based plotline and as a glimpse of the end of the world itself, as a parallel universe's Project Inferno runs out of control, unleashing the forces of nature in a cataclysm the third Doctor can only barely avoid. Settling into his exile and experimenting with the non-functional TARDIS console, the Doctor manages, entirely by accident, to cross over into the parallel world 'Republic of Great Britain': a fascist country in which the royal family had been executed years before. Script editor Terrance Dicks had added the parallel dimension element to Don Houghton's script for 'Inferno' at a late stage, and this inclusion created a path-breaking opportunity for *Doctor Who* to explore MWT several years before the most significant publications by Brandon Carter and G.F.R. Ellis in the mid-1970s. In particular, the Doctor is fascinated by the differences between events in his own universe and those at the end of the Project Inferno of fascist Britain, running on a faster timetable. 'Yes, of course, of course,' he muses after returning from the cataclysm on the alternate Earth. 'An infinity of universes, ergo an infinite number of choices. So free will is not an illusion after all. The pattern can be changed.' Of course, it's not at all clear that this is what the Doctor's multiple-world experiences prove at all. Rather, what they do show is that, given certain starting conditions, one result will occur, while given sufficiently different conditions, a different result will probably come about. Despite the perverse replication of the Doctor's friends in the form of Brigade Leader Lethbridge-Stewart and Section Leader Elizabeth Shaw, there are enough significant differences between the 'parallel' worlds to challenge the Doctor's speculation about the significance of free will. 'Inferno' tells us more about the working of the aforementioned 'consistency principle' in different worlds than it does anything else.

Because they convert the necessities of our world into what seem to be new possibilities, alternate universes have their drawbacks as well as their insights. In the first episode to feature MWT in the new *Doctor Who*, 'Rise of the Cybermen', the tenth Doctor counsels his companions Rose and Mickey, 'Parallel world, it's like a gingerbread house. All those temptations calling out.' If there are an infinite number of parallel universes, each related to the next but different in subtle ways, then this fact could even be subversive of morality in general, As Bud Foote points out by claiming that if all possibilities exist somewhere, choice becomes meaningless: 'Plot, like morality, depends upon acts having consequences.'[26] But the likelihood of just such an infinite number of alternatives is precisely what the multiple-worlds interpretation of quantum mechanics implies.

Among other interpretations, MWT as it ties into quantum mechanics was first proposed by Hugh Everett in 1957, and it challenges the definition of determinism we encountered earlier in this chapter: *'Classical determinism is a logical equivalence between two propositions of Newtonian dynamics with respect to two different instants of time.'*[27] At the quantum level, no logical, one-to-one equivalence between propositions in Newtonian physics – most famously, those concerning the speed and velocity of a particle à la Heisenberg's indeterminacy principle – will necessarily obtain in every case. This means that certain observations cannot be predicted absolutely, so physicists – beginning with Everett – concluded that in such cases they could specify only a *range* of possible observations, each with a different probability. Of course, in the long run, determinism still obtains: 'as applied to the multiverse, quantum theory is deterministic – it predicts the subjective probability of each outcome by prescribing the proportion of universes in which that outcome occurs'.[28] According to the 'many-worlds' interpretation of quantum mechanics, each of these possible observations corresponds to a different universe. SF movies, television and literature have exploited this insight to speculate that, for any contingent change that may be resolved one way or another, a duplicate universe is created in which the unactualised resolution becomes actual.

This is the premise of the intriguing tale 'Turn Left' (2008). In this episode, the apparently trivial decision of Donna Noble (Catherine Tate) to pursue a different job opportunity six months before meeting the Doctor prompts her to take a right rather than left turn at a traffic intersection. A mysterious fortune-teller from the planet Shan Shen prompts her to change her own past after she separates from the Doctor to sightsee a bit. 'Turn right, and never meet that man. Turn right, and change the world,' the fortune-teller urges her compellingly. For most of the rest of the episode, the audience is left in the dark as to whether or not Donna's right turn is actually a change to established history or whether she is merely dreaming or hallucinating.

Although the 'turn right' parallel world is created by Donna's mundane decision, the episode ingeniously explores what would have happened had she not met the Doctor as she did in 'The Runaway Bride'. Writer Russell T. Davies kills the Doctor off right away, an unfortunate victim of his own tactics against the Racnoss queen in that episode. Although Donna is confused about what is going on in and around Chiswick, it's made clear to the viewer that without her involvement with the Doctor – and their efforts to save people from the Judoon ('Smith and Jones', 2007), the crash of the starship *Titanic* ('Voyage of the Damned'), the Adipose ('Partners in Crime'), and the Sontarans ('The Sontaran Strategem'/'The Poison Sky', both 2008) – the world is a much worse place. The 'turn right' universe shows us a Britain decimated and its economy gutted by alien invasions and radioactivity from the *Titanic* crash, its immigrant population forced into labour camps, and even the stars vanishing from the night sky. Only Donna – with the help of Rose Tyler and UNIT – can restore the proper chain of events.

When the situation is resolved and history is on the 'right track' again, the Doctor explains that Donna's memory has been the victim of a powerful giant 'Time Beetle'. The creature apparently feeds off the energy created by a time differential, but has to produce these by changing one person's history – in this case, Donna's:

> **DOCTOR:** Just got lucky, this thing. It's one of the Trickster's Brigade. Changes a life in tiny little ways. Most times, the universe just compensates around it, but with you? Great big parallel world.
> **DONNA:** Hold on. You said parallel worlds are sealed off.
> **DOCTOR:** They are. But you had one created around you. Funny thing is, seems to be happening a lot to you.[29]

The reason why Donna is special is revealed in the ensuing story featuring Davros and the Daleks, but 'Turn Left' is a brilliant extrapolation of MWT. It demonstrates how the 'principle of consistency' of natural laws produces different outcomes when one key decision – or one key player, the Doctor – is changed or removed from the equation.

Many-worlds quantum mechanics also provides an explanation for how the 'autonomy principle' could override the 'consistency principle', which, as discussed above, would never conflict within the world of classical Newtonian physics. Recall that even travelling back into the past by using a closed timelike curve would not necessarily allow someone like Donna to change the past, as logical and physical necessity would have it. But using a CTC in a situation in which quantum indeterminacy leads to the creation of a parallel universe means that when Donna goes backward in time, she doesn't emerge in *her own* past, but instead in that of a roughly parallel universe (call this the 'Trickster' universe). It may have been true in her 'home' universe that the Doctor didn't die in his confrontation with the Racnoss queen, and so events could not be different. But in the Trickster universe, Donna has an open future (the universe was just split off from her 'home' universe) and, in many ways, is a free agent, since she doesn't even hail from this parallel world. In such a case, her autonomy to change the future as she sees fit would trump the normal constraint of the consistency principle. Donna could even send her loud-mouthed mother Sylvia packing without worrying about the fact that she never did so in her home universe – in the Trickster universe, that hasn't happened yet.

It's About Time

Stephen Moffat's 'Whoniverse' has, ever since the landmark episode 'Blink', been a universe depicted not as structured by a 'web of time' but by 'wibbley-wobbley, timey-wimey *stuff*'. Not only does this explicit effort to disavow a theory of time and time travel smack of the Romanticism we discussed all the way back in Chapter 1; it works surprisingly well with what quantum physics tells us about the nature of time. The Doctor's own theory about the nature of time is fundamentally different from most of the views we have examined so far in this chapter. We must assume that it is informed by intellectual intuitions about time, change and history similar to those discussed throughout the book; in the Doctor's own words from 'Time and the Rani', he has 'a unique conceptual understanding of the properties of time'. The tenth Doctor's theory from 'The Waters of Mars', recall, is roughly encapsulated in the ideas that 'certain moments in time are fixed', while 'everything else is in flux, anything can happen'. We took to calling fixed moments in time – like the destruction of Bowie Base One – 'Jonbar Struts'. Although our favourite Time Lord doesn't here mention anything like 'Jonbar Hinges', it's intimated that there are such things in tales such as 'Genesis of the Daleks', 'Frontios' and 'Attack of the Cybermen'.

Causal determinism refutes the Doctor's theory because, in such a world, every event is a Jonbar Strut. It cannot stomach, in principle, the idea that 'anything can happen'. Similarly, the attribution of logical necessity to all timelessly true and timelessly false statements, which we saw was Aristotle's move, cannot be reconciled with 'everything in flux', unless this flux is mere appearance, merely the way the universe seems to work according to the uneducated or ignorant.

But *can* history be rewritten? The Doctor seems to have changed his mind about this since 'The Massacre of St Bartholomew's Eve'. Elements of his theory are present in the fan-favourite episode 'Blink', starting with the Doctor's description of the Weeping Angels to police detective Billy Shipton:

> **DOCTOR:** Fascinating race, the Weeping Angels. The only psychopaths in the universe to kill you nicely. No mess, no fuss, they just zap you into the past and let you live to death. The rest of your life used up and blown away in the blink of an eye. You die in the past, and in the present they consume the energy of all the days you might have had. All your stolen moments. They're creatures of the abstract. They live off potential energy.
> **BILLY:** What in God's name are you talking about?
> **MARTHA:** Trust me. Just nod when he stops for breath.[30]

The Weeping Angels, also known as 'Lonely Assassins', are, like the Silence from the 2011 series, *Doctor Who* monsters for the quantum age. Their threat of 'living you to death' is unique, but, as Michelle Saint and Peter A. French comment, 'being transported back in time is a far cry from being torn to pieces or having one's brain stuffed into a metallic shell'.[31] When being gazed upon, the Angels are 'quantum-locked' and cannot move, a conceit aimed at capitalising on the 'observer effect' in quantum mechanics, which dictates that precise measurements of extremely small particles cannot be made without affecting the systems of which they are a part. When not thus 'turned to stone', the Angels can move instantaneously and without effort, much like the phenomenon of 'quantum tunnelling'. The science fantasy dimension of *Doctor Who* is uniquely situated to bring out the horrifying implications of a scientific discovery such as this, which tells us that 'potential barriers in the quantum world are fuzzy. They do inhibit the motion of particles, but they are not the solid, impenetrable boundaries of the Newtonian world.'[32] Since the Weeping Angels possess these kinds of powers, why isn't the Doctor more worried about the threat they pose on Earth? With each human that they touch, he faces the possibility of yet another Barbara Wright cast back into history, trying to rewrite the past.

Quantum mechanics (and the Doctor's own theory of time) suggest that while there is considerable order in the universe – particularly at the level of the 'middle-sized dry goods' that we interact with on a daily basis – there is far more room for the malleability of past, present and future than logical necessity or causal determinism would suggest. A robust determinism would fail in the face of quantum indeterminacy, leaving us with descriptions of causes and effects in terms of very high probabilities, not necessities. As mentioned earlier, only at the broadest possible level – across the multiverse of quantum-linked worlds – would determinism obtain, because quantum mechanics become the new 'consistency principle' for *every* world. Meantime, criticisms of Aristotelian logical necessity could note that the level of precision that we can achieve in describing logically necessary truths and falsities about 'middle-sized dry goods' simply doesn't obtain at the quantum level.

The tenth Doctor explains in this first Weeping Angel episode that 'people assume that time is a strict progression of cause to effect, but actually from a non-linear, non-subjective viewpoint, it's more like a big ball of wibbly-wobbly, timey-wimey stuff'. This may be his effort to explain something that is beyond human ken, but one is tempted to say that in dialogue such as this, the tenth and eleventh Doctors often parody the programme's own tendency to substitute pseudo-scientific gobbledygook for genuine explanations. In 'Blink', the Doctor tells Billy Shipton:

> This is my timey-wimey detector. It goes ding when there's stuff. Also, it can boil an egg at thirty paces, whether you want it to or not, actually, so I've learned to stay away from hens. It's not pretty when they blow.

This story and later Moffat-scripted episodes like 'The Big Bang' and 'The Wedding of River Song' (2011) insinuate that when changes to history occur, even massive changes, the effects are felt instantaneously and the shift typically goes unnoticed except for one central character. In 'The Big Bang', this is young Amelia Pond, while in 'The Wedding of

River Song', it's the bearded Doctor in the '5.02' paratime universe. The Doctor is often shown to be resistant to the effect of major, or even catastrophic, changes to the fabric of space-time – what he calls an 'eye of the storm effect'. In 'The Time Monster' (1972), the Master's experiments with TOMTIT produce a 'crack in time' with any number of freak effects, and in 'Cold Blood' the Doctor resists the inimical effects of a similar crack (which persists throughout the episodes of that year's series) that erases Rory Williams from time (only the second of his many deaths!). Rory's effacement from Amy Pond's memory splits the difference between an instantaneous causal 'quantum shift' and the slow fading-out of the no-longer-actual future (sometimes called the 'Back to the Future' effect); in the time remaining to him, the Doctor urges Amy to keep him in memory:

> **DOCTOR:** Keep him in your mind. Don't forget him. If you forget him, you'll lose him forever.
> **AMY:** When we were on the *Byzantium*, I still remembered the Clerics because I am a time traveller now, you said.
> **DOCTOR:** They weren't part of your world. This is different. This is your own history changing.
> **AMY:** Don't tell me it's going to be okay. You have to make it okay.
> **DOCTOR:** It's going to be hard, but you can do it, Amy. Tell me about Rory, eh? Fantastic Rory. Funny Rory. Gorgeous Rory. Amy, listen to me. Do exactly as I say. Amy, please. Keep concentrating. You can do this.
> **AMY:** I can't.[33]

However, Amy's fighting a losing battle against quantum field theory, classical physics and brain biochemistry combined. 'Quantum entanglement', is the feature of quantum mechanics that poses the greatest challenge to the tradition of metaphysics, because it fundamentally undermines our notion of cause and effect as requiring a necessary connection of transfer of energy over relatively short distances. When objects as small as electrons or photons – or as large as carbon buckyballs or tiny diamonds – have interacted with each other, they become 'entangled', or share one or more of the same quantum states. These states can be seen to vary correlatively in both objects, despite distances between them; the objects seem to 'communicate' with each other, even though there is no energy transfer between them. Although in reality it is small-scale experiments which produce observable entanglements under laboratory conditions, a large-scale change of particles at one point in the universe could create a 'ripple' effect in their entangled partners elsewhere in the cosmos, producing a seemingly instantaneous change of great magnitude.

To produce one of these quantum shifts that reorder reality, action on the part of the time traveller in the past or future would not be sufficient; after all, any decision that a non-time traveller makes, any action they take, by definition creates change in their world, the material aspect of which will always involve quantum mechanical transformations. It is the fact that the time traveller *doesn't belong* – according to the consistency principles of the world and time they've arrived in – that makes all the difference. For physicist Stephen Hawking, this fact is enough to prove that time travel isn't possible. Hawking has claimed that something like historical inertia – but with a valid scientific explanation – could prevent time travel into the past in the first place:

> There seems to be a Chronology Protection Agency that makes the world safe for historians by preventing travel into the past. What happens is that the uncertainty principle implies that space-time is full of pairs of particles and antiparticles that appear together, move part, and come back together again, and annihilate. These particles and antiparticles are said to be virtual because one does not normally notice their existence and one cannot observe them with a particle detector. However, if space-time is warped so that particles can come back to earlier points in their histories, the density of virtual particles will go up because one could have many copies of a given particle at the same time. This extra density of virtual particles would either distort space-time so much that it was not possible to go back in time, or it would cause space-time

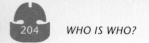

to come to an end in a singularity, like the Big Bang or the Big Crunch.[34]

Such an event seems to have occurred when the eleventh Doctor piloted the Pandorica into his own exploding TARDIS in the finale to the 2010 series. Having transmitted the Pandorica's restoration field to every particle of space and time simultaneously to produce 'Big Bang Two', the Doctor has either restored the universe before the stars went out, or has created a new and very similar one. This latter option might have prompted some viewers to ask, 'Is the Doctor now god?' A number of long-time *Doctor Who* fans, however, were satisfied to ask, 'Does this mean that Matt Smith is now the *first* Doctor?'

The Doctor has repeatedly asserted that fundamental changes have come about in the multiverse now that the Time Lords have no sway over it. Is it possible that when we compare classic *Who*'s vague presuppositions about 'linear time' or the 'web of time' to post-2005 *Who*, the lack of a 'Chronology Protection Agency' makes all the difference? And if the warping of space-time is minimal – if it's only the Doctor whipping about the universe and a few other misguided mad scientists whose experiments produce ripples in time 'up to point four on the Bocher scale' ('The Two Doctors'), what effect would that produce? The entanglement between philosophy, quantum mechanics and *Doctor Who* has only begun, and it is impossible to see precisely where it may take us.

One fact – take it as frightening or invigorating as you please – does remain clear: with the new wrinkles on the viability of time travel put by quantum theory, it's possible that the past is already being changed rather frequently by our reality's equivalent of Time Lords and their dastardly foes. We would probably be completely unaware of this if instantaneous quantum shifts occur, changing histories and memories in a flash through quantum entanglement. Perhaps history is being changed right now – on Wimbledon Common and the Eye of Orion, in Tooting Bec or Charing Cross Underground Station or Totter's Lane, perhaps in a town called Mercy. As the Doctor reminds us: 'The universe is big. It's vast and complicated and ridiculous, and sometimes, very rarely, impossible things just happen and we call them miracles, and that's the theory. Nine hundred years, never seen one yet, but this would do me' ('The Pandorica Opens', 2010).

Anything could happen.

NOTES

Preface

1 John Tulloch and Manuel Alvarado, *Doctor Who: The Unfolding Text* (New York, 1983), p. 76.
2 See Lance Parkin, 'Canonicity Matters: Defining the *Doctor Who* Canon', in David Butler (ed.), *Time and Relative Dissertations in Space: Critical Perspectives on Doctor Who* (Manchester, 2007), pp. 246–62. For the 1963–89 series and the 1996 telemovie, I have found David J. Howe and Stephen James Walker's *Doctor Who: The Television Companion* (London, 1998) and Howe, Stammers and Walker's *Doctor Who – The Handbook* series (London, 1992–8) to be invaluable. For the 'reboot' of the programme beginning in 2005, Gary Russell's *Doctor Who: The Encylopedia*, 2nd edn (London, 2011) has served me in good stead.

Introduction

1 Plato, *Theatetus* 155d 2–4, in John M. Cooper (ed.), *Plato: Complete Works* (Indianapolis, IN, 1997), p. 173.
2 Aristotle, *Metaphysics* 982b 12–13, in Jonathan Barnes (ed.), *The Complete Works of Aristotle*, vol. 2 (Princeton, NJ, 1984), p. 1554.
3 Lao Tzu, *Tao Te Ching*, 'The Book of Tao', ch. 1, trans. Douglas Allchin, http://my.pclink.com/~allchin/tao/contents.htm; accessed 27 October 2011.
4 'The Eleventh Hour', writer Stephen Moffat, director Adam Smith (2010).
5 Justin Richards, *Doctor Who: The Legend* (London, 2003), p. 9.
6 David J. Howe, Mark Stammers and Stephen James Walker, *Doctor Who – The Handbook: The First Doctor* (London, 1995), p. 15.
7 David J. Howe, Mark Stammers and Stephen James Walker, *Doctor Who: The Sixties* (London, 1992), p. 3.
8 Sydney Newman, quoted in Peter Haining, *Doctor Who: The Key to Time, A Year-by-Year Record* (London, 1984), p. 12.

9   Peter Haining, *Doctor Who: The Early Years* (London, 1986), pp. 29–30.

10 Ibid., p. 35.

11 Alexei and Cory Panshin, *The World Beyond the Hill: Science Fiction and the Quest for Transcendence* (Los Angeles, CA, 1989), p. 194. 'Taylor', Charlton Heston's character in the 1968 film *Planet of the Apes*, represents a more nihilistic, less optimistic version of this trope.

12 Cited in Howe, Stammers and Walker, *Doctor Who – The Handbook*, p. 8.

13 Ibid., p. 8.

14 Howe, Stammers and Walker, *Doctor Who: The Sixties*, pp. 67–8.

15 Quoted in David J. Howe and Stephen James Walker, *Doctor Who – The Handbook: The Third Doctor* (London, 1996), p. 18.

16 'The Three Doctors', writers Bob Baker and Dave Martin, director Lennie Mayne (1973).

17 Quoted in David J. Howe, Mark Stammers and Stephen James Walker, *Doctor Who: The Seventies* (London, 1994), p. 59.

18 Howe and Walker, *The Third Doctor*, p. 43.

19 A fan-revered 'classic' episode, this serial reintroduced the Master after the death of Roger Delgado and was written by one of *Doctor Who*'s finest script talents, Robert Holmes, who would continue to write for the programme right up until his death in 1986.

20 David J. Howe, Mark Stammers and Stephen James Walker, *Doctor Who: The Eighties* (London, 1996), p. 11.

21 Terrance Dicks, *Doctor Who: Four to Doomsday* (London, 1983), p. 9.

22 Howe, Stammers and Walker, *Doctor Who: The Eighties*, p. 68.

23 The case of the sixth Doctor and the planet Kolpasha is an example of this. One thing that everyone seems able to agree to is the extremely bad taste of this Doctor's coat, which he claims was tailored on this planet, the 'fashion capital of the universe' ('The Year of the Pig', writer Matthew Sweet, Big Finish audio, 2006). If this is true, then the Doctor's claim to be a trendsetter as stylish as Beau Brummell is true – but probably only on Kolpasha.

24 Howe, Stammers and Walker, *Doctor Who: The Eighties*, pp. 94–8.

25 Philip Segal, with Gary Russell, *Regeneration: The Story Behind the Revival of a Television Legend* (London, 2000), p. 6.

26 David J. Howe and Stephen James Walker, *Doctor Who – The Handbook: The Seventh Doctor* (London, 1998), pp. 30–1. 'Silver Nemesis', writer Kevin Clarke, director Chris Clough (1988); 'The Curse of Fenric', writer Ian Briggs, director Nicholas Mallett (1989).

27 Kim Newman, *Doctor Who: A Critical Reading of the Series* (London, 2008), p. 112.

28 David Butler, 'How to Pilot a TARDIS: Audiences, Science Fiction and the Fantastic in *Doctor Who*', in David Butler (ed.), *Time and Relative Dissertations in Space: Critical Perspectives on* Doctor Who (Manchester, 2007), p. 28.

29 Jonathan I. Israel, *Radical Enlightenment* (New York, 2001), p. 3.

30 Robert B. Brandom, *Perspectives on Pragmatism: Classical, Recent, & Contemporary* (Cambridge, MA, 2011), p. 41.

31 Segal and Russell, *Regeneration*, p. 100.

32 Matthew Jacobs, *Doctor Who: The Script of the Film* (London, 1996), p. 81.

33 However, this has been challenged at least three times by the reappearance of the Daleks, the Master, and the Time Lords *en masse*.

34   Gary Russell, *Doctor Who: The Inside Story* (London, 2006), p. 6.
35   Tranter, quoted in ibid., p. 18.
36   Harlan Ellison, 'Introducing *Doctor Who*', in Terrance Dicks (ed.), *Doctor Who and the Revenge of the Cybermen* (New York, 1979), p. xii.

Chapter 1: Lost in Time

1   Lance Parkin, 'Canonicity Matters: Defining the *Doctor Who* Canon', in David Butler (ed.), *Time and Relative Dissertations in Space: Critical Perspectives on Doctor Who* (Manchester, 2007), p. 253. In this regard, there is a significant difference between the tenor of the show in its 1963–89 form and in its 2005-to-the-present incarnation, the positions of head writer and producer having been combined in the latter period to give Russell T. Davies and Stephen Moffat primary responsibility for the direction of the programme.
2   Quoted in Gary Gillatt, *Doctor Who from A to Z* (London, 1998), p. 11.
3   A.N. Whitehead, *Modes of Thought* (New York, 1968), p. 168.
4   Jeremy Bentham, *Doctor Who: The Early Years* (London, 1986), p. 60.
5   Ibid., p. 61.
6   Ibid., p. 30.
7   'Science Fiction—BBC Report', BBC Archives, http://www.bbc.co.uk/archive/doctorwho/6400.shtml; accessed 25 April 2012; see also David Butler, 'How to Pilot a TARDIS: Audiences, Science Fiction and the Fantastic in *Doctor Who*', in Butler (ed.), *Time and Relative Dissertations*.
8   John Tulloch and Manuel Alvarado, *Doctor Who: The Unfolding Text* (New York, 1983), p. 40.
9   Ibid.
10   Ibid., p. 41.
11   In the first episode of the programme, the Doctor's granddaughter Susan claims, 'I made up the name TARDIS from the initials. Time And Relative Dimension In Space.' This seems to suggest that the Doctor had a hand in creating the vehicle, and also contradicts later continuity in which the Time Lords, the Doctor's people, use the term in much the way we use 'automobile'. When we next hear the name of the machine explained (in 1965's 'The Time Meddler'), 'Dimension' has changed to 'Dimensions', which it remained for most of the classic series.
12   I do not contend that *Doctor Who* is clearly and unproblematically positivistic, a qualification that I make good in the next section.
13   Alan Lacey, 'Positivism', in Ted Honderich (ed.), *The Oxford Companion to Philosophy* (Oxford, 1995), p. 705.
14   Comte, *The Positive Philosophy of August Comte*, vol. III, trans. Harriet Martineau (London, 1896), p. 245.
15   A.J. Ayer, *Language, Truth and Logic* (New York, 1952), p. 48.
16   Ibid.
17   Kingsley Amis, *New Maps of Hell: A Survey of Science Fiction* (New York, 1960), p. 77.
18   Hartwell, 'Hard Science Fiction', in David G. Hartwell and Kathryn Cramer (eds), *The Ascent of Wonder: The Evolution of Hard SF* (New York, 1994), p. 34.
19   Ibid., p. 35.

20 Ibid., pp. 35–6.
21 'An Unearthly Child' transcript, writers Anthony Coburn and C.E. Webber (uncredited), director Waris Hussein, *The* Doctor Who *Transcript Project*, http://dwtpscripts.tripod.com/1stdoc/a/a1.html; accessed 1 March 2012.
22 Terrance Dicks, *Doctor Who and the Dalek Invasion of Earth* (London, 1977), p. 45.
23 'The Dæmons', writers Robert Sloman and Barry Letts, director Christopher Barry (1971).
24 Oswald Hanfling, 'Logical Positivism', in Stuart G. Shanker (ed.), *Routledge History of Philosophy*, vol. IX: *Philosophy of Science, Logic and Mathematics in the Twentieth Century* (London, 1966), p. 195.
25 Moritz Schlick, in Henk L. Mulder and Barbara F.B. van de Velde-Schlick (eds), *Moritz Schlick: Philosophical Papers, 1923–1936*, vol. II (Dordrecht, Holland, 1979), p. 311.
26 Richard Creath, 'Quine's Challenge to Carnap', in Michael Friedman and Richard Creath (eds), *The Cambridge Companion to Carnap* (Cambridge, UK, 2007), p. 319.
27 Ayer, *Language, Truth and Logic*, p. 31.
28 Ayer, quoted in Hanfling, 'Logical Positivism', p. 194.
29 'The Tomb of the Cybermen' transcript, episode 4, writers Kit Pedler and Gerry Davis, director Morris Barry, *The* Doctor Who *Transcript Project*, http://dwtpscripts.tripod.com/2nddoc/mm/mm4.html; accessed 17 April 2012.
30 Arthur C. Clarke, 'Hazards of Prophecy: The Failure of Imagination', *Profiles of the Future: An Enquiry into the Limits of the Possible* (New York, 1962), p. 36. In 'Battlefield' (1989), the seventh Doctor states that the reverse of Clarke's Third Law – that any sufficiently advanced magic is indistinguishable from science – is also true.
31 Ibid., p. 14.
32 Ian Stuart Black, *The Macra Terror* (London, 1987), p. 47.
33 An excellent book that traces the common history of both traditions is Michael Friedman's *A Parting of the Ways: Carnap, Cassirer, and Heidegger* (Chicago, IL, 2000).
34 Alec Charles, 'The Crack of Doom: The Uncanny Echoes of Steven Moffat's Doctor Who', *Science Fiction Film and Television* 4:1 (2011), p. 9.
35 'Earthshock' transcript, writer Eric Saward, director Peter Grimwade; 'The Doctor Who Transcripts', http://www.chakoteya.net/DoctorWho/19-6.htm; accessed 16 April 2012.
36 Edmund Husserl, *Ideas: General Introduction to Pure Phenomenology*, trans. W.R. Boyce Gibson (London, 1962), p. 94.
37 Dermot Moran, *Introduction to Phenomenology* (London, 2000), pp. 181–2.
38 Amis, *New Maps of Hell*, p. 69.
39 'Uncanny' is derived from a Scots usage referring to the occult, while 'canny', like the German *heimlich*, can imply 'snug and cosy'. *Unheimlich* implies the unsettledness of 'not being at home' in a certain situation.
40 Martin Heidegger, *History of the Concept of Time: Prolegomena*, trans. Theodore Kisiel (Bloomington, IN, 1985), pp. 284, 289.
41 Bentham, *Doctor Who*, p. 98.
42 Jim Leach, *Doctor Who* (Detroit, MI, 2009), p. 7.
43 'The Robots of Death' transcript, writer Chris Boucher, director Michael Briant;

'The *Doctor Who* Transcripts', http://www.chakoteya.net/DoctorWho/14-5. htm; accessed 11 April 2012.

44 'The Aztecs', writer John Lucarotti, director John Crockett (1964).

45 This is itself a metaphor for a theme common to Wells's SF: the observer who is helpless to prevent degenerative evolution around him and who despairs when his entire world is changed.

46 Martin Heidegger, *Ontology—The Hermeneutics of Facticity*, trans. John van Buren (Bloomington, IN, 1999), p. 13.

47 Martin Heidegger, *Being and Time*, trans. John MacQuarrie and Edward Robinson (London, 1962), p. 102.

48 In particular, see the serials 'The Deadly Assassin' (1976), 'Arc of Infinity' (1983), episode 13 of 'Trial of a Time Lord' (1986) and David Tennant's swansong as the Doctor, 'The End of Time', Parts One and Two (2009–10).

49 Gary Russell, *Doctor Who: The Inside Story* (London, 2006), p. 29.

50 Simone de Beauvoir, *The Ethics of Ambiguity* (New York, 1976), p. 34.

51 Pierre-Simon Laplace, *A Philosophical Essay on Probabilities*, trans. Frederick Wilson Truscott and Frederick Lincoln Emory (New York, 1951), p. 4.

52 Heidegger, *Being and Time*, p. 147.

53 'An Unearthly Child' transcript, writers Anthony Coburn and C.E. Webber (uncredited); 'The *Doctor Who* Transcripts', http://www.chakoteya.net/ DoctorWho/1-1.htm; accessed 6 May 2012.

Chapter 2: Exterminate!

1 Quoted in Jeremy Bentham, *Doctor Who: The Early Years* (London, 1986), pp. 210–11.

2 Susan Neiman, *Evil in Modern Thought* (Oxford, 2004), p. xvi.

3 Some of these tropes reappear, merely coincidentally, in *Doctor Who*. For example, aside from the original 'creation' of the universe, the Doctor has been involved in two other cosmic 'creations' (or 'recreations') in the episodes 'Terminus' (1983) and 'The Big Bang' (2010). A malevolent entity called 'The Great Intelligence' figures in the eerie Patrick Troughton tales 'The Abominable Snowmen' (1967) and 'The Web of Fear' (1968). The Great Intelligence resurfaces to play a major role in Series 7 of the new show.

4 David J. Howe, *Doctor Who: A Book of Monsters* (London, 1997), p. 7.

5 David J. Howe, Mark Stammers and Stephen James Walker, *Doctor Who: The Sixties* (London, 1992), p. 96.

6 Per Schelde, *Androids, Humanoids, and Other Science Fiction Monsters: Science and Soul in Science Fiction Films* (London, 1993), pp. 13–14.

7 Neiman, *Evil in Modern Thought*, p. 1.

8 St Augustine, *City of God*, ed. Vernon J. Bourke, Bk XII, ch. 6 (London, 1958), p. 251.

9 Immanuel Kant, *Religion within the Limits of Reason Alone*, trans. T.M. Greene and H.H. Hudson (New York, 1960), p. 29.

10 Ibid., p. 39.

11 Richard Bernstein, *Radical Evil: A Philosophical Interrogation* (Cambridge, UK, 2002), p. 32.

12 Michael Ignatieff, *The Lesser Evil: Political Ethics in an Age of Terror* (Oxford, 2004), p. 14.

13 Ibid., p. 15.

14 'Time and the Rani' transcript, writers Pip and Jane Baker, director Andrew Morgan; 'The *Doctor Who* Transcripts', http://www.chakoteya.net/DoctorWho/24-1.htm; accessed 17 July 2012. One wonders how the Silurian people, who kept dinosaurs as pets, will take to this proposition.

15 Colin McGinn, *Ethics, Evil, and Fiction* (Oxford, 1997), p. 61.

16 Gary Gillatt, *Doctor Who from A to Z* (London, 1998), p. 49.

17 Augustine, *City of God*, Bk XII, ch. 3, p. 248.

18 See *St Irenaeus of Lyons: Against the Heresies*, trans. Dominic J. Unger (New York, 1992).

19 See John Hick, *An Interpretation of Religion: Human Responses to the Transcendent*, 2nd edn (New Haven, CT, 2004).

20 'Daleks', in Gary Russell, *Doctor Who: The Encyclopedia*, 2nd edn (London, 2011), p. 81.

21 Mark Bould, 'Science Fiction Television in the United Kingdom', in J.P. Telotte (ed.), *The Essential Science Fiction Television Reader* (Lexington, KY, 2008), p. 218.

22 Howe, Stammers and Walker, *Doctor Who: The Sixties*, p. 125.

23 Howe, *Doctor Who: A Book of Monsters*, p. 81.

24 Howe, Stammers and Walker, *Doctor Who: The Sixties*, p. 31.

25 Bentham, *Doctor Who*, p. 120.

26 Ibid., p. 215.

27 Paul Ricoeur, *Oneself as Another*, trans. Kathleen Blamey (London, 1992), p. 343.

28 'Genesis of the Daleks' transcript, writer Terry Nation, director David Maloney; 'The *Doctor Who* Transcripts', http://www.chakoteya.net/DoctorWho/12-4.htm; accessed 15 July 2012.

29 John Tulloch and Manuel Alvarado, *Doctor Who: The Unfolding Text* (New York, 1983), p. 137.

30 Published near the peak of the original programme's popularity in the United States, *The Official Doctor Who and the Daleks Book* by John Peel and Terry Nation (New York, 1988) sets the events of 'Genesis' a few hundred years before that of 'The Daleks', but implies they are part of a continuous history (p. 121). Tribe and Goss's *The Dalek Handbook* (London, 2011) claims that the Doctor actually changed history in 'Genesis', and that the Dalek future examined in all the preceding televised stories before 1974 had been overwritten by a 'new timeline' (p. 65).

31 Ignatieff, *The Lesser Evil*, p. 61.

32 Tribe and Goss, *The Dalek Handbook*, p. 99.

33 Jacqueline Rayner, et al., *Doctor Who: The Visual Dictionary*, rev. edn (London, 2009), p. 44. Something similar is suggested in the entry 'Time War, the Last Great' in Russell, *Doctor Who*, p. 354. Tribe and Goss's *Dalek Handbook* claims that 'Genesis' was the beginning of merely a 'phoney war' between the two parties played out behind the scenes of televised Dalek stories in the late 1970s and 80s.

34 Created by Lawrence Miles, Faction Paradox is a cross between a time-travelling voodoo cult and a crime syndicate, and is conceived as the antithesis of the Time Lords, wanting the disruption of established history for its own

sake. Several books, from Miles's *Alien Bodies* (London, 1997) to Stephen Cole and Peter Anghelides' *The Ancestor Cell* (London, 2000), feature the Faction.

35 Hordes of Daleks are shown in 'The Evil of the Daleks' (1967) and 'Planet of the Daleks', but the effects (achieved by the use of commercially available toy Daleks on a miniature set) do not exactly encourage the suspension of disbelief.

36 'Dalek' transcript, writer Robert Shearman, director Joe Ahearne; '*Doctor Who* 2005+ Transcripts', http://who-transcripts.atspace.com/2005/transcripts/106_dalek.html; accessed 16 July 2012.

37 James Chapman, *Inside the TARDIS: The Worlds of* Doctor Who (London, 2006), p. 190.

38 Robert Shearman, 'Bringing Back the Daleks', in Tribe and Goss, *The Dalek Handbook*, p. 105.

39 Ignatieff, *The Lesser Evil*, p. 22.

40 Chapman, *Inside the TARDIS*, p. 196.

41 'Bad Wolf' transcript, writer Russell T. Davies, director Joe Ahearne; '*Doctor Who* 2005+ Transcripts', http://who-transcripts.atspace.com/2005/transcripts/112_badwolf.html; accessed 17 July 2012.

42 Søren Kierkegaard, *The Sickness Unto Death*, trans. Alastair Hannay (Harmondsworth, 1989), pp. 62–3.

Chapter 3: We All Depend on the Beast Below

1   St Augustine, *City of God*, abridged, Bk XVI, ch. 8, ed. Vernon J. Bourke (London, 1958), p. 365.

2   Ibid., pp. 365, 367.

3   Colin McGinn, *Ethics, Evil, and Fiction* (Oxford, 1997), p. 65.

4   G.W.F. Hegel, *Phenomenology of Spirit*, trans. A.V. Miller (Oxford, 1977), p. 111.

5   Ibid.

6   McGinn, *Ethics, Evil, and Fiction*, p. 66.

7   John Tulloch and Manuel Alvarado, *Doctor Who: The Unfolding Text* (New York, 1983), p. 77.

8   Barbara S. Andrew, 'Beauvoir's Place in Philosophical Thought', in Claudia Card (ed.), *The Cambridge Companion to Simone de Beauvoir* (Cambridge, UK, 2003), p. 27.

9   Moira Gatens, 'Beauvoir and Biology: A Second Look', in Card (ed.), *The Cambridge Companion*, p. 269.

10 The naming and history of the Earth-native 'Silurians' represent one of the more bizarre and interesting tales of the development of a non-human race in *Doctor Who* through the interpenetration of various media, including novels and comics featuring the creatures, and even fan views reconstructing the coherency of their history. These creatures, inaccurately called 'Silurians' in reference to their time of origin in both the title of their première story, in the media, and in official treatments of the series like Howe's *Doctor Who: A Book of Monsters*, were named 'reptile men' or *Homo reptilia* by the Doctor in 'Doctor Who and the Silurians'. They hail in fact from the Eocene epoch. This origin of 56 to 34 million years ago (much closer to the present than the Silurian period, which was slightly more than 400 million years ago) would take into

account the fact that the creatures appear to have evolved intelligence as the descendants of non-dinosaur reptiles that flourished in the earlier Jurassic or Cretaceous periods. It would not, however, explain how they had managed to keep alive tyrannosaurs – as guards or mounts – long after they were thought to have died out, or how they suffered competition from fairly intelligent, chimp-like primates before going into hibernation ('Twilight of the Silurians', *Doctor Who Weekly* 21–2, March 1980; reprinted and colourised in Marvel Comics' *Doctor Who* 18, March 1986, pp. 23–30). Adding to the confusion is the reason for their underground and undersea hibernation: the approach to ancient Earth of a 'little planet' that threatens to plummet to the ground and cause mass devastation. The astronomical visitor – identified by Malcolm Hulke in his novelisation of 'Doctor Who and the Silurians' as the Moon – in reality had already taken up orbit several billion years before the events in Hulke's prologue (*Doctor Who and the Cave-Monsters*, London, 1974, pp. 7–11). The Doctor identifies the reptiles as 'Eocenes' in 'The Sea Devils', an episode in which we meet a completely different-looking, sea-dwelling version of *Homo reptilian*, which is more naturally aggressive to humans. Further biological subgroups of the creatures appear in 1984's 'Warriors of the Deep' and Gary Russell's novel *The Scales of Injustice* (London, 1996). The current iteration of Silurian creatures reintroduced in 'The Hungry Earth' in 2010 is much more human-looking, and is distinctive in having at least one member (Madame Vastra) who is a personal friend of the Doctor's ('A Good Man Goes to War', 2011).

11 Gerry Davis, 'How the Cybermen were Created', introduction to David Banks, *Cybermen* (London, 1988), pp. 7–8.

12 Gerry Davis, *Doctor Who and the Cybermen* (London, 1974), pp. 23, 26.

13 Jean-Paul Sartre, *Being and Nothingness*, trans. Hazel E. Barnes (New York, 1956), p. 262.

14 The 2002 Big Finish audio drama 'Spare Parts' by Marc Platt is a brilliant and frightening realisation of what life on Mondas around the birth of the Cybermen would have been like.

15 'The Waters of Mars' transcript, writers Russell T. Davies and Phil Ford, director Graeme Harper; 'The *Doctor Who* Transcripts', http://www.chakoteya.net/DoctorWho/30-16.htm; accessed 22 July 2012.

16 Judith Halberstam, *Skin Shows: Gothic Horror and the Technology of Monsters* (London, 1995), p. 3.

17 Paul Goetsch, *Monsters in English Literature: From the Romantic Age to the First World War* (Oxford, 2002), p. 9.

18 Ibid.

19 Ibid., pp. 9–10.

20 McGinn, *Ethics, Evil, and Fiction*, p. 145.

21 Hulke, *Doctor Who and the Cave-Monsters*, p. 19.

22 Quoted in David J. Howe and Stephen James Walker, *Doctor Who: The Television Companion* (London, 1998), p. 188.

23 Emmanuel Lévinas, 'Philosophy and the Idea of Infinity', in Matthew Calarco and Peter Atterton (eds), *The Continental Ethics Reader* (London, 2003), p. 43; republished from *Collected Philosophical Papers*, trans. Alphonso Lingis (Pittsburgh, PN, 1998), pp. 47–59.

24 Hulke, *Doctor Who*, p. 59.

25 Ibid., p. 52.

26 Ibid., p. 97.

27 Ibid., p. 121.

28 'The Hungry Earth' transcript, writer Chris Chibnall, director Ashley Way; 'The *Doctor Who* Transcripts', http://www.chakoteya.net/DoctorWho/ 31-8.htm; accessed 23 July 2012.

29 Lévinas, 'Philosophy', p. 45.

30 'Cold Blood' transcript, writer Chris Chibnall, director Ashley Way; 'The *Doctor Who* Transcripts', http://www.chakoteya.net/DoctorWho/31-8.htm; accessed 23 July 2012.

31 'The Celestial Toymaker', 1966; 'The Invasion', 1968; 'Inferno', 1970; 'The Three Doctors', 1973 and 'Arc of Infinity', 1983; 'Genesis of the Daleks', 1975 onward; 'The Talons of Weng-Chiang', 1977; various episodes, 1979–83; 'Mark of the Rani', 1984 and 'Time and the Rani', 1987; 'Human Nature'/'The Family of Blood', 2007; various episodes, 2011; various episodes, 1971–2010.

32 Andrew Blair, '*Doctor Who*: A Celebration of Death', *Den of Geek*, http://www. denofgeek.com/tv/doctor-who/21876/doctor-who-a-celebration-of-death; published 6 July 2012, accessed 24 July 2012.

33 In particular, see Richard Rorty, *Contingency, Irony, and Solidarity* (Cambridge, UK, 1989).

34 Emmanuel Lévinas, 'Useless Suffering', in Robert Bernasconi and David Wood (eds), *The Provocation of Levinas: Rethinking the Other* (London, 1988), p. 161.

35 Benedict Spinoza, *Ethics*, ed. and trans. G.H.R. Parkinson (Oxford, 2000), Part I, prop. 11, p. 82.

36 Matthew Stewart, *The Courtier and the Heretic: Leibniz, Spinoza, and the Fate of God in the Modern World* (London, 2006), pp. 158–9.

37 Spinoza, 'To the Most Noble and Learned Henry Oldenburg', in Michael L. Morgan (ed.), *Spinoza: Complete Works* (Cambridge, UK, 2002), p. 849.

38 John Peel, *The Gallifrey Chronicles* (London, 1991), p. 59.

39 Spinoza, *Treatise on the Emendation of the Intellect*, trans. Samuel Shirley, in Morgan (ed.), *Spinoza: Complete Works*, p. 5.

40 Tulloch and Alvarado, *Doctor Who*, p. 137.

41 Readers interested in how this depiction of the Doctor might have unfolded over time are urged to read Paul Cornell's *Love and War* (London, 1992) and listen to the trilogy of Big Finish audios 'Protect and Survive' by Jonathan Morris (July 2012); 'Black and White' by Matt Fitton (August 2012); and 'Gods and Monsters' by Mike Maddox and Alan Barnes (September 2012).

42 Andrew Cartmel, quoted in David J. Howe and Stephen James Walker, *Doctor Who – The Handbook: The Seventh Doctor* (London, 1998), p. 130.

43 Ibid.

44 'The Curse of Fenric' transcript, writer Ian Briggs, director Nicholas Mallett; 'The *Doctor Who* Transcripts Project', http://dwtpscripts.tripod .com/7thdoc/7m/7m4ex.html; accessed 25 July 2012.

45 This means 'under a species of eternity', or with the use of reason.

46 Spinoza, *Ethics*, Part I, Appendix, p. 110.

47 Ibid., Part IV, prop. 26, p. 244.

48 Richard Bernstein, *Radical Evil: A Philosophical Interrogation* (Cambridge, UK, 2002), p. 91.

49 Spinoza, *Ethics*, Part IV, prop. 37, schol. 2, p. 254.

50 Bernstein, *Radical Evil*, p. 94.

51   Joseph P. Lawrence, 'Philosophical Religion and the Quest for Authenticity', in Jason M. Wirth (ed.), *Schelling Now: Contemporary Readings* (Bloomington, IN, 2005), p. 20.
52   'Utopia' transcript, writer Russell T. Davies, director Graeme Harper; 'The *Doctor Who* Transcripts', http://www.chakoteya.net/DoctorWho/29-11.htm; accessed 25 July 2012.
53   Tulloch and Alvarado, *Doctor Who*, p. 137.

Chapter 4: The Ethics of the Last of the Time Lords

1   Gary Gillatt, *Doctor Who from A to Z* (London, 1998), p. 51.
2   Terrance Dicks, *The Eight Doctors* (London, 1997), p. 103.
3   See David Rafer, 'Mythic Identity in *Doctor Who*', in David Butler (ed.), *Time and Relative Dissertations in Space: Critical Perspectives on* Doctor Who (Manchester, 2007), p. 128.
4   The only other reasonable contender for this title is the set of BBC novels published in 2000 forming a story arc in which the eighth Doctor has lost his memory and is awaiting the slow regrowth of his TARDIS. The first of these, *The Burning* (by Justin Richards), takes place in England in the 1890s. Five novels later, the Doctor has reached *Escape Velocity* (by Colin Brake) to leave Brussels, Belgium and Earth in 2001. This will clearly be a longer period of 'exile' than the UNIT years.
5   David J. Howe, Mark Stammers and Stephen James Walker, *Doctor Who – The Handbook: The Second Doctor* (London, 1997), p. 303.
6   This is something of a problem for the Doctor: the same thing has occurred in each of the first instalments for Paul McGann's and Matt Smith's Time Lord.
7   Piers D. Britton and Simon J. Barker, *Reading between Designs: Visual Imagery and the Generation of Meaning in* The Avengers, The Prisoner, *and* Doctor Who (Austin, TX, 2003), p. 149.
8   Thomas Nagel, 'The Objective Basis for Morality', in *What Does It All Mean?* (Oxford, 1987); excerpted in Peter Singer (ed.), *Ethics* (Oxford, 1994), p. 158.
9   'School Reunion' transcript, writer Toby Whithouse, director James Hawes; '*Doctor Who* 2005+ Transcripts', http://who-transcripts.atspace.com/2006/transcripts/203_schoolreunion.html; accessed 21 June 2012.
10   Simone de Beauvoir, *The Ethics of Ambiguity* (New York, 1976), p. 44.
11   Stacy Keltner, 'Beauvoir's Idea of Ambiguity', in Margaret A. Simons (ed.), *The Philosophy of Simone de Beauvoir* (Bloomington, IN, 2006), p. 201.
12   Kim Newman, *Doctor Who: A Critical Reading of the Series* (London, 2008), p. 112.
13   Lance Parkin, quoted in David Howe and Stephen James Walker, *Doctor Who – The Handbook: The Seventh Doctor* (London, 1998), p. 200; originally published in *Matrix* 53 (autumn 1996).
14   M.H. Abrams, 'English Romanticism: The Spirit of the Age', in Harold Bloom (ed.), *Romanticism and Consciousness: Essays in Criticism* (New York, 1970), p. 95.
15   Condorcet, quoted in Abrams, 'English Romanticism', p. 95.
16   Norman Ashby, *A Comprehensive History of Western Ethics*, ed. W. Allen Ashby (Amherst, NY, 1997), p. 441.

17 Ibid., p. 444.
18 William Wordsworth, *The Prelude*; excerpted in Abrams, 'English Romanticism', pp. 109–10.
19 In *Shelley: Selected Poems*, ed. Timothy Webb (London, 1977), pp. 100–1.
20 Shelley, quoted in Peter J. Kitson, 'Beyond the Enlightenment: The Philosophical, Scientific and Religious Inheritance', in Duncan Wu (ed.), *A Companion to Romanticism* (Oxford, 1998), p. 40.
21 Jane Stabler, 'The Literary Background', in Nicholas Roe (ed.), *Romanticism: An Oxford Guide* (Oxford, 2005), pp. 29–30.
22 Adela Pinch, 'Sensibility', in Roe, *Romanticism*, p. 53.
23 Novalis, 'Miscellaneous Remarks', excerpted in J.M. Bernstein (ed.), *Classical and Romantic German Aesthetics* (Cambridge, UK, 2003), p. 210.
24 Gerald Izenberg, 'The Politics of Song in Wordsworth's *Lyrical Ballads*', in Kevin Sharpe and Steven N. Zwicker (eds), *Refiguring Revolutions: Aesthetics and Politics from the English Revolution to the Romantic Revolution* (London, 1998), p. 118.
25 James Baldwin, *Giovanni's Room* (New York, 1985), p. 10.
26 The significant obstacle to this freedom for the Doctor in his first three incarnations is, of course, his spotty knowledge of how to work the ship (the knowledge is actively repressed by the Time Lords during his exile on Earth). In 'An Unearthly Child', the Doctor explains to Barbara and Ian why he can't use the TARDIS to take them back to their own time: 'You see, this isn't working properly. Or rather the code is still a secret.'
27 Charles Taylor, *Sources of the Self: The Making of the Modern Identity* (Cambridge, MA, 1989), p. 384.
28 Immanuel Kant, *Groundwork of the Metaphysics of Morals*, Ak. 4:462, in Mary Gregor (trans. and ed.), *The Cambridge Edition of the Works of Immanuel Kant: Practical Philosophy* (Cambridge, 1996), p. 107.
29 Friedrich Schiller, *Letters on the Aesthetic Education of Man*; excerpted in Georg Mohr and Brian O'Connor (eds), *German Idealism: An Anthology and Guide* (Chicago, IL, 2007), p. 235.
30 Ibid., p. 239.
31 Ibid., p. 238.
32 For an examination of how Kant's understanding of autonomy or self-governance contradicts itself, see Robert Arp and Kevin S. Decker, '"That Fatal Kiss": Bond, Ethics, and the Objectification of Women', in James South and Jacob Held (eds), *James Bond and Philosophy* (Chicago, IL, 2006).
33 Jean-Paul Sartre, *Existentialism is a Humanism*, trans. Bernard Flechtman (New York, 1947), pp. 29–30.
34 Fyodor Dostoevsky, *Notes from Underground* (New York, 1993), p. 28.
35 De Beauvoir, *The Ethics of Ambiguity*, p. 12.
36 James Chapman, *Inside the TARDIS: The Worlds of Doctor Who* (London, 2006), p. 7.
37 Jean-Paul Sartre, *War Diaries* (London, 1984), p. 113.
38 'Rise of the Cybermen' transcript, writer Tom McCrae, director Graeme Harper; '*Doctor Who* 2005+ Transcripts', http://who-transcripts.atspace.com/2006/transcripts/205_riseofthecybermen.html; accessed 29 June 2012.
39 This Greek name has two etymologies, both of which are telling in the context of *Doctor Who*. In its more linguistically certain meaning, it means 'to steal'. But another etymology relates it to the Greek word for 'foresight'.

Chapter 5: Not the Man He Was

1   They are the final televised lines of the fifth Doctor ('Caves of Androzani', 1984); the fourth Doctor ('Logopolis', 1981); the tenth Doctor ('The End of Time', Part Two, 2009); and the sixth Doctor ('Trial of a Time Lord', 1986).

2   David J. Howe and Stephen James Walker, *Doctor Who: The Television Companion* (London, 1998), p. 98.

3   David J. Howe, Mark Stammers and Stephen James Walker, *Doctor Who: The Sixties* (London, 1992), p. 68.

4   Ibid.

5   'TV Tropes', http://tvtropes.org/pmwiki/pmwiki.php/Main/TheNthDoctor; accessed 28 July 2012.

6   Harry Frankfurt, 'Freedom of the Will and the Concept of a Person', in Kim Atkins (ed.), *Self and Subjectivity* (Oxford, 2005), p. 145; originally published in *The Journal of Philosophy* 68:1 (1971), pp. 5–16.

7   'The Power of the Daleks' transcript, writers David Whitaker and Dennis Spooner, director Christopher Barry; 'The *Doctor Who* Transcripts', http://www.chakoteya.net/DoctorWho/4-3.htm; accessed 28 July 2012.

8   See Paul Parsons, *The Science of* Doctor Who (Baltimore, MD, 2010), ch. 4.

9   Robert C. Sleigh, Jr, 'Identity of Indiscernibles', in Jaegwon Kim and Ernest Sosa (eds), *A Companion to Metaphysics* (Oxford, 1995), p. 234.

10 Ibid.

11 G.W. Leibniz, *New Essays on the Human Understanding*, Bk II, ch. 7, sect. 8; excerpted in William O. Stephens (ed.), *The Person: Readings in Human Nature* (Upper Saddle River, NJ, 2006), p. 100.

12 John Locke, *An Essay Concerning Human Understanding*, ed. Roger Woolhouse (London, 1997), Bk IV, ch. 3, sect. 6.

13 'For, since we must allow He has annexed effects to motion which we can no way conceive motion able to produce, what reason have we to conclude that He could not order them as well to be produced in a subject we cannot conceive capable of them, as well as in a subject we cannot conceive the motion of matter can any way operate upon? I say not this, that I would any way lessen the belief of the soul's immateriality: I am not here speaking of probability, but knowledge'; ibid.

14 Ibid., Bk II, ch. xxvii, sect. 1; p. 296.

15 Ibid., Bk II, ch. xxvii, sect. 3; p. 298.

16 Eli Hirsch, 'Identity', in Kim and Sosa, *A Companion*, p. 233.

17 Locke, *An Essay*, Bk II, ch. xxvii, sect. 4; p. 298. I am following Paul Dawson in calling the second kind of identity in Locke's scheme that of 'organisms'; see his 'And Before I Go ...', in Courtland Lewis and Paula Smithka (eds), *Doctor Who and Philosophy: Bigger on the Inside* (Chicago, IL, 2010), p. 230.

18 Locke, *An Essay*, Bk II, ch. xxvii, sect. 26; p. 312.

19 Ibid., Bk II, ch. xxvii, sect. 9; p. 302.

20 Ibid., Bk II, ch. xxvii, sect. 10; p. 303.

21 Douglas Adams gives a nod to this problem in *The Restaurant at the End of the Universe*: 'The major problem is simply one of grammar, and the main work to consult in this matter is Dr. Dan Streetmentioner's *Time Traveler's Handbook of 1001 Tense Formations*. It will tell you, for instance, how to describe something that was about to happen to you in the past before you avoided it by time-

jumping forward two days in order to avoid it. The event will be described differently according to whether you are talking about it from the standpoint of your own natural time, from a time in the further future, or a time in the further past and is further complicated by the possibility of conducting conversations while you are actually traveling from one time to another with the intention of becoming your own mother or father. Most readers get as far as the Future Semiconditionally Modified Subinverted Plagal Past Subjunctive Intentional before giving up; and in fact in later editions of the book all pages beyond this point have been left blank to save on printing costs'; *The Restaurant at the End of the Universe* (New York, 1980), pp. 87–8.

22 The same could be said of characters in 'The Trial of a Time Lord' (1986), but the less said about this instance the better, at least for viewers who haven't seen it yet.

23 Richard Hanley, 'Who's Who on Gallifrey?', in Lewis and Smithka (eds), *Doctor Who and Philosophy*, p. 35.

24 The scenario in 'The Rebel Flesh' and its sequel closely mirrors Derek Parfit's discussion of duplicated and divided selves in a series of thought experiments using a 'teletransporter' machine; see his *Reasons and Persons* (Oxford, 1984), ch. 10.

25 Hanley, 'Who's Who on Gallifrey?', p. 38.

26 In Big Finish audio dramas featuring Paul McGann, the historical Mary Shelley has become a travelling companion for the eighth Doctor. Shelley, played by Julie Cox, features in 'The Company of Friends: Mary's Story' (2009), 'The Silver Turk', 'The Witch from the Well' and 'Army of Death' (all 2011).

27 Mary Whitehouse, founder of the National Viewers' and Listeners' Association, and an evangelical Christian and social conservative, was an outspoken critic of television horror and violence in the 1970s. Her complaint about *Doctor Who* during these years was that it was screened too early (5.15 p.m.) and could cause 'nightmares and bed-wetting among the under-sevens'; David J. Howe, Mark Stammers and Stephen James Walker, *Doctor Who: The Seventies* (London, 1994), p. 108.

28 'The Brain of Morbius' transcript, writer Robin Bland (Terrance Dicks and Robert Holmes), director Christopher Barry; 'The *Doctor Who* Transcripts', http://www.chakoteya.net/DoctorWho/13-5.htm;accessed1August2012.

29 This is not true of the earliest 'Tenth Planet'-era Cybermen, who, in that serial and in early *Doctor Who* comic stories, had names and rudimentary personalities; see also the comic strip 'Junkyard Demon', writer Steve Parkhouse, artists Mike McMahon and Adolfo Buylla, *Doctor Who Monthly* 58–9 (November–December 1981).

30 Of particular interest, see Maurice Merleau-Ponty, *Phenomenology of Perception*, trans. Colin Smith (London, 2002).

31 Sydney Shoemaker, 'Persons and Personal Identity', in Kim and Sosa, *A Companion*, p. 381.

32 Richard J. Bernstein, 'In Defence of American Philosophy', in John E. Smith (ed.), *Contemporary American Philosophy*, second series (London, 1970), pp. 304–5.

33 Derek Parfit, 'Divided Minds and the Nature of Persons', in Susan Schneider, *Science Fiction and Philosophy: From Time Travel to Superintelligence* (Oxford, 2009), p. 92.

34 William James, *Principles of Psychology*, vol. 1 (New York, 1950), p. 299.

35   Donald Davidson, 'The Irreducibility of the Concept of the Self', in Davidson, *Subjective, Intersubjective, Objective* (Oxford, 2001), pp. 87–8.

36   Daniel C. Dennett, 'Conditions of Personhood', in Stephens (ed.), *The Person*, pp. 228–9.

37   'The Doctor Dances' transcript, writer Steven Moffat, director James Hawes; 'The *Doctor Who* Transcripts', http://www.chakoteya.net/DoctorWho/27-10. htm; accessed 2 August 2012.

38   George Herbert Mead, *Mind, Self and Society from the Standpoint of a Social Behaviourist*, ed. Charles S. Morris (Chicago, IL, 1934), p. 138.

39   John Dewey, 'Time and Individuality', in Jo Ann Boydston (ed.), *The Collected Works of John Dewey: The Later Works*, vol. 14 (Carbondale, IL, 1988), p. 107.

40   Ibid., p. 109.

41   C.I. Lewis, *Collected Papers* (Stanford, CA, 1970), p. 108.

42   John Dewey, *Construction and Criticism*, in Jo Ann Boydston (ed.), *The Collected Works of John Dewey: The Later Works*, vol. 5 (Carbondale, IL, 1984), p. 128.

Chapter 6: Speaking Treason Fluently

1   See Marc Platt, *Lungbarrow* (London, 1997); Peter Anghelides and Stephen Cole, *The Ancestor Cell* (London, 2000).

2   Alfred Schutz, *Collected Papers*, vol. 1, ed. Maurice Natanson (The Hague, 1962), p. 53.

3   Aristotle, *Politics* 1253a7–18, in Jonathan Barnes (ed.), *The Complete Works of Aristotle*, vol. 2 (Princeton, NJ, 1984), p. 1988.

4   Richard J. Bernstein, *The Restructuring of Social and Political Theory* (Philadelphia, PN, 1976), p. 104.

5   Ibid.

6   John Tulloch and Manuel Alvarado, *Doctor Who: The Unfolding Text* (New York, 1983), pp. 143, 145.

7   'The Pirate Planet' transcript, writer Douglas Adams, director Pennant Roberts; 'The *Doctor Who* Transcripts', http://www.chakoteya.net/DoctorWho/16-2. htm; accessed 10 August 2012.

8   David J. Howe and Stephen James Walker, *Doctor Who: The Television Companion* (London, 1998), p. 319.

9   'The Robots of Death' transcript, writer Chris Boucher, director Michael Briant; 'The *Doctor Who* Transcripts', http://www.chakoteya.net/Doctor Who/14-5.htm; accessed 10 August 2012.

10   Ibid.

11   Benjamin R. Barber, *Strong Democracy: Participatory Politics for a New Age* (London, 2003), p. 120; italics original.

12   Ibid., p. 34.

13   Karl Marx, *Economic and Philosophical Manuscripts*, in David McLellan (ed.), *Karl Marx: Selected Writings*, 2nd edn (Oxford, 2000), p. 85.

14   Barber, *Strong Democracy*, pp. 64–5.

15   Claude LeFort, *Democracy and Political Theory* (Oxford, 1988), p. 19.

16   Aristotle, *Politics* 1260b35–30, in Barnes (ed.), *Complete Works*, p. 2000.

17   Aristotle, *Politics* 1290b17–18, in Barnes (ed.), *Complete Works*, p. 2048.

18 Plato, *Laws* 636d6–e4, in John M. Cooper (ed.), *Plato: Complete Works* (Cambridge, UK, 1997), p. 1331.

19 Plato, *Republic* 2.370c3–5, in Cooper (ed.), *Complete Works*; p. 1009.

20 Plato, *Euthydemus* 292b4–c1, in Cooper (ed.), *Complete Works*, p. 731.

21 David Keyt, 'Plato on Justice', in Hugh H. Benson (ed.), *A Companion to Plato* (Oxford, 2009), p. 346.

22 Aristotle, *Politics*, 1264b15–25, in Barnes (ed.), *Complete Works*, p. 2006.

23 Ian Shapiro, *The Moral Foundations of Politics* (New Haven, CT, 2003), p. 193.

24 Howe and Walker, *Dr Who*, p. 472.

25 Philip Martin, *Vengeance on Varos* (London, 1988), p. 36.

26 Quoted in Gary Gillatt, *Doctor Who from A to Z* (London, 1998), p. 137.

27 Ibid.

28 Martin, *Vengeance on Varos*, p. 116.

29 Plato, *Republic* 1.348c4–d3, in Cooper (ed.), *Complete Works*, p. 991.

30 Barber, *Strong Democracy*, p. 120.

31 'The Beast Below' transcript, writer Stephen Moffat, director Andrew Gunn; 'The *Doctor Who* Transcripts', http://www.chakoteya.net/DoctorWho/31-2. htm; accessed 13 August 2012. Incidentally, the twenty-ninth century is also the period during which the incidents of 'The Robots of Death' took place, according to Lance Parkin, *Ahistory: An Unauthorised History of the Doctor Who Universe*, 2nd edn (Des Moines, IA, 2007), p. 308.

32 'The Beast Below' transcript, op. cit.

33 Hannah Arendt, *The Origins of Totalitarianism*, new edn (London, 1973), p. 245.

34 Henry Farrell, 'Socialist Surrealism: China Miéville's New Crobuzon Novels', in Donald M. Hassler and Clyde Wilcox (eds), *New Boundaries in Political Science Fiction* (Columbia, SC, 2008), p. 274.

Chapter 7: Did I Mention It Also Travels in Time?

1 Jeremy Bentham, *Doctor Who: The Early Years* (London, 1986), p. 61.

2 Bud Foote, *The Connecticut Yankee in the Twentieth Century: Travel to the Past in Science Fiction* (Westport, CT, 1991), p. 12.

3 David Lewis, 'The Paradoxes of Time Travel', *American Philosophical Quarterly* 13 (April 1976), p. 145.

4 'An Unearthly Child' transcript, writer Anthony Coburn, director Waris Hussein; *The Doctor Who Transcript Project*, http://dwtpscripts.tripod.com/1stdoc/a/ a1.html; accessed 18 August 2012.

5 Theodore Sider, 'Time', in Susan Schneider (ed.), *Science Fiction and Philosophy: From Time Travel to Superintelligence* (Oxford, 2009), p. 301.

6 Parmenides, fr. 19, I.68, in Nicholas Smith, Fritz Allhof and Anand Jayprakash Vaidya (eds), *Ancient Philosophy: Essential Readings with Commentary* (Oxford, 2008), p. 35.

7 Parmenides, fr. 6, I.57, in Smith, Allhof and Vaidya (eds), *Ancient Philosophy*, p. 32.

8 Aristotle, *Physics* 191a23–191b27, in Jonathan Barnes (ed.), *The Complete Works of Aristole*, vol. 1 (Princeton, NJ, 1984), pp. 326–7.

9 Aristotle, *De Interpretatione* 18a29–35, in Barnes (ed.), *Complete Works*, p. 28.

10 Aristotle, *De Interpretatione* 18b10–13, in Barnes (ed.), *Complete Works*, p. 29.

11   Aristotle, *De Interpretatione* 19a1–4, in Barnes (ed.), *Complete Works*, p. 29.

12   J.O. de La Mettrie, *Man a Machine*, http://cscs.umich.edu/~crshalizi/LaMettrie/ Machine/; accessed 19 August 2012. Web version is from *Man a Machine, by Julien Offray de La Mettrie. French-English. Including Frederick the Great's "Eulogy" on La Mettrie and extracts from La Mettrie's "The Natural History of the Soul"; Philosophical and Historical Notes by Gertrude Carman Bussey* (La Salle, IL, 1912).

13   Ibid.

14   Richard Taylor, *Metaphysics*, 3rd edn (Englewood Cliffs, NJ, 1983), p. 53.

15   Roland Omnès, *Quantum Philosophy: Understanding and Interpreting Contemporary Science*, trans. Arturo Sangalli (Princeton, NJ, 1999), pp. 168–9.

16   Lance Parkin dates 'The Aztecs' as circa 1454 in *Ahistory*, p. 62.

17   Contrast this situation with something that Barbara might clearly find *logically* impossible, such as drawing a square circle or proving that 1 equals 2. She might find it *physically* or *causally* impossible to intervene in the Aztecs' customs if she were paralysed, or simply watching the events (as if on television) on the 'Time Scanner' that the Doctor procures in 'The Space Museum' (1965).

18   David Deutsch and Michael Lockwood, 'The Quantum Physics of Time Travel', in Schneider (ed.), *Science Fiction and Philosophy*, p. 327.

19   Ibid., p. 328.

20   Paul Horwich, 'On Some Alleged Paradoxes of Time Travel', *The Journal of Philosophy* 72:14 (14 August 1975), pp. 435–6.

21   'Time Crash' transcript, writer Stephen Moffat, director Graeme Harper; '*Doctor Who* 2005+ Transcripts', http://who-transcripts.atspace.com/2007/ transcripts/CIN2007_timecrash.html; accessed 20 August 2012.

22   Ibid.

23   Deutsch and Lockwood, 'Quantum Physics', p. 329.

24   George Gale, 'Cosmological Fecundity: Theories of Multiple Universes', in John Leslie (ed.), *Modern Cosmology and Philosophy*, 2nd edn (Amherst, NY, 1998), p. 199.

25   Ibid.

26   Foote, *The Connecticut Yankee*, p. 11.

27   Omnès, *Quantum Philosophy*.

28   Deutsch and Lockwood, 'Quantum Physics', p. 331.

29   'Turn Left' transcript, writer Russell T. Davies, director Graeme Harper; 'The *Doctor Who* Transcripts', http://www.chakoteya.net/DoctorWho/30-11.htm; accessed 20 August 2012.

30   'Blink' transcript, writer Stephen Moffat, director Hettie MacDonald; 'The *Doctor Who* Transcripts', http://www.chakoteya.net/DoctorWho/29-10.htm; accessed 20 August 2012.

31   Michelle Saint and Peter A. French, 'The Horror of the Weeping Angels', in Lewis and Smithka (eds), *Doctor Who and Philosophy*, p. 301.

32   James Trefil, *The Nature of Science* (New York, 2003), p. 336.

33   'Cold Blood' transcript, writer Chris Chibnall, director Ashley Way; 'The *Doctor Who* Transcripts', http://www.chakoteya.net/DoctorWho/31-9.htm; accessed 21 August 2012.

34   Stephen Hawking, 'The Future of the Universe', in Leo Howe and Alan Wain (eds), *Predicting the Future* (Cambridge, UK, 1993), p. 22.

BIBLIOGRAPHY

Publications: Books, Journals and Magazines

Abrams, M.H., 'English Romanticism: The Spirit of the Age', in Harold Bloom (ed.), *Romanticism and Consciousness: Essays in Criticism* (New York: W.W. Norton, 1970).

Adams, Douglas, *The Restaurant at the End of the Universe* (New York: Harmony Books, 1980).

Amis, Kingsley, *New Maps of Hell: A Survey of Science Fiction* (New York: Harcourt Brace & Co., 1960).

Andrew, Barbara S., 'Beauvoir's Place in Philosophical Thought', in Claudia Card (ed.), *The Cambridge Companion to Simone de Beauvoir* (Cambridge, UK: Cambridge University Press, 2003).

Arendt, Hannah, *The Origins of Totalitarianism*, new edn (London: Harcourt, Brace & Co., 1973).

Aristotle, *De Interpretatione*, in Jonathan Barnes (ed.), *The Complete Works of Aristotle*, vol. 1 (Princeton, NJ: Princeton University Press, 1984).

———, *Metaphysics*, in Jonathan Barnes (ed.), *The Complete Works of Aristotle*, vol. 2 (Princeton, NJ: Princeton University Press, 1984).

———, *Physics*, in Jonathan Barnes (ed.), *The Complete Works of Aristotle*, vol. 1 (Princeton, NJ: Princeton University Press, 1984).

———, *Politics*, in Jonathan Barnes (ed.), *The Complete Works of Aristotle*, vol. 2 (Princeton, NJ: Princeton University Press, 1984).

Arp, Robert and Kevin S. Decker, '"That Fatal Kiss": Bond, Ethics, and the Objectification of Women', in James South and Jacob Held (eds), *James Bond and Philosophy* (Chicago, IL: Open Court, 2006).

Ashby, Norman, *A Comprehensive History of Western Ethics*, ed. W. Allen Ashby (Amherst, NY: Prometheus Books, 1997).

Augustine, St, *City of God*, abridged, ed. Vernon J. Bourke (London: Image Books/Doubleday, 1958).

Ayer, A.J., *Language, Truth and Logic* (New York: Dover Publications, 1952).

Baldwin, James, *Giovanni's Room* (New York: Laurel, 1985).

Banks, David, with Adrian Rigelsford, *Doctor Who: Cybermen* (London: W.H. Allen, 1988).

Barber, Benjamin R., *Strong Democracy: Participatory Politics for a New Age* (London: University of California Press, 2003).

Bentham, Jeremy, *Doctor Who: The Early Years* (London: W.H. Allen, 1986).

Bernstein, Richard J., 'In Defence of American Philosophy', in John E. Smith (ed.), *Contemporary American Philosophy*, 2nd series (London: George Allen & Unwin, 1970).

————, *The Restructuring of Social and Political Theory* (Philadelphia, PN: University of Pennsylvania Press, 1976).

————, *Radical Evil: A Philosophical Interrogation* (Cambridge, UK: Polity Press, 2002).

Black, Ian Stuart, *The Macra Terror* (London: Target Books, 1987).

Bould, Mark, 'Science Fiction Television in the United Kingdom', in J.P. Telotte (ed.), *The Essential Science Fiction Television Reader* (Lexington, KY: The University of Kentucky Press, 2008).

Blum, Jonathan, 'Model Train Set', in Stephen Cole (ed.), *Short Trips* (London: BBC Books, 1998).

Brake, Colin, *Doctor Who: Escape Velocity* (London: BBC Books, 2001).

Brandom, Robert B., *Perspectives on Pragmatism: Classical, Recent, & Contemporary* (Cambridge, MA: Harvard University Press, 2011).

Britton, Piers D. and Simon J. Barker, *Reading between Designs: Visual Imagery and the Generation of Meaning in* The Avengers, The Prisoner *and* Doctor Who (Austin, TX: University of Texas Press, 2003).

Butler, David, 'How to Pilot a TARDIS: Audiences, Science Fiction and the Fantastic in *Doctor Who*', in David Butler (ed.), *Time and Relative Dissertations in Space: Critical Perspectives on* Doctor Who (Manchester: Manchester University Press, 2007).

Chapman, James, *Inside the TARDIS: The Worlds of Doctor Who – A Cultural History* (London: I.B.Tauris, 2006).

Charles, Alec, 'The Crack of Doom: The Uncanny Echoes of Steven Moffat's *Doctor Who*', *Science Fiction Film and Television* 4:1 (2011), pp. 1–24.

Clark, Andy, 'Time and Mind', *Journal of Philosophy* 95:7 (1998), pp. 354–76.

Clarke, Arthur C., 'Hazards of Prophecy: The Failure of Imagination', in *Profiles of the Future: An Enquiry into the Limits of the Possible* (New York: Harper & Row, 1962).

Cole, Stephen and Peter Anghelides, *Doctor Who: The Ancestor Cell* (London: BBC Books, 2000).

Comte, Auguste, *The Positive Philosophy of August Comte*, vol. III, trans. Harriet Martineau (London: George Bell & Sons, 1896).

Cornell, Paul, *Doctor Who: Love and War* (London: Virgin Publishing, 1992).

Creath, Richard, 'Quine's Challenge to Carnap', in Michael Friedman and Richard Creath (eds), *The Cambridge Companion to Carnap* (Cambridge, UK: Cambridge University Press, 2007).

Davidson, Donald, 'The Irreducibility of the Concept of the Self', *Subjective, Intersubjective, Objective* (Oxford: Clarendon Press, 2001).

Davis, Gerry, *Doctor Who and the Cybermen* (London: Target Books, 1974).

Dawson, Paul, 'And Before I Go ...', in Courtland Lewis and Paula Smithka (eds), *Doctor Who and Philosophy: Bigger on the Inside* (Chicago, IL: Open Court, 2010).

De Beauvoir, Simone, *The Ethics of Ambiguity* (New York: Citadel Press, 1976).

Dennett, Daniel C., 'Conditions of Personhood', in William O. Stephens (ed.), *The Person: Readings in Human Nature* (Upper Saddle River, NJ: Pearson Prentice Hall, 2006).

Deutsch, David and Michael Lockwood, 'The Quantum Physics of Time Travel', in Susan Schneider (ed.), *Science Fiction and Philosophy: From Time Travel to Superintelligence* (Oxford: Wiley-Blackwell).

Dewey, John, *Construction and Criticism*, in *The Collected Works of John Dewey: Later Works*, vol. 5, ed. Jo Ann Boydston (Carbondale, IL: Southern Illinois University Press, 1984).

————, 'Time and Individuality', in *The Collected Works of John Dewey: The Later Works*, vol. 14, ed. Jo Ann Boydston (Carbondale, IL: Southern Illinois University Press, 1988).

Dicks, Terrance, *Doctor Who and the Dalek Invasion of Earth* (London: Target Books, 1977).

————, *Doctor Who: Four to Doomsday* (London: Target Books, 1983).

————, *Doctor Who: The Eight Doctors* (London: BBC Books, 1997).

Dicks, Terrance and Malcolm Hulke, *The Making of Doctor Who* (London: Tandem, 1976).

Dostoevsky, Fyodor, *Notes from Underground* (New York: Alfred A. Knopf, 1993).

Ellison, Harlan, 'Introducing *Doctor Who*', in Terrance Dicks, *Doctor Who and the Revenge of the Cybermen* (New York: Pinnacle Books, 1979).

Farrell, Henry, 'Socialist Surrealism: China Miéville's New Crobuzon Novels', in Donald M. Hassler and Clyde Wilcox (eds), *New Boundaries in Political Science Fiction* (Columbia, SC: University of South Carolina Press, 2008).

Foote, Bud, *The Connecticut Yankee in the Twentieth Century: Travel to the Past in Science Fiction* (Westport, CT: Greenwood Press, 1991).

Frankfurt, Harry, 'Freedom of the Will and the Concept of a Person', in Kim Atkins (ed.), *Self and Subjectivity* (Oxford: Blackwell, 2005); originally published in *The Journal of Philosophy* 68:1 (1971), pp. 5–16.

Friedman, Michael, *A Parting of the Ways: Carnap, Cassirer, and Heidegger* (Chicago, IL: Open Court Publishers, 2000).

Gale, George, 'Cosmological Fecundity: Theories of Multiple Universes', in John Leslie (ed.), *Modern Cosmology and Philosophy*, 2nd edn (Amherst, NY: Prometheus Books, 1998).

Gatens, Moira, 'Beauvoir and Biology: A Second Look', in Claudia Card (ed.), *The Cambridge Companion to Simone de Beauvoir* (Cambridge, UK: Cambridge University Press, 2003).

Gillatt, Gary, *Doctor Who from A to Z* (London: BBC Books, 1998).

Goetsch, Paul, *Monsters in English Literature: From the Romantic Age to the First World War* (Oxford: Peter Lang, 2002).

Haining, Peter, *Doctor Who: A Celebration – Two Decades Through Time and Space* (London: W.H. Allen, 1983).

————, *Doctor Who: The Key to Time, A Year-by-Year Record* (London: W.H. Allen, 1984).

————, *Doctor Who: The Early Years* (London: W.H. Allen, 1986).

Halberstam, Judith, *Skin Shows: Gothic Horror and the Technology of Monsters* (London: Duke University Press, 1995).

Hanfling, Oswald, 'Logical Positivism', in Stuart G. Shanker (ed.), *Routledge History of Philosophy*, vol. IX: *Philosophy of Science, Logic and Mathematics in the Twentieth Century* (London: Routledge, 1966).

Hanley, Richard, 'Who's Who on Gallifrey?', in Courtland Lewis and Paula Smithka (eds), *Doctor Who and Philosophy: Bigger on the Inside* (Chicago, IL: Open Court, 2010).

Hartwell, David G., 'Hard Science Fiction', in David G. Hartwell and Kathryn Cramer (eds), *The Ascent of Wonder: The Evolution of Hard SF* (New York: TOR Books, 1994).

Hawking, Stephen, 'The Future of the Universe', in Leo Howe and Alan Wain (eds), *Predicting the Future* (Cambridge, UK, Cambridge University Press, 1993).

Hegel, G.W.F., *Phenomenology of Spirit*, trans. A.V. Miller (Oxford: Oxford University Press, 1977).

Heidegger, Martin, *Being and Time*, trans. John MacQuarrie and Edward Robinson (London: Harper Perennial, 1962).

————, *History of the Concept of Time: Prolegomena*, trans. Theodore Kisiel (Bloomington, IN: Indiana University Press, 1985).

————, *Ontology: The Hermeneutics of Facticity*, trans. John van Buren (Bloomington, IN: Indiana University Press, 1999).

Hick, John, *An Interpretation of Religion: Human Responses to the Transcendent*, 2nd edn (New Haven, CT: Yale University Press, 2004).

Hirsch, Eli, 'Identity', in Jaegwon Kim and Ernest Sosa (eds), *A Companion to Metaphysics* (Oxford: Blackwell, 1995).

Horwich, Paul, 'On Some Alleged Paradoxes of Time Travel', *The Journal of Philosophy* 72:14 (14 August 1975), pp. 432–44.

Howe, David J., *Doctor Who: A Book of Monsters* (London: BBC Books, 1997).

Howe, David J. and Stephen James Walker, *Doctor Who: The Handbook – The Fifth Doctor* (London: Doctor Who Books, 1995).

————, *Doctor Who: The Handbook – The Third Doctor* (London: Doctor Who Books, 1996).

————, *Doctor Who: The Handbook – The Seventh Doctor* (London: Doctor Who Books, 1998).

————, *Doctor Who: The Television Companion* (London: BBC Books, 1998).

Howe, David J., Stephen James Walker and Mark Stammers, *Doctor Who: The Handbook – The Fourth Doctor* (London: Doctor Who Books, 1992).

————, *Doctor Who: The Sixties* (London: Doctor Who Books, 1992).

————, *Doctor Who: The Handbook – The Sixth Doctor* (London: Doctor Who Books, 1993).

————, *Doctor Who: The Handbook – The First Doctor* (London: Doctor Who Books, 1994).

————, *Doctor Who: The Eighties* (London: Doctor Who Books, 1996).

————, *Doctor Who: The Handbook – The Second Doctor* (London: Doctor Who Books, 1997).

————, *Doctor Who: The Seventies* (London: Doctor Who Books, 1994).

Hulke, Malcolm, *Doctor Who and the Cave-Monsters* (London: Target Books, 1974).

Husserl, Edmund, *Ideas: General Introduction to Pure Phenomenology*, trans. W.R. Boyce Gibson (London: Collier, 1962).

Ignatieff, Michael, *The Lesser Evil: Political Ethics in an Age of Terror* (Princeton, NJ: Princeton University Press, 2004).

Irenaeus, St, *Against the Heresies*, trans. Dominic J. Unger (New York: Paulist Press, 1992).

Israel, Jonathan I., *Radical Enlightenment* (Oxford: Oxford University Press, 2001).

Izenberg, Gerald, 'The Politics of Song in Wordsworth's *Lyrical Ballads*', in Kevin Sharpe and Steven N. Zwicker (eds), *Refiguring Revolutions: Aesthetics and Politics from the English Revolution to the Romantic Revolution* (London: University of California Press, 1998).

Jacobs, Matthew, *Doctor Who: The Script of the Film* (London: BBC Books, 1996).

James, William, *Principles of Psychology*, vol. 1 (New York: Dover Publications, 1950).

Kant, Immanuel, *Religion within the Limits of Reason Alone*, trans. T.M. Greene and H.H. Hudson (New York: Harper Torchbooks, 1960).

————, *Groundwork of the Metaphysics of Morals*, in Mary Gregor (trans. and ed.), *The Cambridge Edition of the Works of Immanuel Kant: Practical Philosophy* (Cambridge, UK: Cambridge University Press, 1996).

Keltner, Stacy, 'Beauvoir's Idea of Ambiguity', in Margaret A. Simons (ed.), *The Philosophy of Simone de Beauvoir* (Bloomington, IN: Indiana University Press, 2006).

Keyt, David, 'Plato on Justice', in Hugh H. Benson (ed.), *A Companion to Plato* (Oxford: Wiley-Blackwell, 2009).

Kierkegaard, Søren, *The Sickness Unto Death*, trans. Alastair Hannay (Harmondsworth: Penguin, 1989).

Kitson, Peter J., 'Beyond the Enlightenment: The Philosophical, Scientific and Religious Inheritance', in Duncan Wu (ed.), *A Companion to Romanticism* (Oxford: Blackwell, 1998).

Kurzweil, Ray, 'Who Am I? What Am I?', in Susan Schneider (ed.), *Science Fiction and Philosophy: From Time Travel to Superintelligence* (Oxford: Blackwell, 2009); originally published in Kurzweil, *The Singularity is Near: When Humans Transcend Biology* (London: Viking, 2005).

Lacey, Alan, 'Positivism', in Ted Honderich (ed.), *The Oxford Companion to Philosophy* (Oxford: Oxford University Press, 1995).

Laplace, Pierre-Simon, *A Philosophical Essay on Probabilities*, trans. Frederick Wilson Truscott and Frederick Lincoln Emory (New York: Dover Publications, 1951).

Lawrence, Joseph P., 'Philosophical Religion and the Quest for Authenticity', in Jason M. Wirth (ed.), *Schelling Now: Contemporary Readings* (Bloomington, IN: Indiana University Press, 2005).

Leach, Jim, *Doctor Who* (Detroit, MI: Wayne State University Press, 2009).

LeFort, Claude, *Democracy and Political Theory* (Oxford: Oxford University Press, 1988).

Leibniz, G.W., *New Essays on the Human Understanding*, excerpted in William O. Stephens (ed.), *The Person: Readings in Human Nature* (Upper Saddle River, NJ: Pearson Prentice Hall, 2006).

Lem, Stanislaw, 'The Time-travel Story and Related Matters of Science-fiction Structuring', *Microworlds: Writings on Science Fiction and Fantasy* (London: Harcourt Brace Jovanovich, 1984).

Lévinas, Emmanuel, 'Useless Suffering', in Robert Bernasconi and David Wood (eds), *The Provocation of Levinas: Rethinking the Other* (London: Routledge, 1988).

————, 'Philosophy and the Idea of Infinity', in Matthew Calarco and Peter Atterton (eds), *The Continental Ethics Reader* (London: Routledge, 2003), republished from *Collected Philosophical Papers*, trans. Alphonso Lingis (Pittsburgh, PN: University of Duquesne Press, 1998).

Lewis, C.I., *Collected Papers* (Stanford, CA: Stanford University Press, 1970).

Lewis, David, 'The Paradoxes of Time Travel', *American Philosophical Quarterly* 13 (April 1976), pp. 145–52.

Locke, John, *An Essay Concerning Human Understanding*, ed. Roger Woolhouse (London: Penguin Books, 1997).

Martin, Philip, *Vengeance on Varos* (London: Target Books, 1988).

Marx, Karl, *Economic and Philosophical Manuscripts*, in David McLellan (ed.), *Karl Marx: Selected Writings*, 2nd edn (Oxford: Oxford University Press, 2000).

McGinn, Colin, *Ethics, Evil, and Fiction* (Oxford: Clarendon Press, 1997).

Mead, George Herbert, *Mind, Self and Society from the Standpoint of a Social Behaviourist*, ed. Charles S. Morris (Chicago, IL: University of Chicago Press, 1934).

Merleau-Ponty, Maurice, *Phenomenology of Perception*, trans. Colin Smith (London: Routledge, 2002).

Miles, Lawrence, *Doctor Who: Alien Bodies* (London: BBC Books, 1997).

Moore, Steve and David Lloyd, 'Twilight of the Silurians', *Doctor Who Weekly* 21–2 (March 1980), reprinted and colourised in Marvel Comics' *Doctor Who* 18 (March 1986), pp. 23–30.

Moran, Dermot, *Introduction to Phenomenology* (London: Routledge, 2000).

Nagel, Thomas, 'The Objective Basis for Morality', in Peter Singer (ed.), *Ethics* (Oxford: Oxford University Press, 1994).

Neiman, Susan, *Evil in Modern Thought* (Oxford: Princeton University Press, 2004).

Newman, Kim, *Doctor Who: A Critical Reading of the Series* (London: Palgrave MacMillan, 2008).

Novalis, 'Miscellaneous Remarks', in J.M. Bernstein (ed.), *Classical and Romantic German Aesthetics* (Cambridge, UK: Cambridge University Press, 2003).

Omnès, Roland, *Quantum Philosophy: Understanding and Interpreting Contemporary Science*, trans. Arturo Sangalli (Princeton, NJ: Princeton University Press, 1999).

Panshin, Alexei and Cory Panshin, *The World Beyond the Hill: Science Fiction and the Quest for Transcendence* (Los Angeles, CA: Jeremy P. Tarcher, 1989).

Parfit, Derek, *Reasons and Persons* (Oxford: Clarendon Press, 1984).

————, 'Divided Minds and the Nature of Persons', in Susan Schneider (ed.), *Science Fiction and Philosophy: From Time Travel to Superintelligence* (Oxford: Blackwell, 2009).

Parkhouse, Steve, Mike McMahon and Adolfo Buylla, 'Junkyard Demon', *Doctor Who Monthly* 58–9 (November–December 1981).

Parkin, Lance, *Ahistory: An Unauthorised History of the* Doctor Who *Universe*, 2nd edn with additional material by Lars Pearson (Des Moines, IA: Mad Norwegian Press, 2007).

————, 'Canonicity Matters: Defining the *Doctor Who* Canon', in David Butler (ed.), *Time and Relative Dissertations in Space: Critical Perspectives on* Doctor Who (Manchester: Manchester University Press 2007), pp. 246–62.

Parmenides, fragments, in Nicholas Smith, Fritz Allhof and Anand Jayprakash Vaidya (eds), *Ancient Philosophy: Essential Readings with Commentary* (Oxford: Blackwell Publishing, 2008).

Parsons, Paul, *The Science of* Doctor Who (Baltimore, MD: Johns Hopkins University Press, 2010).

Peel, John, *The Gallifrey Chronicles* (London: Virgin Publishing, 1991).

Peel, John and Terry Nation, *The Official Doctor Who and the Daleks Book* (New York: St Martin's Press, 1988).

Pinch, Adela, 'Sensibility', in Nicholas Roe (ed.), *Romanticism: An Oxford Guide* (Oxford: Oxford University Press, 2005).

Plato, *Euthydemus*, in John M. Cooper (ed.), *Plato: Complete Works* (Indianapolis, IN: Hackett, 1997).

————, *Laws*, in John M. Cooper (ed.), *Plato: Complete Works* (Indianapolis, IN: Hackett, 1997).

————, *Republic* 2.370c3-5, in John M. Cooper (ed.), *Plato: Complete Works* (Indianapolis, IN: Hackett, 1997).

————, *Theatetus*, in John M. Cooper (ed.), *Plato: Complete Works* (Indianapolis, IN: Hackett, 1997).

Platt, Marc, *Lungbarrow* (London: Virgin Books, 1997).

Rafer, David, 'Mythic Identity in *Doctor Who*', in David Butler (ed.), *Time and Relative Dissertations in Space: Critical Perspectives on* Doctor Who (Manchester: Manchester University Press, 2007).

Rayner, Jacqueline, Andrew Darling, Kerrie Dougherty, David John and Simon Beecroft, *Doctor Who: The Visual Dictionary*, rev. edn (London: Dorling-Kindersley, 2009).

Richards, Justin, *Doctor Who: The Burning* (London: BBC Books, 2000).

————, *Doctor Who: The Legend – 40 Years of Time Travel* (London: BBC Books, 2003).

Ricoeur, Paul, *Oneself as Another*, trans. Kathleen Blamey (Chicago, IL: University of Chicago Press, 1992).

Rorty, Richard, *Contingency, Irony, and Solidarity* (Cambridge, UK: Cambridge University Press, 1989).

Russell, Bertrand, 'On the Experience of Time', *The Monist* 25 (1915), pp. 212–33.

Russell, Gary, *Doctor Who: The Scales of Injustice* (London: Virgin Books, 1996).

————, *Doctor Who: The Inside Story* (London: BBC Books, 2006).

————, *Doctor Who: The Encylopedia*, 2nd edn (London: BBC Books, 2011).

Saint, Michelle and Peter A. French, 'The Horror of the Weeping Angels', in Courtland Lewis and Paula Smithka (eds), *Doctor Who and Philosophy* (Chicago, IL: Open Court, 2010).

Sartre, Jean-Paul, *Existentialism is a Humanism*, trans. Bernard Flechtman (New York: Citadel, 1947).

————, *Being and Nothingness*, trans. Hazel E. Barnes (New York: Gramercy Books, 1956).

————, *War Diaries* (London: Verso, 1984).

Segal, Philip, with Gary Russell, *Regeneration: The Story Behind the Revival of a Television Legend* (London: HarperCollins Entertainment, 2000).

Schelde, Per, *Androids, Humanoids, and Other Science Fiction Monsters: Science and Soul in Science Fiction Films* (London: New York University Press, 1993).

Schiller, Friedrich Schiller, *Letters on the Aesthetic Education of Man* in *German Idealism: An Anthology and Guide*, ed. Georg Mohr and Brian O'Connor (Chicago, IL: University of Chicago Press, 2007).

Schlick, Moritz, *Philosophical Papers*, vol. II, ed. Henk L. Mulder and Barbara F.B. van de Velde-Schlick (Dordrecht, Holland: D. Reidel, 1979).

Schutz, Alfred Schutz, *Collected Papers*, vol. 1, ed. Maurice Natanson (The Hague: Martinus Nijhoff, 1962).

Shapiro, Ian, *The Moral Foundations of Politics* (New Haven, CT: Yale University Press, 2003).

Shoemaker, Sydney, 'Persons and Personal Identity', in Jaegwon Kim and Ernest Sosa (eds), *A Companion to Metaphysics* (Oxford: Blackwell, 1995).

Sider, Theodore, 'Time', in Susan Schneider (ed.), *Science Fiction and Philosophy: From Time Travel to Superintelligence* (Oxford: Wiley-Blackwell).

Sleigh, Robert C., Jr, 'Identity of Indiscernibles', in Jaegwon Kim and Ernest Sosa (eds), *A Companion to Metaphysics* (Oxford: Blackwell, 1995).

Spinoza, Benedict, *Ethics*, ed. and trans. G.H.R. Parkinson (Oxford: Oxford University Press, 2000).

———, 'To the Most Noble and Learned Henry Oldenburg', in Michael L. Morgan (ed.), *Spinoza: Complete Works* (Indianapolis, IN: Hackett, 2002).

———, *Treatise on the Emendation of the Intellect*, trans. Samuel Shirley, in Michael L. Morgan (ed.), *Spinoza: Complete Works* (Indianapolis, IN: Hackett, 2002).

Stabler, Jane, 'The Literary Background', in Nicholas Roe (ed.), *Romanticism: An Oxford Guide* (Oxford: Oxford University Press, 2005).

Stadler, Friedrich, 'The Vienna Circle: Context, Profile, and Development', in Alan Richardson and Thomas Uebel (eds), *The Cambridge Companion to Logical Empiricism* (Cambridge, UK: Cambridge University Press, 2007).

Stewart, Matthew, *The Courtier and the Heretic: Leibniz, Spinoza, and the Fate of God in the Modern World* (London: W.W. Norton & Company, 2006).

Taylor, Charles, *Sources of the Self: The Making of the Modern Identity* (Cambridge, MA: Harvard University Press, 1989).

Taylor, Richard, *Metaphysics*, 3rd edn (Englewood Cliffs, NJ: Prentice Hall, 1983).

Trefil, James, *The Nature of Science* (New York: Houghton Mifflin, 2003).

Tribe, Steve and James Goss, *The Dalek Handbook* (London: BBC Books, 2011).

Tulloch, John and Henry Jenkins, *Science Fiction Audiences: Watching 'Doctor Who' and 'Star Trek'* (London: Routledge, 1995).

Tulloch, John and Manuel Alvarado, *Doctor Who: The Unfolding Text* (New York: St Martin's Press, 1983).

Webb, Timothy (ed.), *Shelley: Selected Poems* (London: Dent, 1977).

Whitehead, Alfred North, *Modes of Thought* (New York: Free Press, 1968).

Internet Sources

Blair, Andrew, '*Doctor Who*: A Celebration of Death', *Den of Geek*, http://www.denofgeek.com/tv/doctor-who/21876/doctor-who-a-celebration-of-death; published 6 July 2012, accessed 24 July 2012.

'*Doctor Who* 2005+ Transcripts', http://who-transcripts.atspace.com/.

The Doctor Who Transcript Project (Mirror Site), http://dwtpscripts.tripod.com/index.html.

'The *Doctor Who* Transcripts', http://www.chakoteya.net/DoctorWho/.

Frick, Alice and Donald Bull, 'Science Fiction: BBC Report', BBC Archives, http://www.bbc.co.uk/archive/doctorwho/6400.shtml; accessed 25 April 2012.

La Mettrie, J.O. de, *Man a Machine*, http://cscs.umich.edu/~crshalizi/LaMettrie/ Machine/; accessed 19 August 2012. Web version is from *Man a Machine, by Julien Offray de La Mettrie. French-English. Including Frederick the Great's "`Eulogy" on La Mettrie and extracts from La Mettrie's "The Natural History of the Soul"; Philosophical and Historical Notes by Gertrude Carman Bussey* (La Salle, IL: Open Court, 1912).

Lao Tzu, *Tao Te Ching*, 'The Book of Tao', ch. 1, trans. Douglas Allchin, http:// my.pclink.com/~allchin/tao/contents.htm; accessed 27 October 2011.

'TV Tropes', http://tvtropes.org/pmwiki/pmwiki.php/Main/TheNthDoctor; accessed 28 July 2012.

INDEX